IN SEARCH OF SHAKESPEARE

This engraving of Shakespeare, by Martin Droeshout, is probably based on a drawing from life. The famous Hamlet quotation—"To be or not to be That ys the question"—and the signature—"Willm Shackspeare of Stratford upon Avon"—are a composite formed from Shakespeare's handwriting in his holographic will.

IN SEARCH
of
SHAKESPEARE

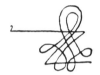

A RECONNAISSANCE INTO THE POET'S

LIFE AND HANDWRITING

Charles Hamilton

HARCOURT BRACE JOVANOVICH, PUBLISHERS

SAN DIEGO · NEW YORK · LONDON

Library of Congress Cataloging in Publication Data
Hamilton, Charles, 1913–
    In search of Shakespeare.
    Bibliography: p.
    Includes index.
    1. Shakespeare, William, 1564–1616—Autographs.
2. Shakespeare, William, 1564–1616—Biography.
3. Dramatists, English—Early modern, 1500–1700—
Biography. I. Title.
PR2949.H34 1985 822.3'3 [B] 85-797
ISBN 0-15-144534-6

Printed in the United States of America

First edition

A B C D E

*To my wife, Diane,
who helped me to express
many of the ideas in this
book*

CONTENTS

PREFACE

THIS book is an exploratory probe into the mysteries of Shakespeare's life and creative art.

Come with me, step by step, as we unlock new doors and discover fresh, startling facts about the poet and the world he lived in, all based upon original manuscripts in his handwriting.

No manuscript expert has ever before delved into Shakespeare's script and its significance in revealing his career as a man and as an author. True, vast numbers of skilled researchers, some of them seasoned paleographers, have tried to solve the puzzle of his six signatures and to use them to uncover other writings in Shakespeare's hand, but their success was limited because they were primarily scholars, not manuscript professionals.

I certainly do not profess to be a great Shakespearean scholar; but I am an experienced handwriting expert and historian. I shall merely present the evidence, suggest its implications and leave its importance for you to judge.

And now I invite you to join me in this adventure into the unknown world of William Shakespeare.

A FEW WORDS OF THANKS

DURING the writing of this book I left in my wake a host of obligations to many people who went far out of their way to help me.

At least a dozen members of the staff at the New York Public Library, Fifth Avenue and 42nd Street, in the manuscript and rare book rooms, in the stacks and reading rooms, and in the photographing department gave without stint their time and knowledge to help me locate and make photocopies from the rare books in their custody. I am grateful to them and welcome this chance to acknowledge their aid.

Dr. Levi Fox and the Shakespeare Birthplace Trust in Stratford-upon-Avon went to much trouble to furnish speedily all the photocopies I required. On one occasion, merely on the chance it might prove useful, Dr. Fox mailed me a photocopy of a manuscript that I had not seen or asked for. To my delight, I found that it incorporated a signature of Shakespeare's. The manuscripts reproduced by courtesy of The Shakespeare Birthplace Trust are on pages 120, 121, 124 (illus. 100, 101, 103, 104, 105).

I am grateful to The Folger Shakespeare Library for permission to reproduce the photographs on pages 140, 142, 241 (illus. 120, 121, 190) and to Longleat and the Courtauld Institute of Art, University of London for the *Titus Andronicus* photograph on page 149 (illus. 130).

Among other generous contributors to this book are the British Library, Department of Manuscripts; the College of Arms; the Marquis of Bath; the Bodleian Library, Oxford; the Dulwich College Picture Gallery, London; The National Picture Gallery, London; the Public Record Office, London; and the British Museum.

I am especially indebted to my publishers for their courage in undertaking this book in the face of possible controversy regarding some of its contents.

Finally, my deep appreciation goes to my friends Susan Miller and Carolyn Compton for their understanding help; to my executive assistant, Dianne Barbaro, for heroic efforts in preparing the glossary of Shakespeare's words and for other aid; to my daughter Carolyn for her valued opinions; and especially to my wife, Diane, not only for her constant, helpful suggestions and assistance, but for her forbearance during my long, preoccupied hours at the typewriter.

IN SEARCH OF SHAKESPEARE

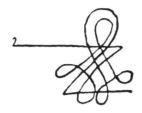

I

SETTING THE STAGE
FOR SHAKESPEARE

"The materials for a life of Shakespeare," wrote Professor Joseph Quincy Adams in the Preface to his 1923 biography of the poet, "have been gradually assembled by the industry of hundreds of scholars, extending through more than two centuries; and probably little new matter of importance remains to be discovered, except through a happy, and at present quite unforeseen, accident."

Professor Adams's remark struck the quintain dead center: Nearly every one of the discoveries I am going to tell you about in this book was a pure accident.

Let me now finish the quotation from Professor Adams's Preface: "The arduous labors of Professor and Mrs. [Charles W.] Wallace in the manuscript archives of England, during the course of which they examined over a million documents [Wallace stated that he had actually looked at five million old papers], recently yielded some fresh information; yet the small number of their 'finds' assures us that nearly all that we are likely to know of the personal affairs of the great dramatist has already been made public. This stagnation in discovery is perhaps responsible for the tendency, especially marked in the last decade, for writers to deal in fanciful speculation, evolving from the slight evidence, or none worthy of the name, bizarre and often elaborately detailed hypotheses regarding Shakespeare's relations with his contemporaries."

Professor Adams was no slouch when it came to "fanciful speculation." There's plenty of it in his biography. And there will necessarily be some of it in this book, although I have tried to place every speculative comment upon a base of granite. Still, Louis Untermeyer put it that any life of Shakespeare must necessarily be "a shaky structure built on a minimum of fact and a maximum of memorials, imaginative interpretations, shrewd deductions and sheer guesswork."

It is now half a century since Professor Adams deplored the lack of fresh material on Shakespeare and very little has turned up. In the Preface to his *William Shakespeare: a Documentary Life* (1975), Professor S. Schoenbaum laments the lack of documentary data but warns against "luxuriating in a sense of deprivation." Of his own book he adds: "Were I to claim any novelty for my narrative, that claim would have to rest on its lack of novelty . . . I have no interesting theories at all to offer. These I leave to more adventurous spirits." Perhaps Professor Schoenbaum realized, without articulating the fact, that many of his fellow Shakespearean scholars are not always receptive to "interesting theories" or new discoveries.

From boyhood my ambition was to find a previously unknown autograph of Shakespeare's. Sixty years ago, when I was nine, I exhumed from my father's tiny library in Flint, Michigan, a copy of Charles and Mary Lamb's *Tales from Shakespeare*. I savored the small volume bound in limp, black leather with colored illustrations and a colored frontispiece of the famous Chandos portrait of Shakespeare. Under the portrait was a facsimile signature. I coveted this portrait and signature. Sometimes I would make believe the signature was real, although I knew it was not, and I would brush it lightly and affectionately with my fingers, pretending that I was touching the same paper that the Great Poet had touched. I looked at the portrait every day for weeks. The more I examined it and felt of it and admired it, the looser it got, and finally it fell right out of the book and into my hands. I hid it in a small box of my treasures where I could look at it whenever I wished. That was the beginning of a lifelong adoration for Shakespeare and quest for his manuscripts. While a graduate student at the University of California, Los Angeles, I had the good fortune to study Shakespeare under Dr. Alfred E. Longueil, a scholar whose iridescent lectures seemed to me to possess more gusto than those of Hazlitt and Coleridge.

A few years later, as a soldier in England during World War II, I visited Holy Trinity Church, in Stratford-upon-Avon, where Shakespeare is buried. The flat stone above him, on which is incised an imprecation on ghouls, was chained off as a protection against exuberant visitors. For a while I stood in reverence. Presently, I took the sexton aside and pressed a ten-shilling note into his hand and asked him to let me stand on the grave of Shakespeare. "It's against regulations," he said, "so wait until everyone is out of the church."

I waited a few minutes and when the church was momentarily empty I hopped over the low chain and stood on the carved stone. Like tens of thousands of aspiring writers and thespians before me, I had a request to make of the poet. I bowed my head and moved my lips in a silent orison: "Dear friend Will, please help me to discover some scrap of handwriting from your pen."

I knew, as do all lovers of Shakespeare, that only six signatures of the poet had survived, and not another bit of his handwriting—except three disputed pages in an old prompt book. For almost three centuries scholars have pressed a bootless quest for any example of his script. Even the sextet of signatures that survives is baffling: every signature is different.

During my half-century as a collector of and expert in handwritten documents, my eye has probed thousands of old Elizabethan and Jacobean indentures, mildewed or clean, faded or clear, written in secretary, courthand or chancery, in my quest for the name Shakespeare or Shaxpar or Saxspere. Wretched old scripts by the thousands, all yielding nothing.

As scholars know, searching for fresh data on Shakespeare is like groping in deepest darkness for the light switch in an unfamiliar room. If you do stumble upon the switch, it's out of order. And if you are lucky enough to find a candle, there's nothing left of it but a wickless puddle of tallow that spurns a flame. You finally get the feeling that all illumination is vanished from the world, leaving not even a flicker of light to cast upon the life and work of Shakespeare.

I've always been an admirer of scholarly detectives and, as a manuscript dealer, I've tried to emulate them. When I was a senior in high school in 1932, I read John Livingston Lowes's *The Road to Xanadu.* I came away dazzled, drenched with its magic. From Leslie Hotson's *The Death of Christopher Marlowe* I learned the basic tenets of all sound scholarship: Ignore established beliefs, keep an open mind and draw your own conclusions. In 1934, I read John Carter's and Graham Pollard's exposé of Thomas J. Wise. Despite some of the detail that I found wearisome, the *Enquiry into the Nature of Certain Nineteenth Century Pamphlets* struck me as a landmark in the investigative method of scholarship.

This book was accidentally launched on Saturday, June 4, 1983, by a casual conversation. I was at a dinner party with my wife, Diane, and four old friends, one of them Dr. Michael Baden, formerly chief medical examiner of New York City. Baden was also the forensic pathologist in charge of the exhumation and examination of John F. Kennedy's body. Dr. Baden was two hours late for dinner because of a corpse that required his immediate scrutiny, so it was eleven o'clock by the time our conversation drifted into one of my favorite subjects—Shakespeare.

"Suppose we dug up Shakespeare's body," I said to Dr. Baden. "Could we learn anything from it?"

Dr. Baden said, "What we'd find would depend upon the condition of Shakespeare's coffin."

My wife asked if his clothes would be intact.

"Well, if water got into the coffin, there wouldn't be much left except a few bones. Maybe a signet ring or a locket."

I said if we could find a way to get Shakespeare's body out of the earth, that might unlock important secrets about his life. It was the custom in Shakespeare's day for fellow poets to toss their manuscript eulogies to the deceased into the coffin. There might be a manuscript of Ben Jonson's in the coffin.

Diane asked, "Is there any way we can legally dig him up?"

Before Dr. Baden could reply, I interrupted. "Remember, he's laid a curse on ghouls. Let me show you the quatrain chiseled on his grave marker." I printed out a copy of this inscription for them:

```
GOOD FREND FOR IESVS SAKE FORBEARE,
TO DIGG THE DVST ENCLOASED HEARE:
BLESE BE Y͏ͤ MAN Y͏ͭ SPARES THES STONES,
AND CVRST BE HE Y͏ͭ MOVES MY BONES.
```

[1] Shakespeare's gravemarker.

The ominous warning seemed to egg Dr. Baden on, because he asked how close the grave was to the Avon River.

"Very close," I said.

"Well, even if we dug the body up, I'm not sure we'd find much of anything except bones. We can't justify exhuming his corpse on medical grounds. At least, I don't think we can."

(In 1796 workmen digging a vault next to Shakespeare's grave stated that the earth above was undisturbed. They accidentally opened one side of the poet's tomb and found nothing except a hollow space where the coffin may have lain. Perhaps the poet was the victim of body snatchers, or perhaps he was never even buried in the church at all. But there are other possible explanations. Because of the proximity of the river Avon, the coffin and the body of the poet may have rotted away, leaving nothing but a hollow space in the packed earth. Or a sexton may have violated the injunction of the dead poet and dug up his skeleton to pitch into the charnel, known as the "bone house," where are heaped the remains from church graves emptied to make way for new corpses. Or the poet's body may actually have been buried, as tradition has it, seventeen feet deep. It is also quite possible that the coffin of Shakespeare may not lie directly under the gravestone, since the original stone had rotted into fragments by the middle of the eighteenth century and was replaced by a duplicate. The workmen who peered into the poet's gaping tomb were so terrified by the threat on his gravestone that they immediately walled up the open side of the hole with mortar and bricks. My own belief is that to find the poet's coffin, or what is left of it, one might have to dig deep and perhaps as far as three or four feet in all directions from the gravestone.)

I had another question for Dr. Baden. "How about starting a movement to transfer his remains to a great national monument in London? Something like a huge marble statue of Shakespeare, with representations of his famous characters around him and his mortal remains enshrined in a great sarcophagus in the center?"

"Before we think about that," said Dr. Baden, who by now was fascinated at the idea of performing a postmortem on the poet's remains, "find out all you can about his death and burial and then let's talk about it again. Maybe there's nothing left worth digging up."

I told Dr. Baden the old story about how Shakespeare supposedly died of a fever after a drinking bout with Ben Jonson and Michael Drayton. In the seventeenth century the word *fever* was loosely used and could apply to many diseases—cholera, for example—in which fever was present at the time of death.

"I've got some thoughts about that," said Dr. Baden. "But get me some more information first, if you can."

All three of us were now excited about the possibility, remote though it was, of making some fresh discovery about Shakespeare.

The next morning I scrambled out of bed at five o'clock. I began a fierce assault on the half a dozen books about Shakespeare in my apartment library. I tried to conduct my research with the punctilious care of a pathologist. I learned that Shakespeare's brother-in-law, William Hart, had been buried on April 15, 1616, only eight days before Shakespeare died, on April 23. Was there a connection? Possibly Shakespeare had contracted a communicable disease on a bedside visit to his sister's husband. Stratford was at one time notorious for its unhealthful environs. Also, I found out that Shakespeare was entombed two days after his death, instead of the usual three. Had his son-in-law and physician, Dr. John Hall, known or suspected something? Then there was a reference to Shakespeare's being buried in a wooden coffin "seventeen feet deep." I discounted this as probably false, likely a tale concocted to discourage any future sexton from moving the poet's bones into the church's charnel house.

As I struggled to find a cord that would bind the fragmentary data I was picking up, an awareness gradually seeped into my phlegmatic wits that I was trying to do the same thing that had been attempted thousands of times by other researchers. Still, Dr. Michael Baden's penetrating mind encouraged me to think that perhaps I could uncover enough information to help him.

I struggled to open up some new line of thought, however tenuous, despite the meager data. I turned to my copy of Schoenbaum's *William Shakespeare: a Documentary Life* and

[2] The "bone house" of the Stratford church, about 1790. This Gothic burial chamber (pulled down about 1835) was located only a few steps from Shakespeare's grave. One early observer said it contained the "greatest assemblage of human bones I ever saw."

began to study the photographs of Shakespeare's will. Here, if anywhere, I might find an overlooked clue. I'd read the will dozens of times, but now I was involved in an earnest quest. I examined with great care the third signature on the will: "By me William Shakspeare." For a few minutes I felt encouraged and then the hopelessness of it all began to grow on me. I got more and more depressed. Here I was, in my seventieth year, and after more than half a century of determined effort to find a document of Shakespeare's I had come up with nothing. I would have settled for a punctuation mark in the poet's hand! As I sat, chin in hand, resigning myself to another failure, my gaze meandered over the two facing pages of the will open before me. I glanced listlessly from Shakespeare's famous "By me" signature in the middle of page three to the leaf opposite, the second page of the will . . . and suddenly I was in the magic land of Serendip. *I perceived that the interlinear notes on page two were in the same handwriting as "By me William Shakspeare."*

A chill shot up my spine and lifted the hair on the back of my neck. Fortune had thrust into my hand a key that was sure to unlock many doors of Shakespeare's life. I leaped from my seat and shouted: "I did it, Will! By God, I did it!"

After a minute or two of exultation I simmered down and returned to the photographs of the will in Schoenbaum's book. First, I turned the text upside down and compared the "feel," or general configuration, of the signature with the interlinear script *(illus. 3)*. The feel was identical. I was now positive that my initial, split-second identification was correct. I then examined the formation of words and letters. The stroke pattern was the same. Oddly, I did not immediately recognize that the entire will was in the poet's hand. It was an hour before I discovered this important fact. Then, for the first time, I understood why the poet had written "By me" in front of his signature at the end of the will: the will was holographic.

In the course of my career I had occasionally run across financial documents of the seventeenth century in which the words "By me" preceded the signature, and I had always supposed that it was merely a pleasant, if redundant, way for the signer to attest his signature. But nobody, and especially a dying man, as Shakespeare was when he signed his will, writes two words without a reason—and these two words do not occur on the other three documents known to have been signed by Shakespeare, simply because they were not in the poet's handwriting. He added only his signature to them. I have since checked every example of handwriting I could locate in which "By me" was used, and in all cases the document was entirely in the hand of the signer. To my chagrin I realized I might have arrived at this discovery some forty years earlier, when I first wondered why Shakespeare's signature bearing the preliminary "By me" was at the end of his will.

The next day I compared the script in the holographic will with the manuscript reproductions of "Writer D" in *The [Prompt] Booke of Sir Thomas Moore* (the spelling of *Moore* is usually corrected to *More*). Most scholars now believe that Writer D was Shakespeare. Although more than two decades separated the handwriting examples, the script in the will (1616) and in the three pages by Writer D (probably about 1592 or 1593) almost exactly agreed, and I concluded that the same person had written both.

With these two examples of Shakespeare's handwriting as guides, I was able during the next nine weeks to uncover more documents in Shakespeare's script.

How do we know that these additional documents are in the poet's hand?

A manuscript expert can usually determine genuineness with almost scientific exactitude. The margin for error is just about zero. Sometimes even a glance is enough for him to take in the feel of a script and render an unqualified judgment.

The feel of handwriting is nothing more than the instantaneous impression it creates upon a practiced eye. Far from being an amorphous test of authenticity, feel is actually the sum total of the viewer's knowledge, the fusion of intuition and an immense amount of experience. After the manuscript expert has made a feel judgment, his split-second impression can be crystallized by a detailed examination of the script.

The manuscript expert nearly always comes to a definite conclusion. It would be improper for him to say "I think" or "I believe" or "in my opinion," implying a degree of uncertainty when there is none. To make qualifying remarks when one is certain is unprofessional and intrudes a discordant note of false modesty into the world of science. Does a ballistics expert say "I *think* these two bullets were fired from the same gun" after he examines their striations and finds them to be identical? No. He says, without equivo-

[3] The "feel" of Shakespeare's handwriting. To get the feel, or overall impression [a], of the interlinear words in Shakespeare's will that first caught my eye and convinced me that the writing was in the poet's hand, study the signature [b] for a moment, then look at the seven words above it: "my will & towardes the p[er]formans thereof." These words, from the dying Shakespeare's interlinear writing near the center of page 2 of the will, have the same tortured, palsied character as the signature. Despite the fact that the poet wrote *By me* and his name in a slightly larger script and spaced the words farther apart (he had ample room to do so at the end of the will), there is a startling consanguinity between the signature and the scrawled interlinear lines.

Compare the *kspeare* of Shakespeare's surname with *thereof* directly above it. The feel is so similar that at a glance you might take them for the same word. Notice that the letters rise in an uncertain crescendo. The pen-stroke pattern, pen pressure, and slant of the writing are identical. The undisciplined script is almost indecipherable, suggesting that the quill has seized control of the penman. Compare the *y* in *By me* with the *y* in *my*, directly above it: In the interlinear *y* the lower stroke is slightly cramped (the poet had very little room to write between lines). Compare the *m* in *William* with the *m* in *p[er]formans*, and the *a* in *William* and *Shakspeare* with the *a* in *towardes*. Compare the second *l* in *William* with the second *l* in *will*: Both are stubby and the nib of the writer's quill makes an identical spread at the base.

cation, "These two bullets were fired from the same gun." Thus, when handwriting is obviously from the same penman, and a scrutiny of two examples reveals the fact that they were written by the same person, the fact can and should be so stated—without equivocation or qualification.

Occasionally in this volume I will use the word *feel* in connection with handwriting. Feel is the key factor in comparing scripts or in judging authenticity. The occasional examiner of questioned handwriting may be impervious to feel. He may study laboriously the formation of individual letters in a document. He may, if he has had some experience, notice how "key" words—words that seldom vary in a person's script—such as *and* (or the ampersand), *the, of, in, by, with, for, to, from* and similar common words are formed. He will observe the capital letters to see if they conform with other, known-to-be-authentic examples. This method of comparing scripts to determine authenticity is, in my opinion, a rather oblique way to approach a suspect document. Many people constantly vary the formation of their words (Shakespeare was one who did), so that such a comparison, without considering the preliminary feel, might be very misleading. In the case of forgery, a skilled fabricator may imitate individual letters and words so perfectly that only an expert with years of experience can detect his fakery. But feel, on the other hand, is a subtle, telltale clue that mocks the most adroit forger.

Some of the factors that contribute to the feel of a manuscript are: the amount of space between words and between lines; the size of the script; the ease, or lack of ease, with which the script flows; the pressure of the pen in forming strokes, especially descending strokes; the length of the descending strokes, as in *y*'s and *g*'s; the overall legibility of the script; the position of the dots over the *i*'s and the crossbars of the *t*'s; the thickness of the pen strokes; and the haste, or lack of haste, with which the words and letters have been formed.

You can often take in the feel of documents very quickly by examining or comparing them upside down. Whenever I have any initial doubts about the authenticity of a manuscript, or wish to compare it with another example of handwriting, I upend the papers so that the words become obscured and only the feel is perceptible.

Once a manuscript passes the feel test, a thorough examination of individual words and letters is in order. For this type of examination I have prepared charts so that you can easily make comparisons between key words in the various documents written by Shakespeare.

Throughout this book I may from time to time question the dogmas of modern scholarship. Whenever I set myself at odds with established opinion, I shall assemble all the available, fresh evidence and state the case for the old beliefs as well. Readers with a literary-detective bent can examine and weigh the facts, new and old, consider all the possible implications and hypotheses, review my conclusions, and then make their own decision.

II

THE POET'S SWEET-FLOWING SCRIPT

FOR any Elizabethan bard who wished to dig the rowels into the flanks of his Pegasus and put the beast to a mad gallop, the Elizabethan "secretary," or "running," hand was a perfect style of penmanship. It could pile words on foolscap with swiftness and ease. It was a natural partner to abbreviation. And there was beauty in its sweeping curves.

The secretary hand was a favorite with authors. Marlowe used it. So did Bacon. Shakespeare could apparently write this sweet-flowing script with speed, pausing only for a second now and then to cross out an inexact word or false start. This appears evident from the three surviving pages from an old play that he collaborated on. Had Shakespeare been a more deliberate writer, the italic script, that voluptuous expression of beauty in ink, would better have suited his genius. But it is my belief that Shakespeare never stayed his quill when the fine frenzy was upon him. I doubt if he even paused to dine or drink.

Before venturing into Shakespeare's variant handwriting as it appears in his holographic will and many other papers, I should first like to say a few words about the secretary, or running-hand, style that Shakespeare found so compatible. For readers unfamiliar with the secretary hand, illustrations 4, 5 and 6 will "learn you," as our friend from Stratford would say, to read it with some success. Still, Shakespeare lived in the glorious days when whim and caprice were the guides to spelling and penmanship. There were some Elizabethan scribblers whose handwriting is so execrable that to decipher it calls for infinite patience and more than a tithe of imagination. Happily, Shakespeare was not often an inkpot maniac.

The secretary alphabet taught in the grammar schools or by tutors provided a lot of leeway. A writer could pick his own style for each letter. The earliest book on penman-

[4] Secretary and court hands from the 1891 edition of Thomas Wright's *Court Hand Restored.*

[5] Secretary, or running, hand from Thomas Astle's *The Origin and Progress of Handwriting* (1784). Note the contractions, which could create problems if not precisely understood.

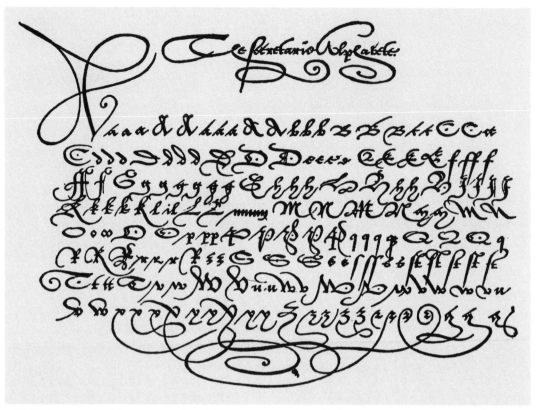

[6] This example of the secretary hand is contained in a penmanship book by John de Beau Chesne and John Baildon published in 1571, when Shakespeare was 7—and is possibly the very alphabet he used to practice from as a student in the Stratford Grammar School.

ship in English was *A Booke Containing Divers Sortes of Hands* (London, 1570), by John de Beau Chesne and John Baildon. It was illustrated with thirty-seven styles of handwriting, including the bastard secretary, the small bastard secretary, the secretary, the small secretary and even the secretary written with the left hand for mirror reading (a favorite device of Leonardo da Vinci's).

Most writers of the Elizabethan era improvised from the somewhat bewildering array of shapes and sizes and developed their own script, and their idiosyncrasies enable us to recognize their handwriting. Some devised a hand that combined the best, or worst, features of the italic and secretary alphabets. Ben Jonson created an eclectic script that is beautiful and legible.

Occasionally, two secretary scripts may look somewhat alike, but there are always distinguishing features that can be discovered by a cock of the head or squint of the eye. Shakespeare's chirography—when on "good behavior"—is pretty close to the copybook style. Maybe, as tradition has it, the poet was at one time a schoolteacher and never got very far away from the hornbook.

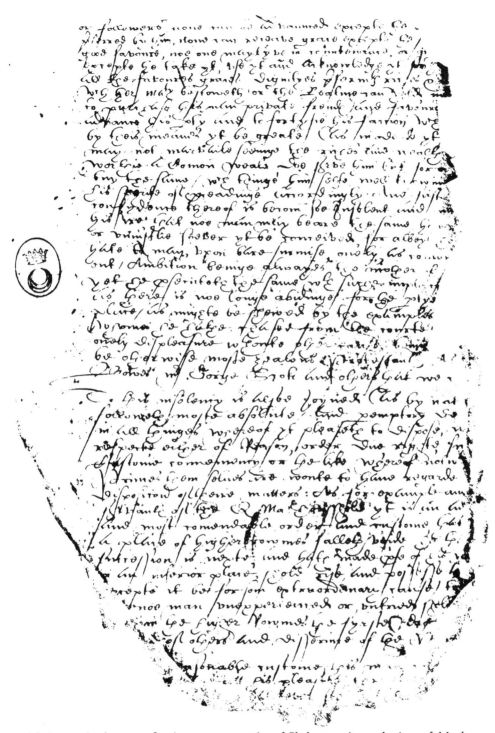

[7] A page in the sweet-flowing secretary script of Shakespeare's youth. A careful look shows it to be quite different from the variant handwritings of other celebrated Elizabethans. This page is folio 65 from *Leicester's Commonwealth* in the *Northumberland Manuscript,* copied out by the poet sometime between 1592 and 1594. (A transcript of this page will be found in Chapter 14.)

[8] Stratford Grammar School and the Guild Hall (about 1860).
Shakespeare may have been a student here until he was about 15.

Rather than intrude upon you a technical discussion of the secretary hand that might run to forty or fifty pages, let me refer you for fastidious details to Dr. Samuel A. Tannenbaum's *The Handwriting of the Renaissance* (1930). Dr. Tannenbaum's book is a superb exposition of the type of handwriting used by Shakespeare. I recommend highly, also, *Elizabethan Handwriting, 1500–1650* (1966) by Giles E. Dawson and Laetitia Kennedy-Skipton, a valuable manual with interesting introductory chapters and many excellent illustrations accompanied by transcriptions. Of great interest and value is Walter W. Greg's classic three-volume work, *English Literary Autographs* (1932), crammed with examples of early English handwriting, all with full transcriptions. For those who wish only to lean on my shoulder, there are more details on the secretary hand in chapters XV, "Notes on Shakespeare's Penmanship," and XVII, "Glossary of Shakespeare's Words."

For the handwriting illustrated in this chapter I have provided no transcriptions. The variant scripts are furnished only so you can examine the multitude of hands used in Shakespeare's day and thus perceive that the poet's handwriting is very distinctive and not easily confused with anyone else's script. This book is concerned, of course, only with the penmanship of Shakespeare and what we can learn from the surviving documents in his hand about his life and literary work.

Please look at the chart from the schoolbook dated 1571. You may be examining a reproduction of the very page studied by William Shakespeare when he was a boy in Stratford. The poet's handwriting is similar to that depicted in this and the other charts.

Examine the chirography of Shakespeare's contemporaries *(illus. 10 through 57)*. If you care to look over the scripts that illustrate variations of the same person's penmanship, you may be amazed at how greatly a writer's handwriting can change. Queen Elizabeth, for example, could use with delicacy and skill the beautiful italic hand she learned from her toxophilitic tutor, Roger Ascham; but a hastily penned, informal letter from her quill reveals far more of the gusto and enthusiasm that made her one of the world's great sovereigns. For an illustrated discussion of the volatile script of Sir Francis Bacon, see Chapter XIV, "Ghostwriter for Francis Bacon."

The mutable pattern frequently occurs in Shakespeare's writing. He has a beautiful, stately script for important occasions; a sweeping, rolling penmanship for his poetic compositions; and a dynamic, swift, devil-may-care hand for everyday scrawls.

A brief perusal of the handwriting examples that follow—all are by the poet's English contemporaries—will help you to recognize and understand Shakespeare's script.

[9] A Stratford Grammar School room (about 1860), where Shakespeare may have studied the secretary hand.

[10] Ben Jonson's dedicatory epistle shows his formal writing style, an elaborate, graceful fusion of the secretary and italic scripts. Jonson (1573?–1637), poet, dramatist and actor, was a close friend of Shakespeare's and an associate of Francis Bacon's.

[11] Ben Jonson's less elaborate hand, used for informal writing.

I have sent you herewith a petition
I deliuered vnto mee in the behalf of cer=
tayne poore men dwellinge att Gosport
who have been hardly vsed by Winter,
who vnder collor of beeinge Captayne
of the Kinges pinnace hath comitted many
insolencies, as also a noate of divers other
his misdeamenors wth the neglect of his
duty & charge, all wch & much more
(as I am enformed) will bee proued
against him, if it will please my lo:
priuy Seale to appointe some to examen
the parties that complayne, & some other
dwellinge theraboutes, who will bee redy
to iustify these thinges & more, but
they beinge poore men would bee vtterly
vndoone if they should goe to London to
bee examined, wherfore my lo: weare
best to appoint suh: who hee shall thinke
fitt to take their examinations heere in
the contry. My lo: Shandos hath gaylsd
for I heaue no newes of him & am therfore
vncertayne of my cominge into the contry,
but if I come, you shall heare from mee
otherwise I hope wee shall meete att your
returne till when wishinge you good sport
I rest
                    your assured frend
                    H SOUTHAMPTON

the 1- of Octob.

[12] Henry Wriothesley's legible script marks a transition from modified secretary hand to the modern form of writing. Wriothesley (1573–1624) was Earl of Southampton, Shakespeare's patron and probable lover, to whom the poet dedicated *Venus and Adonis* (1593) and *Lucrece* (1594). Southampton was also an intimate friend of Robert Devereux, second Earl of Essex, Bacon's patron. After the unsuccessful Essex Rebellion, in which Southampton took part, Essex was executed and Southampton condemned to die. He was ultimately pardoned and freed from prison by James I. A man of courage, taste and integrity, Southampton contributed lavishly to the arts, especially poetry.

[13] John Donne (1573–1631), metaphysical poet. A note to Sir Robert Cotton in Donne's clear, legible script.

[14] John Lyly (1554?–1606), author of *Euphues* (1579), a romance written in affected, overblown style. In this last page of a letter to Lord Burghley, Lyly's script is crabbed and spastic.

[15] Christopher Marlowe (1564–1593), poet and dramatist; friend and literary rival of Shakespeare's. Until recently, not a single pen scratch in Marlowe's hand was known. His signature (Christofer Marley), third from the top, is as witness to a will in 1583. (Kent County Archives.)

[16]

[17]

[16] William Cecil, Lord Burghley (1520–1598), statesman, adviser to Elizabeth I. His busy script pushes words together in an economy of paper that makes his writing a little hard to read.

[17] Anne Clifford, Countess of Pembroke (1590–1676), was educated by the poet Samuel Daniel and keenly interested in architecture and the arts. Conclusion of the letter is in later italic script.

[18]

[18] Edmund Spenser (1552–1599), poet who wrote *The Faerie Queene* (1590), in my opinion penned this document—granting custody of a house and grounds about 1589—as well as the signature, "Ed: Sp(en)ser."

[19] Spenser authenticated this clerical document at lower left as a *Copia Vera* ("true copy").

[20] Celebrated sonnet believed by some to be in Spenser's hand. It was uncovered by A. S. W. Rosenbach, bibliophile and manuscript dealer. In his *Books and Bidders* he writes that a distinguished scholar "placed in my hands a volume in its original binding of old calf . . . Spenser's own copy of *The Faerie Queene*, dated 1590, with an inscription on the title page in Greek: 'From the author to himself.' He had also presented this volume to Elizabeth Boyle, whom he married four years later. On a blank page toward the back of the book he gallantly wrote in French, 'A sa mistresse,' and under this elegant heading had inscribed the complete first sonnet from his glorious *Amoretti*. . . .'" The sonnet appears as a grotesque patchwork of Elizabethan and modern scripts. The first two lines have a totally different feel from the rest of the writing and the whole poem has a forced, awkward look that instantly suggests a fabrication. The use of the open thorn to make the words *the* and *that* in an inscription of this type is gratuitous and bizarre. Script has none of the virility of the 1589 house grant document accepted as holographic of Spenser by me and other authorities.

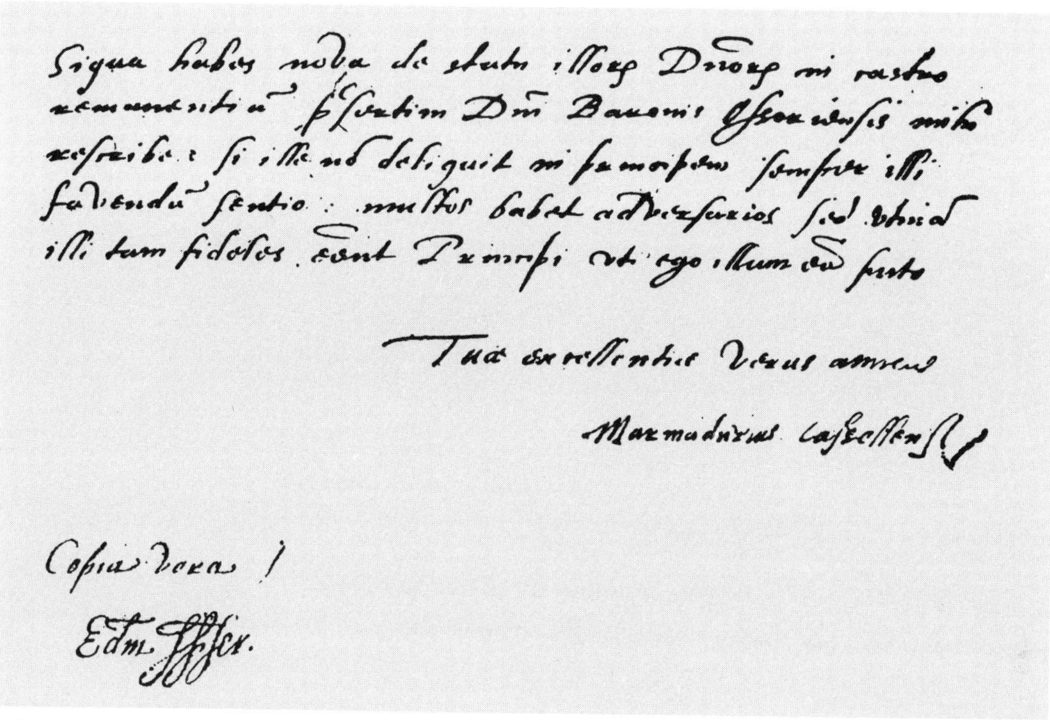

Siqua habes noua de statu illorum Dominorum in nostro commemoratione praesertim Domini Baronis Chesterdensis mihi rescribe: si ille non deliquit in Principem semper illi faciendum sentio: multos habet adversarios sed vidi illi tam fideles erga Principem ut ego illum esse puto

Tuae excellentiae verus amicus

Marmaducus Castellensis

Copia vera!

Edm. Ussher.

[19]

[20]

A sa mistresse

Happy ye leaves whenas those lilly hands
That holds my life in her deadly might
Shall handle you and hold in loves sweet bands
Like captives trembling at the victors sight.
Happy ye lines wherein with starry light
Those lamping eyes shall deigne on you to looke
And reade the sorrowes of my dying spright
written with teares in harts close bleeding booke.
Happy ye rymes bathed in the sacred brooke
of Helicon whence she derived is
when ye shall behold that angells looke
my soules long lacked foode my heavens blisse
Leaves, lines and rymes seeke her to please alone
whome if ye please I care for other none!

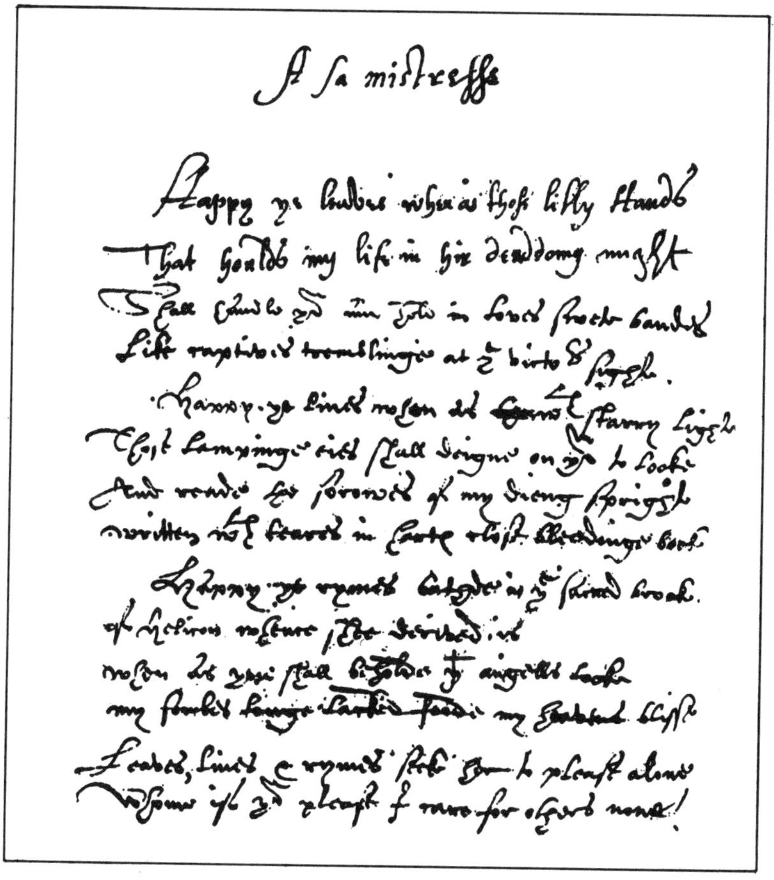

1ᵗ August · 1599

[facsimile of handwritten receipt in secretary hand]

Thomas Dekker.

[21] Receipt for twenty shillings, from dramatist Thomas Dekker (1572?–1632) to Philip Henslowe (theater manager and producer), penned in a secretary script that bears a slight similarity to Shakespeare's.

[22] Philip Massinger (1583–1640), dramatist. Dedicatory poem to Sir Francis Feljambe, written in handsome, legible secretary hand and accompanied by a variant signature.

Philip Massinger

Philip massinger

[23] George Chapman (1559–1634), poet, dramatist and Ben Jonson collaborator whose translation of Homer inspired Keats's famous sonnet. Handwritten receipt—for forty shillings received from Philip Henslowe in 1599—is excellent example of secretary script.

[24] Josuah Sylvester (1563–1618), poet and translator. Handwritten letter signed in italic.

My a very good friend, mr Camden

Coventry . 25 . August . 1609

Ph . Holland

[25] Philemon Holland (1552–1637), Translator General. Shakespeare used his translations of Pliny's *Natural History* and Livy.

[26] Sir Francis Drake (1540?–1596), navigator and privateer, circumnavigated the globe in the *Golden Hind* (1577–1580). Conclusion of handwritten letter (example of bad scrawl) signed in secretary script.

[27] Sir Walter Raleigh—or Ralegh, his own spelling—born about 1552. Career as explorer led him into what are now Florida and Virginia. While a prisoner in Tower of London, for treason, he wrote *History of the World* (1614). His secretary hand is loose, disjointed, somewhat difficult to decipher.

[28] John Dee (1527–1608), mathematician, astrologer, chronic delver into crystal gazing and magic. Tried on charge of practicing sorcery against Mary I and acquitted (1555). In beautiful copybook italic hand, Dee here congratulates Elizabeth I on defeat of the Spanish Armada (1588).

§ Most Gratious Soueraine Lady, The God of Heauen and earth, (Who hath mightilie, and euidently, giuen vnto your most excellent Royall Maiestie, this wunderfull Triumphant victorie,) be allwaies, thanked, praysed, and glorified: A Dm: 1588: § John Dee

[29] Thomas Sackville, first Earl of Dorset and Baron Buckhurst (1536–1608), poet, diplomat and, with Thomas Norton, author of the earliest English tragedy, *Gorboduc* (1561). This note is in the legible style of script that preceded the secretary hand in popular usage.

[30] Sir John Harington (Haryngton) (1561–1612), satirist, banished from court for *The Metamorphosis of Ajax* (1596). The word ajax is a pun on the vulgar Elizabethan word for privy, jack or jacks (today, john). A handwritten note to Lady Russell, accompanied by a variant signature. Like Shakespeare, Bacon, Jonson and other Elizabethans, Harington used several styles of script.

My Lorde I haue a requeste to make vnto your grace wiche feare has made me
omitte til this time for two causes, the one bicause I sawe that my request for the
rumors wiche were sprede abrode of me toke so litel place wiche thinge whan
I considered I thoughty shulde litel profit in any other sute, howbeit now I
vnderstande that ther is a proclamacion for them (for the wiche I giue your
grace and the rest of the counsel most humble thankes) I am the bolder
to speake for a nother thinge. And the other was bicause parauenture
your Lordeship, and the rest of the counsel wil thinke that I fauor her wel
doinge for whome I shal speake for, Wiche is for Kateryn Aschiley, that it
wolde please your grace and the rest of the counsel to be good vnto her
wiche thinge I do not to fauor her in any iuel (for that I wolde be sorye to
do) but for thes consideracions wiche folowe the wiche hope dothe teache
me in same that I ougth not to doute but that your grace and the rest of
the counsel wil thinke that I do it for thre other consideracions, first bi=
cause that she hathe bene with me a longe time, and manye years, ann
hathe taken great labor, and paine in brinkinge of me vp in lerninge and
honestie, and therfore I ougth of very dewtye speke for her, for Saint
Gregorie sayeth that we ar more bounde to them that bringeth us up wel
than to our parents, for our parents do that wiche is natural for them, that
is bringeth us into this worlde but our brinkers up ar a cause to make us
liue wel in it. The seconde is bicause I thinke that whatsoeuer she hathe
done in my Lorde Admirals matter as concerninge the marynge of me
she dide it bicause knowinge him to be one of the counsel she thooth he
wolde not go aboute any suche thinge without he had the counsels con=
sent therunto, for I haue harde her manye times say that she wolde ne=
uer in any place without your Graces and the counsels consente.
The thirde cause is bicause that it shal and doth make men thinke that
I am not clere of the dide myselfe, but that it is pardoned in me bicause
of my youthe, bicause that she I loued so wel is in suche a place. Thus
hope preuailinge more with me than feare hathe wone the battel, and
I haue at this time gone furth with it. Wiche I pray God be taken
no other wais that it is mente, Writen in hast. Frome Hatfilde
this 7 day of Marche. Also if I may be so bolde not offendinge I beseche
your grace and the rest of the counsel to be good to master Aschiley her husbode.
Wiche bicause he is my kindesman I wold be glad he shulde do wel.

Your assured frende to my litel
power. Elizabeth

[31] Early letter in the elegant italic script taught to Elizabeth I (1533–1603)
by her tutor and, later, secretary, Roger Ascham.

[32] Letter in French penned by
Elizabeth I in early English hand that
predated wide use of the secretary script.

[33] Conclusion of a letter in italic hand
of Elizabeth's youth.

[34] Conclusion of Elizabeth I letter in
the fluent English penmanship used in
most of the queen's correspondence. It
combines the italic and secretary scripts.

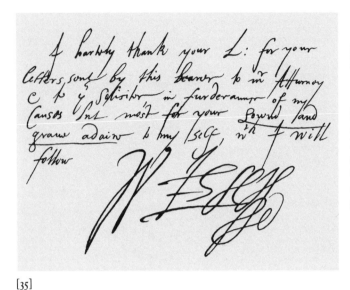

[35] Note written and signed by Walter Devereux, first Earl of Essex (1541?–1576)

[36] Signature of Robert Devereux, second Earl of Essex (1566–1601), favorite and lover of Elizabeth I, and Francis Bacon's patron. After an abortive rebellion against the queen, Essex was tried by the queen's counsel, Francis Bacon (who owed his position and success to Essex), found guilty of treason and beheaded.

[35]

[36]

[37]

[37] Beautifully penned epistle in italic, possibly to Elizabeth I, by James I (formerly James VI of Scotland). A pious believer in witchcraft, about which he wrote a pamphlet, and staunch friend of the arts, James was benefactor of Shakespeare and his acting group.

[38] Elizabeth I, from a rare crayon sketch by F. Zuccero, an Italian artist who visited London in

1575. Elizabeth sponsored Shakespeare and his acting group, the Lord Chamberlain's Men (later the King's Men). Her cordiality toward Shakespeare cooled after his patron, the Earl of Southampton, joined Essex in his rebellion against the queen. On the eve of the rebellion, Shakespeare and his company performed *Richard II*, a play abhorred by Elizabeth because of its suggestion of treason.

[38]

[39] James I, in a rare, early portrait. Friend and
sponsor of Shakespeare, the astute monarch
appreciated and encouraged literary excellence
and was himself an author of some distinction.
Sir John Harington reported that in a brief
conversation he had with the sovereign, he was
impressed with James's knowledge of the classics
and his probing intellect. When Shakespeare was
at court, he and the king most likely had many
stimulating conversations.

[40] Note written by James I in a variant script.
In the old Roman fashion, the words are locked
together with virtually no lacunae; the weaviness
of the lines is the result of James's intense
concentration on the formation of the individual
letters, rather than on the entire word. These
two factors constitute a part of the feel of the
script, an extremely important consideration in
judging authenticity—and often the explanation
for an expert's being able to make an
instantaneous verification. If the feel is wrong—
nearly always the case in a forgery—the
document is a fake. It is relatively easy for a
forger to imitate the size and shape of letters and
words; to capture the feel is extremely difficult,
almost impossible.

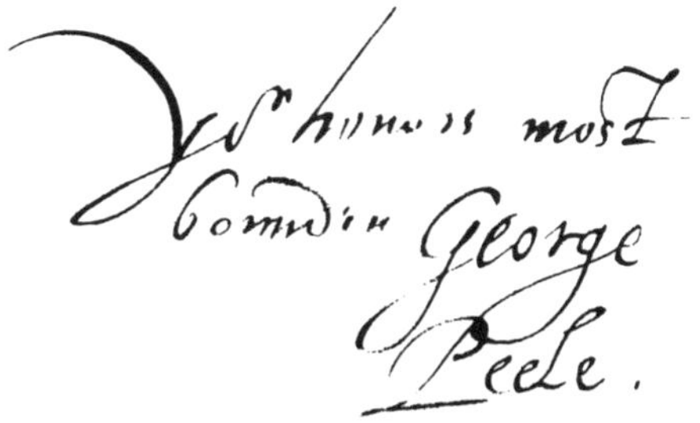

[image of George Peele's signature]

[41] George Peele (1558?–1597), poet, dramatist, actor, probably a friend of Shakespeare's. Conclusion of a letter indited in a delicate, almost effeminate script.

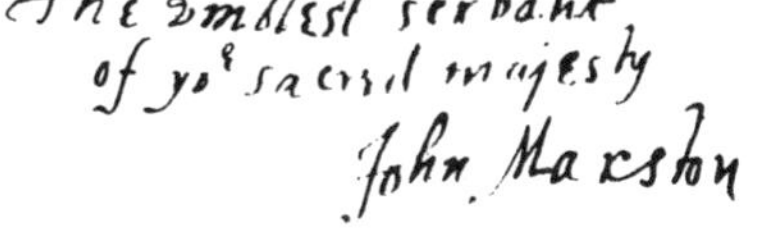

[image of John Marston's signature]

[42] John Marston (1575?–1634), satiric dramatist. Marston quarreled with Ben Jonson, later collaborated with him. Likely knew Shakespeare. Conclusion of a letter in punctilious italic hand.

[43] Sir Francis Walsingham (153?–1590), statesman, Elizabeth's secretary of state, developer of elaborate espionage system. The poet Marlowe may have been a spy for Walsingham and quite possibly was murdered at Walsingham's orders because he "knew too much." Conclusion of a letter in a secretary script, with Walsingham's characteristically flamboyant signature.

[44] Sir Thomas Chaloner (1521–1565), diplomat, poet. This fine italic hand is not characteristic of Sir Thomas's hard-to-read script. (Fifty years ago, as an impecunious college freshman, I saved for over a month in order to buy a lengthy holographic document of Sir Thomas Chaloner from an autograph dealer—for one dollar. The eight-page document was a report on Chaloner's expenses as British ambassador to Spain. After several weeks of hard work, I was able to decipher every word and every amount in the poorly penned but much treasured document.)

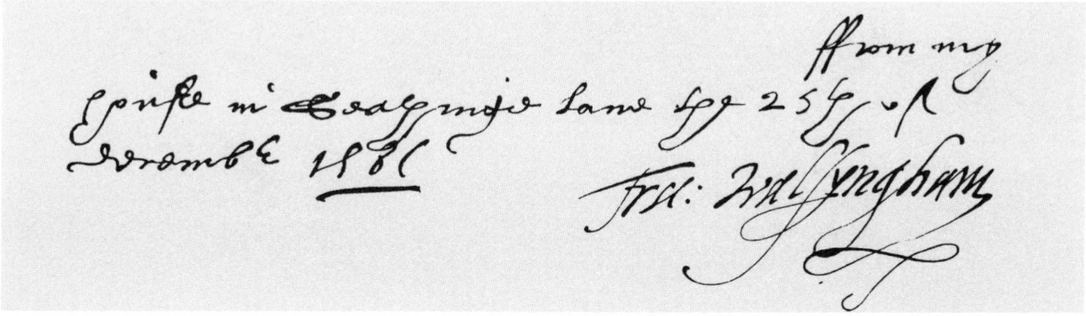

[43]

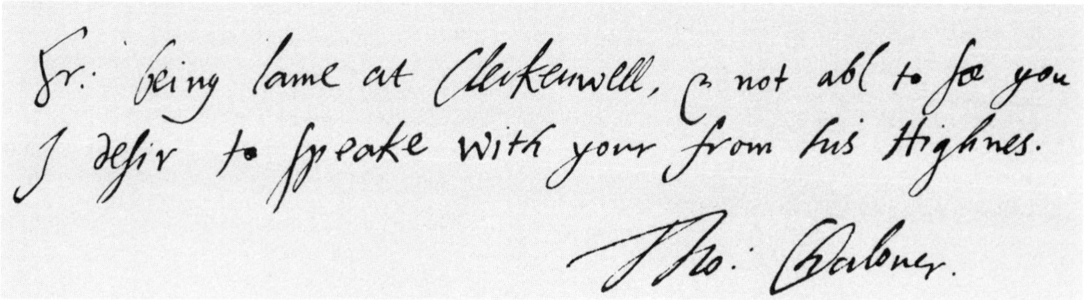

[44]

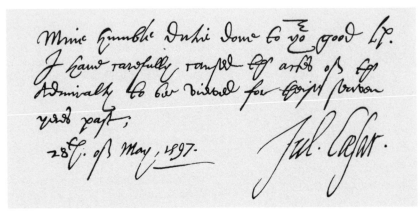

[45] Letter by an English judge, Sir Julius Caesar (1558–1636), is in secretary script.

[46] Sir Fulke Greville, Lord Brooke (1554–1628), poet, dramatist, statesman, close friend of Sir Philip Sidney's. Conclusion of a letter written in secretary script. The identification "F. Brooke" is in another hand.

[47] Sir Philip Sidney (1554–1586), poet, courtier, soldier, famed for his sonnets and pastoral romance, *Arcadia* (1581). Sidney was mortally wounded in battle. This letter was written in a beautiful, swift-moving italic hand.

[48] Sidney note, in Latin, is painstakingly indited in fastidious italic.

[49] Sidney letter, in French, is rather sloppy italic, apparently penned in haste. Compare with the more meticulous penmanship of his letter to "Right honorable my very good Lorde."

Righte honorable my very good Lorde. J am bolde to troble your L. withe these few wordes. humbly to crave yowr Lps favour so furr unto me, as that it will please yow to lett me undrestande, whether J may with yowr Lps. leave, and that J may not offende in wante of my service, remaine absente frome the cowrte this Christmas tyme.
Frome wilton this 16th of December 1577

[47]
            Philippe Sidney.

            Joh. Wier S.
Mi Wier vere vere. Valde te
cupio, de vita periclitor. aut vivus,
aut mortuus non ero ingratus.
sed festinus oro. Plura non possum.
        Tuus
[48]   *Ph. Sidney.*

Monsieur. J'ay receu vos lettres
Et vous remercie infiniement pour
m'avoir este liberall, de vostre
coignoissance et amitie.
[49]   *Ph. Sidnei*

[50] William Lambarde (1536–1601), lawyer and antiquary. Note, penned in italic, is to his friend, historian William Camden, who supported Shakespeare's application for a coat of arms.

[51] Alexander Nowell (1507–1594), divine and educator who endowed thirteen scholarships at Oxford. Penmanship here is a strange union of the secretary and italic hands.

[52] Henry Howard, Earl of Northampton (1539?–1614), scholar known as the "most noble among the learned." His writing is a lazy, indifferent derivative of the italic script.

My noble continuall travayle my lo: is in
finishing the worke of the treasures of Englande
who I have brought unto Henry ye fourth, and
hoope to finishe before Easter next, till which
I only made of yr Lo yt some staye maye be made
of bestowinge those offices till I have fynished
yt booke

December 1593.

Francis Thynne

[53] Francis Thynne (d. 1611), Lancaster herald in the College of Heralds from
1602 until his death. Script combines the secretary and italic hands; signature is
orgiastic.

[54] Charles Blount, Earl of Mountjoy (d. 1606), soldier and scholar. The neat
script of this letter recalls the handwriting of the age of Henry VIII.

If I with all that I have may stopp
the gullfe off theas wars, by throwinge
my selfe to bec swallowed upp therin, I
shall dye a happye and a contented
Curtius,

June 1600

Mountjoy

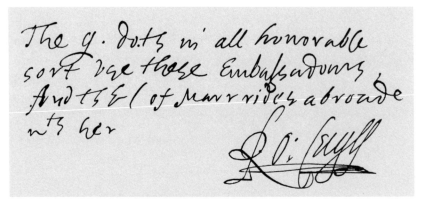

[55] Robert Cecil, Earl of Salisbury (1563?–1612), statesman who aided James I to secure the English throne. Note written in flaccid script; antecedents are indefinite.

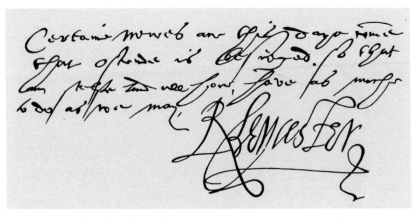

[56] Robert Dudley, Earl of Leicester (1532?–1588), courtier and favorite of Elizabeth I. Handwriting is in secretary script.

[57] Conclusion of a holographic letter by Scottish poet George Buchanan (1506–1582) that fuses secretary and italic hands.

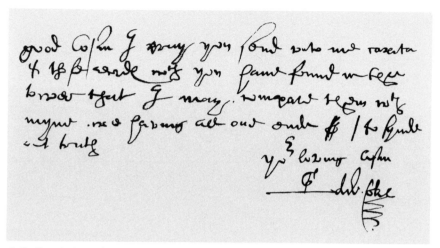

[58] Conclusion of a letter in secretary script by Sir Edward Coke (1552–1634), first chief justice of England, author of *Institutes*.

[59] Signature on the address leaf of a letter to Sir Francis Walsingham from Lancelot Andrewes (1555–1626), prelate, scholar, important contributor to the King James version of the Bible.

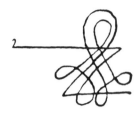

III

THE SIX SIGNATURES
OF SHAKESPEARE

ONLY six known signatures of Shakespeare and every one of them different! Because of the enormous variation in these famous signatures of the poet—it's a challenge to find in them two similar letters of the alphabet—scholars have been unable for nearly three centuries to discover what his real handwriting was like. Some biographers even claimed Shakespeare never learned to hold a quill or write his name properly.

In *The Shakspere Coat-of-Arms* (1908), the distinguished expert on Elizabethan bibliography Samuel A. Tannenbaum reflected the quiet desperation of scholars when he wrote: "Earnest investigators have applied themselves with matchless zeal to the task of unearthing some bit of evidence [about Shakespeare and his handwriting]. Cellars, garrets, storehouses and official records in the most out of the way places have been searched. But all more or less in vain. To the professed Shakspearean nothing is more amazing than the peculiar fatality which has attended almost everything in any way connected with the history of William Shakspere."

There are many examples of Shakespeare's handwriting illustrated in this book, but this chapter is concerned only with the six previously known signatures *(illus. 60)* and their influence on Shakespearean scholarship. The most important of the six signatures are the three affixed to the poet's last will and testament. The will is dated March 25, 1616, but was probably signed around the middle of April, perhaps as late as the day of Shakespeare's death, April 23, 1616. The will was preserved (and *preserved* is not the word I am tempted to use!) in the Prerogative Office at the Doctor's Commons in London for nearly two hundred and fifty years after it was probated on June 22, 1616. In 1747 the Reverend Joseph Greene of Stratford-upon-Avon discovered the document. By the middle of the eighteenth century scholars and admirers of the poet were at work scrutinizing and fondling it. Most documents of 1616 vintage, a fairly modern date as manuscripts go, are in excellent condition. The pure rag paper of the seventeenth century, if not tampered with or abused, wears like sheet metal. And parchment is virtually indestructible. Thousands of Elizabethan indentures, deeds, and wills have passed through my hands in the past forty years and I am always amazed at their excellent state of preservation. Not so with Shakespeare's will, one of the most precious documents in

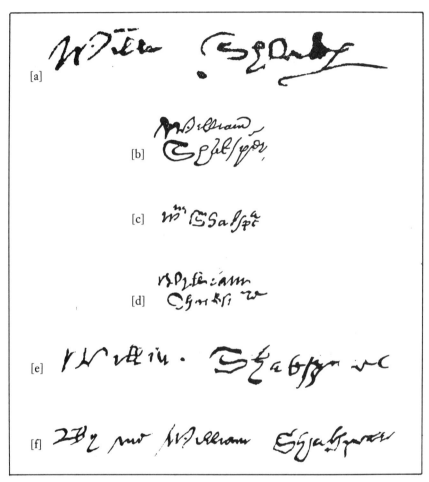

[60] The Six Signatures of Shakespeare. Letters represented by symbols are in italics.

[a] Willia m Shackper. On Belott-Mountjoy deposition, June 19, 1612. (Public Records Office, London)

[b] William Shakspear. On a conveyance for a gatehouse in Blackfriars, London, March 10, 1612/13. (The Guildhall, City of London Library)

[c] Wm Shakspea. On a mortgage to the Blackfriars gatehouse, March 11, 1612/13. (British Museum Library)

[d] William Shackspere. On Shakespeare's will, page 1. (British Museum Library)

[e] Willm. Shakspere. On Shakespeare's will, page 2. (British Museum Library)

[f] By me William Shakspeare. On Shakespeare's will, page 3. (British Museum Library)

[61] The "improved" signatures of Shakespeare. What Shakespeare's six signatures looked like originally—with every minuscule stroke of his goose quill—we will never know, because the documents are now faded or damaged. To give an idea of the monkey business in the Shakespeare world, I've provided a few examples of two of the signatures from his will. The "improved" varieties are frequently reproduced in books about Shakespeare. *Left column:* Notorious forger William Henry Ireland made copy at the top. George Steevens's tracing follows. The descending progression shows, in the various tracings and artists' interpretations, the gradual disintegration of the signature on the first page of Shakespeare's will. The signature has today almost entirely vanished. *Right column:* Again the list begins with Ireland's imitation (certainly as accurate as some of the others), and proceeds down through more recent copies. The *ar* of this signature, which appears on page 2 of the will, is orphaned from the rest of the name because in writing it the dying Shakespeare had to circumvent a lower loop from an *h* in the bottom line on the page.

England. One can scarcely credit the amount of damage inflicted on the poet's last testament. Until recently, a casual visitor could have his way with it upon payment of a modest will-inspection charge: For a shilling he could rub his greasy fingers over the very places where the great poet put his quill, or even kiss the signatures with wet, passionate lips! Luckily, the varlets who permitted this desecration are long dead and can thus escape my wrath.

The first assault on the will was made by well-intentioned George Steevens, an early and distinguished editor of Shakespeare's plays who, accompanied by the brilliant late-eighteenth-century Shakespearean scholar Edmund Malone, visited the Prerogative Office to make tracings of the signatures *(illus. 61)*. Malone described the will: "On the 24th of September, 1776, I went with my friend, Mr. Steevens, to the Prerogative Office on Doctor's Commons, to see Shakespeare's original Will, in order to get a *fac simile* of the handwriting. The Will is written in the clerical hand of that age, on three small [actually about 12' × 16'] sheets, fastened like a lawyer's brief. Shakespeare's name is signed at the bottom of the first and second sheets, and his final signature, 'By me William Shakspear', is in the middle of the third sheet. The name, however, at the bottom of the first sheet is not in the usual place, but in the margin at the left-hand, and so different from the others that we doubted whether it was his handwriting. He appears to have been very ill and weak when he signed his will, for the hand is very irregular and tremulous. I suspect he signed his name at the end of the Will first, and so went backwards, which will account for that on the first page being worse written than the rest, the hand growing gradually weaker."

The tracings made by Steevens are not entirely accurate, but they are a great help to scholars. Especially because the signature on the first page of the will has been so brutally treated by a parade of curiosity-inspired visitors that it has chipped right off at the bottom of the page. I recently evaluated Shakespeare's signature at $1 million, so the worth of each minuscule paper crumb that exfoliates from this precious signature is about $50,000.

From more amorous caressing than any movie queen ever got, the will is now creased and worn. The signatures on pages 2 and 3 have also suffered. By 1848 the deterioration was disconcertingly obvious, but nothing was done to stay it. The Shakespearean scholar James Orchard Halliwell-Phillipps wrote in his *Life of Shakespeare* (1848) that "at present the folding and unfolding requisite on every inspection of the document imperceptibly tend to the deterioration of the fragile substance on which it is written."

In 1861 the will was transferred to Somerset House and in 1962 to the Public Record Office. It is now on display in a splendid wall case. I have not seen it and do not wish to see it. The abuse and disfiguration of any great document distresses me so greatly that I rarely subject my emotions to such an ordeal. It is, of course, a popular belief that examining an original is more illuminating than looking at a good facsimile or Xerox copy. This is certainly not the case with Shakespeare's will, for the facsimiles made by photolithography in 1864 are clearer and more useful than the badly damaged and faded original. (Occasionally, of course, if there is a possibility that a document may be an expert forgery so cunningly contrived that the imposition is not instantly detectable from a photocopy, a study of the original document is imperative, but such cases are rare.) In 1823 the custodian of the American Declaration of Independence permitted a historian, W. J. Stone, to pull a copy of the Declaration by the wet-paper process, a method by which ink is drawn off the original document by pressing against it a blotter-like sheet of tissue paper. Stone made a perfect copy. That is fortunate, because he virtually destroyed the precious original when he drew the impression from it. As I reflect upon the desecration of this symbol of mankind's freedom, I gnash my few remaining teeth and itch to find some punishment adequate for the archivist who permitted it. However, we do have the Stone copies to tell us what the document once looked like. And, like many reproductions, they have a clarity and brilliance that in the original is partially obliterated by foxing, stains, fading and wear. Certainly, the copies of Shakespeare's will made over a century ago are far better than any we can hope to obtain today, even with the most sophisticated modern equipment.

The signatures of Shakespeare on the will, like the three other famous signatures of the poet, are a little world-weary and hard to decipher. The facsimiles made by sundry scholars vary greatly and it is likely we will never know the exact shading by Shakespeare's quill, the tiny gossamer lines that broadened into dramatic strokes. The delicate touches have vanished forever and in their stead we have a selection of tracings and copies that represents the talents of numerous artists but not the true signatures of the poet. I have reproduced some of the conceptions of the signatures on the will *(illus. 62)*. Careful observation of the small but important differences among them will yield an understanding of what sparse evidence scholars had to work with and why it required a fortuitous accident to discover what Shakespeare's handwriting was really like.

The three remaining signatures of Shakespeare all occur on legal documents. One is on the counterpart of a deed of purchase by Shakespeare from Henry Walker for a gatehouse in Blackfriars, London. It is dated March 10, 1613. The document was discovered in a collection of old deeds by Albany Willis, a lawyer, in 1768. Malone printed it

[62] Recent reproductions of Shakespeare's signatures. Variations in the poet's signatures from biography to biography are considerable and at times confusing. At the top of each group of three are the signatures as they appear in Ray Rawlins's *Stein and Day Book of World Autographs,* and are accurate representations based upon the photographs in Sir Sidney Lee's *Life of Shakespeare* (New York, 1899).

The second-line signatures in each figure, from Frayne Williams's *Mr. Shakespeare of The Globe,* are less accurate and obviously copied by an artist who did not understand the secretary style of writing. In [b], for example, the middle signature has closed up the space between the *e* and the *re* in Shakespeare's surname, but the space exists in the original because the poet had to write his name around a word that extended into the space where he had chosen to sign. Every signature in Williams's book contains minor variations from the original.

In the third line of each group appear the signatures (slightly enlarged) as published in Pierre Waleffe's *Shakespeare,* apparently copied from Peter Quennell's *Shakespeare.* The most conspicuous example of the extreme inaccuracy in these signatures is line 3 of [b] which incorporates a *the* in the surname. The signature was originally written directly under the word *the* in the text and the lower loop of the *h* intruded into the signature; the artist who copied it presumed that *the* was part of the name.

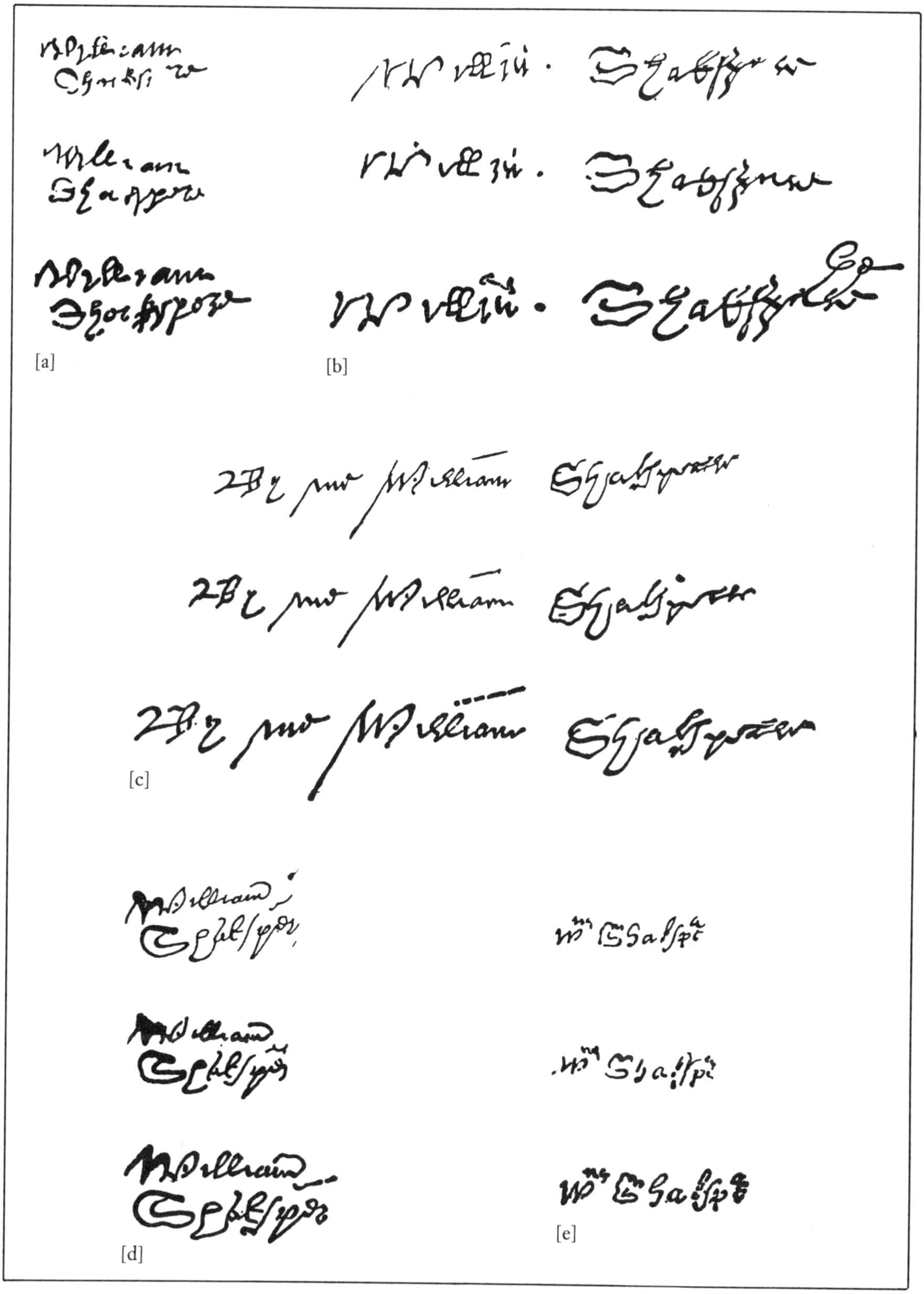
[a]
[b]
[c]
[d]
[e]

in 1796. It was the first and only Shakespeare autograph ever put on the auction block. In 1841 it was sold by Evans of Pall Mall and was knocked down to Elkins, a book dealer, for £162. On May 7, 1843, it was again put under the hammer by Evans. The bidding opened at £10. The Napoleon Museum bid £100. Eventually, the bidding mounted to £140, with Stanbury of the Napoleon Museum the high bidder. On behalf of the City Library (British Museum), R. L. Jones then topped Stanbury with a successful £145 bid. Oddly, the price the document fetched was almost the identical amount (£140) that Shakespeare had paid two hundred and forty years earlier for the gatehouse at Blackfriars. (If this same document were put up at auction today, I venture to predict it would fetch at least $2 million.)

The mortgage to the Blackfriars gatehouse, dated March 11, 1613, provides a fifth signature. The sixth signature, discovered in the Public Record Office, Chancery Lane, London, in 1909 by those indefatigable hounds to the bard, Professor Charles William Wallace and his wife, Hulda, is a deposition signed by Shakespeare in the Belott-Mountjoy suit. It is dated June 19, 1612.

It does not take a practiced eye to see that every one of the six previously known signatures is different. The handwriting is spastic, or very nearly so, and the spelling varies from signature to signature. Some authorities are inclined to the theory that Shakespeare had Bright's disease. The variations in the poet's signatures have brought joy and succor to the Baconians, who insist that Shakespeare was only a shill for Bacon, a semiliterate hayseed who could not possibly have written the sonnets and poems and plays.

The really tragic thing about the wide variation in the six signatures is not that they fortified the Baconian theory, but that their very obvious differences have delayed for more than two hundred years positive knowledge of how Shakespeare wrote when his handwriting was on good behavior. Half of the known signatures were penned when Shakespeare was dying and are of limited use in evaluating his penmanship. Certainly there was no scholar who did not realize even two centuries ago that if we could find out what Shakespeare's handwriting was like we would not only discover new documents written by him and fresh facts about his life; we would also have the ultimate key to detecting printer's errors in the early editions of the poems and plays.

Many brilliant scholars have invested a great deal of time in trying to figure out why the six signatures vary so greatly. In "The Handwriting on the Three Pages" (*Shakespeare's Hand in the Play of Sir Thomas More*, edited by A. W. Pollard), Sir Edward Maunde Thompson discusses the three manuscript leaves attributed to Shakespeare in *The Booke of Sir Thomas More* and quotes some interesting theories: "J. F. Nisbet in his book on *The Insanity of Genius* (1891) concludes, after examination of the signatures to the will, that Shakespeare's ailment was a prostration of the nervous system and that in his later days he was a victim to nerve disorder. In March 1919 the late Dr. R. W. Leftwich delivered before the Royal Society of Medicine a lecture on 'The Evidence of Disease in Shakespeare's Handwriting' in which he analysed the signatures and decided that the writer was subject to the spastic or spasmodic form of writer's cramp . . . I may state that independently there had arisen in my mind, from the time I first entered on an examination of Shakespeare's signatures, a suspicion that he had been afflicted with some nervous complaint which had left its mark upon his writing. . . ."

As already noted, spelling was a matter of personal taste in the Elizabethan era. Sir Walter Raleigh signed his name four different ways but preferred "Ralegh." Christopher Marlowe, the Muses' darling of the mighty line, was known as Marlowe, Marlow, Marley, Marlin, Merling, Morley and Marle. That Shakespeare spelled his name in different ways is not startling. His father, John, appears in documents of the period with seventeen different spellings of Shakespeare. A literary jester named George Wise wrote an amusing monograph (1869) to demonstrate that there were four thousand different possible spellings of *Shakespeare*. If the poet had lived to be as old as Methuselah I'm sure he would have used them all! I have included the whimsical introduction and four pages from Wise's book *(illus. 63)* not only to give an idea of the variety of spellings, but to demonstrate the fallacy in the popular Baconian approach to Shakespeare's writing. Obviously Shakespeare cared little about how he signed and simply whipped his quill deftly over any paper or parchment that required his signature.

It is axiomatic among handwriting experts that an unschooled but literate person rarely varies the way he signs his name. Daniel Boone and Davy Crockett, both ill-educated frontiersmen, wrote with machine-like exactitude. Their handwriting never changed. Sitting Bull and Geronimo, who could scribble nothing except their names, rarely deviated an iota from the pattern they'd learned. On the other hand a great many well-educated persons alter their scripts from day to day, from hour to hour, even during the writing of the same document. A profuse variety of different handwritings and signatures can be the mark of an imaginative and highly intelligent person. In the next chapter, when I try to put the Baconians to the sword, I will illustrate a few of the signatures that could easily deceive scholars, or any of us, if we did not know a lot about the writers. Even the "X" mark, traditionally interpreted as a sign of illiteracy, can be misleading. In earlier times lawyers sometimes readied documents to be signed without delay. A favorite method was to prepare in advance for the possibility that the person or persons whose signature was required might be illiterate. Since not much significance was attached to the skill of writing and there was little or no disgrace in signing with a mark, the lawyer would simply place the document, prepared with a "his mark" or "her mark" space, and say: "Put your mark here, please." Most people would gratefully oblige with an "X" or a swirl of some sort, glad to be spared the onerous task of writing their name. I once acquired a small sheaf of documents, receipts for an annual pension, signed by Whittier's heroine Barbara Fritchie. Most were signed with an "X," but there were a few that bore clear, easily readable signatures. Upon inquiry of the descendant of the lawyer who had owned the papers, I learned that Barbara had merely followed the request of the attorney and signed an "X" when asked, but had signed in full when the lawyer's clerk failed to prepare a "her mark" box.

I suspect that Shakespeare would have signed nothing more than an "X" if he could have got away with it.

THE AUTOGRAPH

OF

WILLIAM SHAKESPEARE,

WITH

Fac Similes of his Signature as appended to various Legal Documents;

TOGETHER WITH

4000 Ways of Spelling the Name according to English
Orthography.

BY GEORGE WISE.

PHILADELPHIA:
PUBLISHED BY PETER E. ABEL.
MDCCCLXIX.

[63] The title page and Author's Note from
George Wise's amusing book on the possible
spellings of Shakespeare's name, and a sampling
of the four thousand possible spellings Wise
compiled in 1869.

AUTHOR'S NOTE.

NEARLY three centuries have passed since William Shaick-
spear lived to write his wondrous dramas and to present them
for the approval of the lords and ladies of the courts of Elizabeth and of James and during that period "tomes on tomes
of learning and of power" have been written to elucidate their
obscure passages, though it must be confessed that the anno-
tators have at times befogged those that would otherwise be
clear. When Washington Irving thought proper (in deference
to custom) to "contribute his mite of homage to the illustrious
bard," he was sorely puzzled as to the manner in which he
should discharge the duty. "I found myself anticipated,"
he says, "in every attempt at a new reading; every doubtful
line had been explained a dozen different ways, and perplexed
beyond the reach of elucidation; and as to fine passages, they
had all been amply praised by previous admirers; nay, so
completely had the bard of late been overlarded with pane-
gyric by a great German critic [Schlegel], that it was difficult
now to find even a fault that had not been argued into a
beauty."

So strong is the hold that Shaickspeare has taken on the
minds of all "who speak the tongue that Shaickspyr spoke"
that not only have labored commentaries been written and
read, and disputed and defended, in other protean volumes;

iv   *AUTHOR'S NOTE.*

not only has a lady had the patience and skill to prepare an
elaborate concordance, but numerous literary forgeries have
been perpetrated in his name, which, in turn, have taxed the
energies of ingenious students for their refutation, and added
thousands of pages to the bulky Shakespeareana that is so
conspicuous in the scholar's library.

Is it possible, then, that anything valuable or novel can be
added to this imposing mass—the aggregation of almost
three centuries? May I keep within the bounds of modesty
in offering my *brochure* as a Literary Curiosity? I hope that
I may. The reader is assured that the *fac similes* of Shaick-
spyrr autographs here given have been faithfully copied from
and compared with the originals, and may be relied on as correct. It would be "flat and unprofitable" to state the analo-
gical arguments that may be brought forward to support the
various orthographies of the poet's name given in this work.
No special merit is claimed for them; but they seem to be
curious.

In introducing my little volume to the notice of the lovers
of the bard who "wrote not for an age, but for all time," it
is proper that I should acknowledge my great indebtedness to
Dr. R. SHELTON MACKENZIE for his invaluable assistance in
preparing the subject matter.

G. W.

46

Schackesspear	Scheickespeirr	Scheakespear	Shayxspeirr
Schackesspeare	Scheickespeirre	Scheakespeare	Shayxspeirre
Schackesspeer	Scheickesper	Scheakespeer	Shayxsper
Schackesspeere	Scheickespere	Scheakespeere	Shayxspere
Schackesspiere	Scheickesperr	Scheakespiere	Shayxsperr
Schackesspier	Scheickesperre	Scheakespier	Shayxsperre
Schackesspeire	Scheickespyr	Scheakespeire	Shayxspyr
Schackesspeir	Scheickespyrr	Scheakespeir	Shayxspyrr
Schackesspaer	Scheickespir	Scheakespaer	Shayxspir
Schackesspaere	Scheickespirr	Scheakespaere	Shayxspirr
Schackesspierr	Scheickespearr	Scheakespierr	Shayxspearr
Schackesspir	Scheickespaerr	Scheakespierre	Shayxspaerr
Schackesspirr	Shiexspear	Scheakespeirr	Shayquesspear
Schackesspaerr	Shiexspeare	Scheakespeirre	Shayquesspeare
Schackesspearr	Shiexspeer	Scheakesper	Shayquesspeere
Schackessperr	Shiexspeere	Scheakespere	Shayquesspeer
Schackessperre	Shiexspiere	Scheakesperr	Shayquesspiere
Schackesspyr	Shiexspier	Scheakesperre	Shayquesspier
Schackesspyrr	Shiexspeire	Scheakespyr	Shayquesspeire
Schackesspierre	Shiexspeir	Scheakespyrr	Shayquesspeir
Schackesspeirr	Shiexspaer	Scheakespir	Shayquesspaer
Schackesspeirre	Shiexspaere	Scheakespirr	Shayquesspaere
Schackessper	Shiexspierr	Scheakespearr	Shayquesspierr
Schackesspere	Shiexspierre	Scheakespaerr	Shayquesspierre
Shayksspear	Shiexspeirr	Shaeckespear	Shayquesspeirr
Shayksspeare	Shiexspeirre	Shaeckespeare	Shayquesspeirre
Shayksspeer	Shiexsper	Shaeckespeer	Shayquessper
Shayksspeere	Shiexspere	Shaeckespeere	Shayquesspere
Shayksspiere	Shiexsperr	Shaeckespiere	Shayquessperr
Shayksspier	Shiexsperre	Shaeckespier	Shayquessperre
Shayksspeire	Shiexspyr	Shaeckespeire	Shayquesspyr
Shayksspeir	Shiexspyrr	Shaeckespeir	Shayquesspyrr
Shayksspaer	Shiexspir	Shaeckespaer	Shayquesspir
Shayksspaere	Shiexspirr	Shaeckespaere	Shayquesspirr
Shayksspierr	Shiexspearr	Shaeckespierr	Shayquesspearr
Shayksspierre	Shiexspaerr	Shaeckespierre	Shayquesspaerr
Shayksspeirr	Scheyxpear	Shaeckespeirr	Scheckespear
Shayksspeirre	Scheyxpeare	Shaeckespeirre	Scheckespeare
Shaykssper	Scheyxpeer	Shaeckesper	Scheckespeer
Shayksspere	Scheyxpeere	Shaeckespere	Scheckesperre
Shaykssperr	Scheyxpier	Shaeckesperr	Scheckespiere
Shaykssperre	Scheyxpiere	Shaeckesperre	Scheckespier
Shayksspyr	Scheyxpeire	Shaeckespyr	Scheckespeire
Shayksspyrr	Scheyxpeir	Shaeckespyrr	Scheckespeir
Shayksspir	Scheyxpaer	Shaeckespir	Scheckespaer
Shayksspirr	Scheyxpaere	Shaeckespirr	Scheckespaere
Shayksspearr	Scheyxpierr	Shaeckespearr	Scheckespierr
Shayksspaerr	Scheyxpierre	Shaeckespaerr	Scheckespierre
Scheickespear	Scheyxpeirr	Shayxspear	Scheckespeirr
Scheickespeare	Scheyxpeirre	Shayxspeare	Scheckespeirre
Scheickespeer	Scheyxper	Shayxspeer	Scheckesper
Scheickespeere	Scheyxpere	Shayxspeere	Scheckespere
Scheickespiere	Scheyxperr	Shayxspiere	Scheckesperr
Scheickespier	Scheyxperre	Shayxspier	Scheckesperre
Scheickespeire	Scheyxpyr	Shayxspeir	Scheckespyr
Scheickespeir	Scheyxpyrr	Shayxspeire	Scheckespyrr
Scheickespaer	Scheyxpir	Shayxspaer	Scheckespir
Scheickespaere	Scheyxpirr	Shayxspaere	Scheckespirr
Scheickespierr	Scheyxpearr	Shayxspierr	Scheckespearr
Scheickespierre	Scheyxpaerr	Shayxspierre	Scheckespaerr

Shakspear	Schalkspeirr	Schalquespear	Scheyckesspeirr
Shakspeare	Schalkspeirre	Schalquespeare	Scheyckesspeirre
Shakspeer	Schalksper	Schalquespeer	Scheyckessper
Shakspeere	Schalkspere	Schalquespeere	Scheyckesspere
Shakspiere	Schalksperr	Schalquespiere	Scheyckessperr
Shakspier	Schalksperre	Schalquespier	Scheyckessperre
Shakspeire	Schalkspyr	Schalquespeire	Scheyckesspyr
Shakspeir	Schalkspyrr	Schalquespeir	Scheyckesspyrr
Shakspaer	Schalkspir	Schalquespaer	Scheyckesspir
Shakspaere	Schalkspirr	Schalquespaere	Scheyckesspirr
Shakspierr	Schalkspearr	Schalquespierr	Scheyckesspearr
Shakspir	Schalkspaerr	Schalquespierre	Scheyckesspaerr
Shakspirr	Scheaxspear	Schalquespeirr	Schayquespear
Shakspaerr	Scheaxspeare	Schalquespeirre	Schayquespeare
Shakspearr	Scheaxspeer	Schalquesper	Schayquespeer
Shaksperr	Scheaxspeere	Schalquespere	Schayquespeere
Shaksperre	Scheaxspiere	Schalquesperr	Schayquespiere
Shakspyr	Scheaxspier	Schalquesperre	Schayquespier
Shakspyrr	Scheaxspeire	Schalquespyr	Schayquespeire
Shakspierre	Scheaxspeir	Schalquespyrr	Schayquespeir
Shakspeirr	Scheaxspaer	Schalquespir	Schayquespaer
Shakspeirre	Scheaxspaere	Schalquespirr	Schayquespaere
Shaksper	Scheaxspierr	Schalquespearr	Schayquespierr
Shakspere	Scheaxspierre	Schalquespaerr	Schayquespierre
Shaykespear	Scheaxspeirr	Sheacksspear	Schayquespeirr
Shaykespeare	Scheaxspeirre	Sheacksspeare	Schayquespeirre
Shaykespeer	Scheaxsper	Sheacksspeer	Schayquesper
Shaykespeere	Scheaxspere	Sheacksspeere	Schayquespere
Shaykespiere	Scheaxsperr	Sheacksspiere	Schayquesperr
Shaykespier	Scheaxsperre	Sheacksspier	Schayquesperre
Shaykespeire	Scheaxspyr	Sheacksspeire	Schayquespyr
Shaykespeir	Scheaxspyrr	Sheacksspeir	Schayquespyrr
Shaykespaer	Scheaxspir	Sheacksspaer	Schayquespir
Shaykespaere	Scheaxspirr	Sheacksspaere	Schayquespirr
Shaykespierr	Scheaxspearr	Sheacksspierr	Schayquespearr
Shaykespierre	Scheaxspaerr	Sheacksspierre	Schayquespaerr
Shaykespeirr	Sheyckspear	Sheacksspeirr	Sheikesspear
Shaykespeirre	Sheyckspeare	Sheacksspeirre	Sheikesspeare
Shaykesper	Sheyckspeer	Sheackssper	Sheikesspeer
Shaykespere	Sheyckspeere	Sheacksspere	Sheikessperre
Shaykesperr	Sheyckspier	Sheackssperr	Sheikesspiere
Shaykesperre	Sheyckspiere	Sheackssperre	Sheikesspier
Shaykespyr	Sheyckspeire	Sheacksspyr	Sheikesspeire
Shaykespyrr	Sheyckspeir	Sheacksspyrr	Sheikesspeir
Shaykespir	Sheyckspaer	Sheacksspir	Sheikesspaer
Shaykespirr	Sheyckspaere	Sheacksspirr	Sheikesspaere
Shaykespearr	Sheyckspierr	Sheacksspearr	Sheikesspierr
Shaykespaerr	Sheyckspierre	Sheacksspaerr	Sheikesspierre
Schalkspear	Sheyckspeirr	Scheyckesspear	Sheikesspeirr
Schalkspeare	Sheyckspeirre	Scheyckesspeare	Sheikesspeirre
Schalkspeer	Sheycksper	Scheyckesspeer	Sheikessper
Schalkspeere	Sheyckspere	Scheyckesspeere	Sheikesspere
Schalkspiere	Sheycksperr	Scheyckesspiere	Sheikessperr
Schalkspier	Sheycksperre	Scheyckesspier	Sheikessperre
Schalkspeire	Sheyckspyr	Scheyckesspeir	Sheikesspyr
Schalkspeir	Sheyckspyrr	Scheyckesspeire	Sheikesspyrr
Schalkspaer	Sheyckspir	Scheyckesspaer	Sheikesspir
Schalkspaere	Sheyckspirr	Scheyckesspaere	Sheikesspirr
Schalkspierr	Sheyckspearr	Scheyckesspierr	Sheikesspearr
Schalkspierre	Sheyckspaerr	Scheyckesspierre	Sheikesspaerr

Schackespear	Shekespeirr	Scheackespear	Shayxpeirr
Schackespeare	Shekespeirre	Scheackespeare	Shayxpeirre
Schackespeer	Shekesper	Scheackespeer	Shayxper
Schackespeere	Shekespere	Scheackespeere	Shayxpere
Schackespiere	Shekesperr	Scheackespiere	Shayxperr
Schackespier	Shekesperre	Scheackespier	Shayxperre
Schackespeire	Shekespyr	Scheackespeire	Shayxpyr
Schackespeir	Shekespyrr	Scheackespeir	Shayxpyrr
Schackespaer	Shekespir	Scheackespaer	Shayxpir
Schackespaere	Shekespirr	Scheackespaere	Shayxpirr
Schackespierr	Shekespearr	Scheackespierr	Shayxpearr
Schackespir	Shekespaerr	Scheackespierre	Shayxpaerr
Schackespirr	Sheixspear	Scheackespeirr	Sheaquespear
Schackespaerr	Sheixspeare	Scheackespeirre	Sheaquespeare
Schackespearr	Sheixspeer	Scheackesper	Sheaquespeere
Schackesperr	Sheixspeere	Scheackespere	Sheaquespeer
Schackesperre	Sheixspiere	Scheackesperr	Sheaquespiere
Schackespyr	Sheixspier	Scheackesperre	Sheaquespier
Schackespyrr	Sheixspeire	Scheackespyr	Sheaquespeire
Schackespierre	Sheixspeir	Scheackespyrr	Sheaquespeir
Schackespeirr	Sheixspaer	Scheackespir	Sheaquespaer
Schackespeirre	Sheixspaere	Scheackespirr	Sheaquespaere
Schackesper	Sheixspierr	Scheackespearr	Sheaquespierr
Schackespere	Sheixspierre	Scheackespaerr	Sheaquespierre
Schayxspear	Sheixspeirr	Sheackespear	Sheaquespeirr
Schayxspeare	Sheixspeirre	Sheackespeare	Sheaquespeirre
Schayxspeer	Sheixsper	Sheackespeer	Sheaquesper
Schayxspeere	Sheixspere	Sheackespeere	Sheaquespere
Schayxspiere	Sheixsperr	Sheackespiere	Sheaquesperr
Schayxspier	Sheixsperre	Sheackespier	Sheaquesperre
Schayxspeire	Sheixspyr	Sheackespeire	Sheaquespyr
Schayxspeir	Sheixspyrr	Sheackespeir	Sheaquespyrr
Schayxspaer	Sheixspir	Sheackespaer	Sheaquespir
Schayxspaere	Sheixspirr	Sheackespaere	Sheaquespirr
Schayxspierr	Sheixspearr	Sheackespierr	Sheaquespearr
Schayxspierre	Sheixspaerr	Sheackespierre	Sheaquespaerr
Schayxspeirr	Schaexspear	Sheackespeirr	Sheckespear
Schayxspeirre	Schaexspeare	Sheackespeirre	Sheckespeare
Schayxsper	Schaexspeer	Sheackesper	Sheckespeer
Schayxspere	Schaexspeere	Sheackespere	Sheckesperre
Schayxsperr	Schaexspier	Sheackesperr	Sheckespiere
Schayxsperre	Schaexspiere	Sheackesperre	Sheckespier
Schayxspyr	Schaexspeire	Sheackespyr	Sheckespeire
Schayxspyrr	Schaexspeir	Sheackespyrr	Sheckespeir
Schayxspir	Schaexspaer	Sheackespir	Sheckespaer
Schayxspirr	Schaexspaere	Sheackespirr	Sheckespaere
Schayxspearr	Schaexspierr	Sheackespearr	Sheckespierr
Schayxspaerr	Schaexspierre	Sheackespaerr	Sheckespierre
Shekespear	Schaexspeirr	Shayxpear	Sheckespeirr
Shekespeare	Schaexspeirre	Shayxpeare	Sheckespeirre
Shekespeer	Schaexsper	Shayxpeer	Sheckesper
Shekespeere	Schaexspere	Shayxpeere	Sheckespere
Shekespiere	Schaexsperr	Shayxpiere	Sheckesperr
Shekespier	Schaexsperre	Shayxpier	Sheckesperre
Shekespeire	Schaexspyr	Shayxpeir	Sheckespyr
Shekespeir	Schaexspyrr	Shayxpeire	Sheckespyrr
Shekespaer	Schaexspir	Shayxpaer	Sheckespir
Shekespaere	Schaexspirr	Shayxpaere	Sheckespirr
Shekespierr	Schaexspearr	Shayxpierr	Sheckespearr
Shekespierre	Schaexspaerr	Shayxpierre	Sheckespaerr

Schakspear	Shalkespeirr	Shalquespear	Scheyckespeirr
Schakspeare	Shalkespeirre	Shalquespeare	Scheyckespeirre
Schakspeer	Shalkesper	Shalquespeer	Scheyckesper
Schakspeere	Shalkespere	Shalquespeere	Scheyckespere
Schakspiere	Shalkesperr	Shalquespiere	Scheyckesperr
Schakspier	Shalkesperre	Shalquespier	Scheyckesperre
Schakspeire	Shalkespyr	Shalquespeire	Scheyckespyr
Schakspeir	Shalkespyrr	Shalquespeir	Scheyckespyrr
Schakspaer	Shalkespir	Shalquespaer	Scheyckespir
Schakspaere	Shalkespirr	Shalquespaere	Scheyckespirr
Schakspierr	Shalkespearr	Shalquespierr	Scheyckespearr
Schakspir	Shalkespaerr	Shalquespierre	Scheyckespaerr
Schakspirr	Sheaxspear	Shalquespeirr	Shayquespear
Schakspaerr	Sheaxspeare	Shalquespeirre	Shayquespeare
Schakspearr	Sheaxspeer	Shalquesper	Shayquespeer
Schaksperr	Sheaxspeere	Shalquespere	Shayquespeere
Schaksperre	Sheaxspiere	Shalquesperr	Shayquespiere
Schakspyr	Sheaxspier	Shalquesperre	Shayquespier
Schakspyrr	Sheaxspeire	Shalquespyr	Shayquespeire
Schakspierre	Sheaxspeir	Shalquespyrr	Shayquespeir
Schakspeirr	Sheaxspaer	Shalquespir	Shayquespaer
Schakspeirre	Sheaxspaere	Shalquespirr	Shayquespaere
Schaksper	Sheaxspierr	Shalquespearr	Shayquespierr
Schakspere	Sheaxspierre	Shalquespaerr	Shayquespierre
Schaykspear	Sheaxspeirr	Schalckespear	Shayquespeirr
Schaykspeare	Sheaxspeirre	Schalckespeare	Shayquespeirre
Schaykspeer	Sheaxsper	Schalckespeer	Shayquesper
Schaykspeere	Sheaxspere	Schalckespeere	Shayquespere
Schaykspiere	Sheaxsperr	Schalckespiere	Shayquesperr
Schaykspier	Sheaxsperre	Schalckespier	Shayquesperre
Schaykspeire	Sheaxspyr	Schalckespeir	Shayquespyr
Schaykspeir	Sheaxspyrr	Schalckespeire	Shayquespyrr
Schaykspaer	Sheaxspir	Schalckespaer	Shayquespir
Schaykspaere	Sheaxspirr	Schalckespaere	Shayquespirr
Schaykspierr	Sheaxspearr	Schalckespierr	Shayquespearr
Schaykspierre	Sheaxspaerr	Schalckespierre	Shayquespaerr
Schaykspeirr	Scheykspear	Schalckespeirr	Sheikespear
Schaykspeirre	Scheykspeare	Schalckespeirre	Sheikespeare
Schayksper	Scheykspeer	Schalckesper	Sheikespeer
Schaykspere	Scheykspeere	Schalckespere	Sheikesperre
Schayksperr	Scheykspier	Schalckesperr	Sheikespiere
Schayksperre	Scheykspiere	Schalckesperre	Sheikespier
Schaykspyr	Scheykspeire	Schalckespyr	Sheikespeire
Schaykspyrr	Scheykspeir	Schalckespyrr	Sheikespeir
Schaykspir	Scheykspaer	Schalckespir	Sheikespaer
Schaykspirr	Scheykspaere	Schalckespirr	Sheikespaere
Schaykspearr	Scheykspierr	Schalckespearr	Sheikespierr
Schaykspaerr	Scheykspierre	Schalckespaerr	Sheikespierre
Shalkespear	Scheykspeirr	Scheyckespear	Sheikespeirr
Shalkespeare	Scheykspeirre	Scheyckespeare	Sheikespeirre
Shalkespeer	Scheyksper	Scheyckespeer	Sheikesper
Shalkespeere	Scheykspere	Scheyckespeere	Sheikespere
Shalkespiere	Scheyksperr	Scheyckespiere	Sheikesperr
Shalkespier	Scheyksperre	Scheyckespier	Sheikesperre
Shalkespeire	Scheykspyr	Scheyckespeir	Sheikespyr
Shalkespeir	Scheykspyrr	Scheyckespeire	Sheikespyrr
Shalkespaer	Scheykspir	Scheyckespaer	Sheikespir
Shalkespaere	Scheykspirr	Scheyckespaere	Sheikespirr
Shalkespierr	Scheykspearr	Scheyckespierr	Sheikespearr
Shalkespierre	Scheykspaerr	Scheyckespierre	Sheikespaerr

IV

SO LONG, FRANCIS BACON!

T H E theory that Bacon wrote Shakespeare's plays and poems has for the past one hundred years provided a lot of fun and games for ersatz scholars. If you're into cryptograms and ciphers, you can set yourself to the jocular task of proving that Bacon wrote *Hamlet* or Martin Tupper's *Proverbial Wisdom* or, for that matter, the New York telephone directory. With cryptograms you can prove almost anything. Handwriting has fascinated the Baconians. They are addicted to charts and graphs and elaborate arrangements of the alphabet.

The first hints that Shakespeare was just a shill for Bacon came from Herbert Lawrence (1769) and the Reverend James Wilmot (about 1785), but it wasn't until 1856 that Delia Bacon, an American, made a concerted effort to establish Bacon's authorship of the plays. She even planned to dig up Shakespeare's bones to prove her point but backed out at the last moment. Delia's tome, *The Philosophy of the Plays of Shakespere Unfolded* (1857) is, judged solely upon the basis of its enormous length, the bible of the Baconians. It has a literary style reminiscent of Hegel and Fichte at their least lucid. Nathaniel Hawthorne, United States consul at Liverpool in 1857, was conned into writing the preface for this attack upon Shakespeare. Hawthorne broke the world's record for prolixity. After a lengthy, nomadic disquisition on Delia's philosophy, he came to the conclusion that he could not come to a conclusion. He probably tried hard to read Delia's book, as I did, and failed, as I did. The reason for our failure will perhaps be obvious from an example of her prose. I opened the book at random (to be fair) and plucked out the first sentence my eye lit upon: "That sanguinary passion which the heat of conflict proves is but the incident; it is the natural principle of absorption, it is the instinct that nature is full of, that nature is alive with; but the one that she is at war with, too—at war with in the parts

—one that she is for ever opposed to, and conquering in the members, with her mathematical axioms—with her law of the whole, of 'the worthier whole,' of 'the great congregation'; it is that principle of acquisition which it is the business of the state to set bounds to in the human constitution—which gets branded with *other* names, very vulgar ones, too, when the faculty of grasp and absorption is smaller."

Bacon and Shakespeare are somewhere in the book, I'm told, but I couldn't find them. However, a cult grew up around Delia and by 1885 there was a Bacon Society. The sport of "proving" that Bacon was a man of whimsy and wit and that Shakespeare was nothing but a poor player and a walking shadow won a lot of noteworthy adherents. Among those caught up in the Verulam vortex were Mark Twain, Sigmund Freud and Oliver Wendell Holmes Jr. In *Links between Shakespeare and the Law,* Dunbar Plunket Barton alludes to Mark Twain's conviction that Bacon wrote the plays. Sir Dunbar laments that the Baconian theory had "a pernicious effect upon the reasoning power of a vigorous mind." A friend of Twain's, Bartow recalls that the humorist and his secretary, Albert Bigelow Paine, often mortgaged their evenings to the study and creation of ciphers to prove Bacon's authorship of Shakespeare's plays. Twain was so piqued at the Shakespeareans who tried to scuttle his Baconian faith that he unleashed a streak of epithets at them. According to Professor S. Schoenbaum, in *Shakespeare's Lives,* Twain dubbed the devotees of Shakespeare "troglodytes, thugs, Stratfordolators, Shakesperoids, bangalores, herumfrodites, blatherskites, buccaneers, bandoleers and Muscovites."

Sir Francis Bacon, of course, isn't the only nominated pretender to Shakespeare's works. Bacon is certainly touted more often, but there are others. Christopher Marlowe would be a preeminent claimant if he hadn't been stabbed to death in 1593. To establish a claim on his behalf you have to bring him to life for an extra two decades. A number of Marlowe supporters have tried this but he stays as dead as he was the day Ingram Frizer dirked him. Then there's that trio of earls, William Stanley, sixth Earl of Derby, Roger Manners, fifth Earl of Rutland and Edward de Vere, the seventeenth Earl of Oxford. Add to these Sir Walter Raleigh and you bring to seven the total of pretenders. I would be remiss if I failed to push the number to nine by the mention of two fair ladies, Elizabeth I and the beautiful Mary, Countess of Pembroke, both of whom are thought by some to have authored the plays and poems. There are even more claimants but I will not exhaust your patience by cataloging them all.

The touters of the various claimants are always dogmatic about their candidates and speak with contempt of Shakespeare. In his book *Rutland* (1911), Lewis F. Bostelmann contends that Roger Manners, fifth Earl of Rutland, was actually Shakespeare. His book contains a five-act drama entitled *Roger of Rutland* in which he puts a pedestrian touch to his fantasy. Bostelmann calls Shakespeare "Rutland's Dummy." In one interesting passage, Bostelmann alludes to a payment by the sixth Earl of Rutland to Shakespeare and Burbage for designing and painting an impresa: "On the 31st of this month [March 1613] the ex-dummy, Shaksper, collected from Francis, Sixth Earl of Rutland [brother and successor of Roger] the sum of 44 shillings [about $85 of our money today] balance owing the Stratford man as a dummy. The entry in the account book of the Belvoir Steward says this payment was for writing a 'motto' for the new Earl. (Was this motto *Silence is golden?*)."

One of the big reasons why Francis Bacon and the others I've mentioned have their ardent followers is because there's a Tom o' Bedlam tale around that Shakespeare didn't know how to write and couldn't even sign his name. I touched upon this in the last chapter but now I would like to let the Baconians hang themselves.

Edwin Durning-Lawrence writes in his book *Bacon Is Shakespeare:* "The more you examine the whole five [signatures]"—Sir Edwin rejected as secretarial signature number six, discovered in 1909 by Professor and Mrs. Wallace—"the more you will be certain, as the writer is, after the most careful study of the Will and the Deeds, that not one of the five writings is a 'signature,' or pretends to be a 'signature,' and that therefore there is a probability, practically amounting to a certainty, that the Stratford Actor could not so much as manage to scrawl his own name.

"No! We possess not a scrap of writing, not even an attempt at a signature, that can reasonably supposed to be written by the Stratford *gentleman.*"

Sir Edwin is so convinced that his position is invulnerable that he publishes in his book, amid an irrelevant melee of portraits and charts and title pages, a page of the document that bears Shakespeare's sixth known signature discovered by Professor Wallace. The document is a statement by Shakespeare in the Belott-Mountjoy suit that testifies to the reliability and good character of his former landlord, Mountjoy *(illus. 64).* Shakespeare's testimony is in answer to an interrogation by the court. Sir Edwin avers: "An expert in handwriting will at once perceive that 'Willm Shaxpʳ' is written by the same hand that wrote the lower portion of Shakespeare's Answers to Interrogatories. . . ."

I do not perceive this. In fact, I perceive no similarity at all in the handwriting of the body of the document and the signature of Shakespeare, but since Sir Edwin has by this time sprung the trap on the gallows he built himself, I shall allow him to kick in the air for a minute. He continues: "In the case of 'William Shakespeare of Stratford-upon-Avon, Gentleman,' who was . . . unable to write his name, they [the Answers to Interrogatories] are signed with a dot that might quite easily be mistaken for an accidental blot. Our readers will see this mark, which is not a blot but a purposely made mark, just under 'Willm Shaxpʳ' is written by the lawyer or law clerk who wrote the lower part of Shakespeare's deposition . . . The only mark William Shakespeare put to the document was the blot above which the abbreviated name 'Willm Shaxpʳ' was written by the lawyer or law clerk."

Sir Edwin does not make his opinion more tenable by repeating it twice in different words. There are other "signatures of Shakespeare" on this page, including one just below the *e* of the deleted word *some* in line one of this deposition. I'm sure Sir Edwin could explain this apparent flaw in his theory. But I think we've had enough of his crapulous eructations.

Another writer who espouses the authorship of Bacon, Roderick Eagle, writes in his eccentric book *Forgers and Forgeries* (The Bacon Society) that Shakespeare was "not of sufficient importance" to have his portrait painted while he was alive. "Nor is it possible

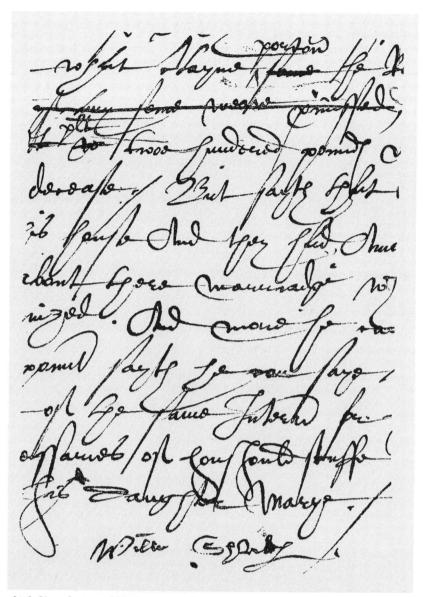

[64] Signed page of Shakespeare's deposition in the Belott-Mountjoy Case. According to Sir Edwin Durning-Lawrence, however, Shakespeare was illiterate and the same clerk who wrote the deposition signed for Shakespeare, who then added his mark—the elliptical blot under the signature.

to connect a man who was practically illiterate with the writing of masterpieces. Any "discovery which may be announced claiming to connect him with the ownership of a book or any scrap of manuscript stated to be in his handwriting, is at once under the greatest suspicion, and little difficulty is found in refuting it."

Some of the Baconians even claim that the interlinear and supralinear additions to Shakespeare's will were criminally added to convince the literary world that Shakespeare, "a mere stage hand" at the Globe Theatre, was personally acquainted with Burbage, Heminges and Condell. The flaw in this argument is that the interlinear additions were known, and commented upon, nearly a century before Delia Bacon got her brainstorm.

One of the most prolix of the Baconians was George Greenwood. In *The Shakspere Signatures and "Sir Thomas More"* (1924), Sir George scourges Edward M. Thompson's brilliant attempt to prove that Writer "D" in *Sir Thomas More* was Shakespeare. Sir George's technical meanderings are tedious forays into sarcasm, so I won't quote them.

You might find amusing an effort by William Henry Burr (1886) to prove that Shakespeare didn't know how to write. It is characteristic of Baconian literature and I have reproduced here the first chapter *(illus. 65).* One of the signatures illustrated by Burr includes the lower loop of an *h* written in the line above it. Evidently Burr could not read the poet's script and mistook this intrusion for part of the signature. There is scarcely a correct statement in Burr's little book. Burr further debunks Shakespeare's authorship by an equally risible chapter on how Francis Bacon wrote the famous sonnets "attributed" to the poet of Stratford.

[65] Title page and first chapter of William Henry Burr's *Bacon and Shakespeare: Proof that William Shakespere Could Not Write* (1886). A characteristic attack by a Baconian. Almost every statement in this chapter is incorrect. At the bottom of page 11, the last of the chapter, an exasperated early reader has written a suggestion to the author: "Oh Shut up."

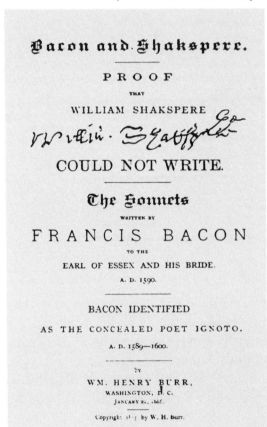

they are so different that an acquaintance with one is little help to the recognition of another.

In the first signature he writes Wm. for William.

The second and third autographs have William written above Shakspere. Who but an illiterate person would sign his name thus?

In the last two signatures (being told perhaps that his name ought to be written on one line) he puts William before Shakspere; but the fourth William reads Willin.

See now how differently each letter is formed in the name Shakspere, beginning with the initial:

Did anybody ever write the first letter of his name so differently? After four attempts to form a capital S he succeeds tolerably well the fifth time. The second S, though of singular shape, appears to have been a customary one as early as 1598. (See examples of that year below.) Shakspere's first attempt to form the crooked letter is a failure, but the second passably good. So again in 1616, when he has a different form to copy, his first attempt is futile, the second is passable, and the third quite successful.

But in attempting the next letter he makes it worse every time:

With the letter a he is more successful, making it legible three times out of five:

But the attempt to form a k is a signal failure:

With the long s he succeeds best the first time, and worst the second and third:

The letter p is legible the first time, but grows worse and worse to the last:

It seems as if in the first attempt to sign his name in 1613 he thought it was complete when he made it end with s p e; but being reminded that it lacked a letter or two he undertook to add one by putting an a over the e thus:

The next time, which was probably the same day,* he seems to have written his name Shaksper, though the terminal letters are uncertain:

The third time he gets it more like Shakspoze:

---

* The deed to Shakspere and two other trustees is dated March 10 and signed Henry Walker. The mortgage *from* Shakspere and the other trustees is dated March 11. But for some unaccountable reason a duplicate verbatim copy of the deed from Henry Walker is signed by William Shakspere. This duplicate is in the Library of the city of London; the mortgage is in the British Museum. The duplicate deed we suspect was signed after the mortgage. Hence the improvement in the autograph; it was probably Shakspere's second attempt to write. Compare it with the third.

The fourth time he seems to have tried to disguise the termination with awkward flourishes, making the letters totally illegible:

Finally, he omits the flourishes and comes nearer legibility, but still it is impossible to tell whether he meant to write *ear*, *ere*, or *eare*:

And now let the reader mark, that notwithstanding the orthodox spelling of the name from 1593 to 1616, and indeed up to the present time, was and is Shakespeare, there is no *e* in the first syllable and no *a* in the last, although some have imagined the letter *a* to exist in the last part of the final autograph.

We have said that these signatures are all that Shakspere is known to have written; we ought to add that he prefixed to the last one the following scrawl:

For a long time we puzzled over this. Could it be an attempt to write " 25th of March," the day of the execution of the will? At last we read the following in Hallowell-Phillipps's Shakspere:

" It may be observed that the words *By me*, which the autograph excepted, are the only ones in the poet's handwriting known to exist, appear to have been penned with ordinary firmness."

Presuming that the signatures were made in a sick bed, the author concedes that the words " By me " were penned with ordinary firmness. Very good; but could not almost any five-year-old boy do as well the first time?

In 1775 certain papers and legal instruments were published, attributed to Shakspere, Queen Elizabeth, and Southampton. In 1796 Edmund Malone proved them to be forgeries. Here is one of the forged autographs of Shakspere:

This is superior to any of the genuine ones, which in some degree it resembles. The letter *a* is pretty clearly written in the last syllable, as if the forger meant to establish the proper spelling of that part of the name. Malone, who at first pronounced the genuine orthography to be Shakspeare, subsequently declared Shakspere to be the poet's own mode of spelling his name beyond all doubt. But others do not accede to this decision, because they think there is an *a* in the last of the five genuine signatures.

The solution of the whole mystery is in the fact that Shakspere was unable to write or even to spell his own name.

In 1598 Richard Quiney addressed a letter to him asking for a loan of £30, and the name was written Shackesper:

In the same year among thirteen names of holders of corn in Stratford the last but one is Shakesper:

The form of the letter *a* in both these fac-similes

was peculiar to that time. It occurs in Shakspere's second autograph. Why did he thus vary the form? Probably because he followed the copy set for him.

Note now the various spellings of his name:

In 1582, as a bridegroom, Shagsper.

In 1593 and 1594, as a poet, Shakespeare; and the same uniformly as a playwright from 1598 to 1623, but sometimes with a hyphen—Shake-speare.

In 1596, as an inhabitant of Southwark, Shaksper.

In 1598, as addressed by letter, Shackesper.

In 1598, as owner of corn, Shakesper.

In 1604, as plaintiff in a suit, Shexpere.

In 1604 and 1605, as author of plays performed at Whitehall before King James, Shaxberd.

In 1609, as plaintiff in a suit, Shackspeare.

In 1612, as plaintiff in a suit, Schackspeare.

In 1614, as written by his cousin, Shakspear.

In 1616, as twice written in his will, Shackspeare; but in signing the same three times he omits the c in the first syllable, and it is impossible to tell what the last three or four letters are. And although in the two Deeds of 1613 the name is written repeatedly Shakespeare in signing them he omits the e in the first syllable both times, and varies the termination of the name, just as an illiterate person would be likely to do.

But there are more of these various spellings. All the records of Shakspere's lifetime have been hunted up and printed. From these documents, consisting of deeds, bills of complaint, letters, poems, plays, etc.,—most of which especially concerned either the father or son or both—we extract the following spellings, giving the dates:

Shakspere 1558, '62, '63, '64, '66, '69, '71, '79, 80, '83, '85, '90, '96, 1616, '17. (John Shakspere and all his offspring so registered, except Richard Shakspeer, baptized 1574.)

Shaxpere 1558, '79, 1607, '08.

Shakspeyr 1567, ("Mr.," meaning John.)

Shaksper 1568, ("Mr. John.")

Shackespere 1573, '89, 1602.

Shakespere 1575, '79, '96, '97, '98, '99, 1602, '04, '06, '08, '09, '10, '11, '13.

Shackspere 1579. (Deed. "Joannis Shaxpere +.") 1608.

Shagsper 1582. (Marriage bond—twice so written.)

Shake-scene 1592. (Greene, the playwright, in derision.)

Shakespeare 1593–1594, (Poems,) 1598, 1603, '05, '13. (and all Plays from 1598 to 1623.)

Shaksper 1596, '98, 1613. (Signature,) 1616.

Shakesper 1598. (Owner of corn.)

Shackesper 1598. (Letter from Quiney to Shakspere.)

Shakspeare 1601, '03, '07, '12, '13, '14, 1623.

Shackespeare 1603, '14. (Agreement.)

Shexpere 1604. (Suit for malt sold.)

Shaxberd 1604, '05. (Dramatist, Whitehall.)

Shakespear 1605. (Conveyance.)

Shakesphear 1605. (Same conveyance.)

Shackspeare 1608, '12, '14, '16.

Schackspeare 1612, '14. (Complaint and agreement.)

Shaksp; 1613. (Signature.)

Shakspear 1614. (Cousin's letter.)

Shaksp • • • 1616. (Signatures to Will.)

Shaxper 1616. ("Bell and pall for Mr. Shaxpers dawghter, viij d.")

If we divide the name between the s and p we have the following variations of each part:

Shaks, Shakes, Shakys, Shacks, Shackes, Schacks, Shags, Shax, Shex; per, pere, peer, pear, peare, peyr, phear, berd, p, p · · · ·

Shakspere's daughter Judith in 1611 witnessed two instruments by making her mark. And his other

daughter Susanna in 1642 disputed the unmistakable handwriting of her deceased husband in such a manner as to betray her illiteracy.

Mr. C. F. Gunther, of Chicago, claims to have obtained a copy of the Shakspere Folio of 1632, (i.e. the second Folio,) containing the author's autograph pasted on a fly-leaf, underneath which is written:

"The works of William Shakespeare. Born in April, 1564, and died in April, 1616. JOHN WARD."

And on the same fly-leaf is pasted a letter from Charles Godwin, of Bath, dated February 16, 1839, to Dr. Charles Severn, of London, who was then editing "The Diary of the Rev. John Ward, A. M.," Vicar of Stratford-upon-Avon from 1648 to 1679.

The book is said to have been owned by a Mormon, and is supposed to have been brought from England by an emigrant to Utah. Aside from the impossibility of such an autograph escaping from England to the wilds of America and remaining undiscovered so many years, the fac-simile in the Chicago Current of May 23, 1885, betrays most certain evidence of fraud. Compare it with the five genuine scrawls of Shakspere. It is so exact a copy of the last signature to the will as to indicate that it was traced therefrom.

Shakspere's last signature:

Pretended autograph in Chicago:

This close resemblance in so clumsy an autograph would be extraordinary, if not impossible: but how easy to forge it by first tracing it lightly with a pencil and then completing it with a pen. Here is a hair-line tracing of the spurious over the genuine autograph:

Even the most illiterate man who is obliged often to sign his name, will do it uniformly, so that when you have seen his signature once you will know it again. For example, take the following autographs:

WASHINGTON, D. C., May 31, 1885.

The undersigned, aged 73 years, wrote the above autographs in presence of the two subscribing witnesses. And he never wrote and cannot write anything but his name, though he can read print with ease. And he further says that he learned to write his name in the course of one month in the administration of President Polk, 1845-49, while serving as a Capitol policeman; otherwise he would have been obliged to sign the pay-roll with his cross.

Witness: A. WATSON.   JOHN W. SMITH.
WM. HENRY BULL.

Bacon required a mask, and he found it in the illiterate play-actor Shakspere.

Since the great variations and illegibility of Shakespeare's six signatures were the sparks that ignited the Baconians, I've decided to set off a counterblast, using the signatures of three famous men—Napoleon I, John F. Kennedy, and Richard Nixon *(illus. 66, 67, 68)*. Presuming the Baconian theory that Shakespeare was semiliterate and could not have written the plays because his signature varies and is hard to read is a sound theory, we would have to question the degree of literacy of all three celebrated men. (There are several humorous attempts to "prove" that Napoleon never even lived. One of the most amusing, *Historic Doubts Relative to Napoleon Bonaparte* [1819] by the Archbishop Richard Whately, exploits a lot of zany "evidence." Yet Whately's "proofs" are more credible than those of the Baconians. The archbishop never mentions Napoleon's erratic signatures. He obviously regarded that line of argument as too preposterous even for a spoof.)

Among the more interesting of the Baconians was Orville Owen who staunchly contended that the pig on the crest of the title page of Sidney's *Arcadia* proved Bacon's authorship. Dr. Owen discovered a cipher that revealed Bacon as the writer of Shake-

[66] Signatures of Napoleon as Emperor of France. Napoleon frequently signed his name in a bewildering variety of ways on a given day, but never legibly.

[67] Signatures of John F. Kennedy, all from the last two years of his life. Although Kennedy employed a huge battery of secretaries and machines to sign his mail, his own signature is easily recognizable because he never signed it twice in the same way.

[68] Signatures of Richard Nixon as President, all affixed to official proclamations or laws. The illegibility and inconsistency are amazing. Signings on the same day varied enormously from document to document. In comparison, Shakespeare's signature is more legible, more consistent.

speare's plays, as well as the works of Marlowe, Greene, Peele, Spenser and even Burton's *Anatomy of Melancholy*. Dr. Owen insisted that Bacon was the bastard son of Elizabeth I. He dug holes along the bank of the river Wye at Chepstow, looking for "pitch-covered boxes" that would contain the evidence of Bacon's noble birth. He didn't find them. Around the year 1895 Dr. Owen published in Detroit a drama called *The Tragical Historie of Our Late Brother Robert, Earl of Essex, by the Author of Hamlet, Richard III, Othello, As You Like It, etc. . . . Deciphered from the Works of Sir Francis Bacon by Orville W. Owen, M.D.* I looked into this drama and found that it is made up of excerpts from Shakespeare's great plays with lengthy fillers by Dr. Owen. Because of the difference in the abilities of the co-authors every member of the cast has a split personality. Sometimes a character speaks in exalted language redolent with word magic and sometimes he rattles along in faltering iambs like a Grub Street balladist. A single line shows how well Shakespeare's collaborator from Detroit had mastered the "bang" (and also adroitly encapsulates my reaction to Dr. Owen's play): "O God! hark! see, see! O heavens forfend!"

This expressive one-liner by Dr. Owen leads me to an equally deft eight-liner by Francis Bacon that has got into a lot of anthologies because of the fame of its author:

> The World's a bubble, and the Life of Man
>   Less than a span;
> In his conception wretched, from the womb
>   So to the tomb;
> Curst from his cradle, and brought up to years
>   With cares and fears.
> Who then to frail mortality shall trust
> But limns on water, or but writes in dust.

This is one of those scraps of doggerel that contributed to the corruption of literary taste in the American and British youth of a few generations ago. True, it beats the Long Island farmer-poet Bloodgood H. Cutter, and Julia A. Moore, the Sweet Singer of Michigan, but it doesn't come up to the jingle standard of Ella Wheeler Wilcox. I don't say this to malign Bacon's poetic skills. I think that with constant candle burning and thoughtful moonlight walks, Bacon might have attained that mastery of English prosody evident in Wilcox's volume of homespun rimes, *Poems of Passion*.

On the morning of August 26, 1983, I expended a fruitless two hours in the New York Public Library in quest of factual information to link the lives of Shakespeare and Bacon. At noon I arrived at my gallery, where a preoccupied young man was waiting to confer with me. He looked as though no gold mines had been discovered in his garden. He also looked as though he hadn't eaten in several days. I know the appearance because I have gone hungry in New York.

"I have some autographs to show you, Mr. Hamilton," he said. "But I need time to get them ready. If you will give me a piece of paper I'll prepare them for you to look at."

My secretary gave him a piece of stationery. He entered our viewing room, sat down at a table, and passed into a state of transcendental meditation during which, from time to time, he made jerky motions with his pen.

When he had finished, half an hour later, he confronted me. "I have just been in touch through the spiritual world with Bacon and Shakespeare. I have their signatures on this sheet of paper." *(Illus. 69.)*

I was amazed that he mentioned the two men who had been on my mind all morning.

The young man continued: "Do you believe in reincarnation?"

"I'm sorry," I said. "I don't believe in anything. Especially reincarnation."

"I used to be Socrates," he said, undismayed by my answer. "I was born again as Leonardo da Vinci. Then I became Jefferson. I returned the last time as Kahlil Gibran."

[69] Spirit writing of Shakespeare, Bacon, Jefferson and others, with a comment by the medium, ". . . some of these signatures I will not sell." The medium told me that he frequently spoke with Bacon, who told him: "I am the author of Shakespeare's plays."

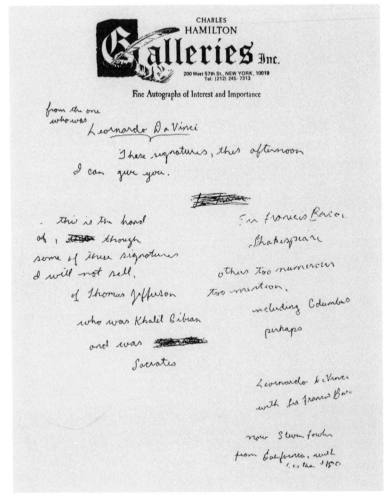

[70] Sir Francis Bacon (1561–1626), essayist and philosopher, who dominated the intellectual life of the late Elizabethan and Jacobean eras. This early portrait of Bacon as Lord Verulam is from his *Sylva Sylvarum* (1627).

I said nothing.

"I thought you might like to communicate with Bacon. You know, the man who wrote the plays of Shakespeare. I know that Bacon wrote Shakespeare's plays because he's told me so many times."

I listened.

The youth handed me a sheet of my stationery on which he'd scrawled a lot of names, including his own and William Shakespeare's. He offered to supply me with all the rare autographs of Bacon and Shakespeare I needed. I said, "Thanks, but I don't want to glut the market and depress the values."

He cast a dolorous look upon me. "I was hoping that meeting you would change my luck," he said. "My luck has been bad lately."

"Maybe this will improve it," I said. And I handed him three dollars. He thanked me with ebullience. But he continued to sit in my reception room, mumbling an occasional remark about a faraway world where things would be better. He asked to use our bathroom, where he remained a considerable while. When he emerged I handed him a cigarette and said, "Well, I'm sorry you have to be leaving now. I hope I meet you again someday."

The youth presented me with the sheet on which he had recorded the "spirit writing." The signatures were remarkably alike.

There is a postscript to this story. After our psychic acquaintance walked out of the gallery, my two young assistants, Dianne Barbaro and Carolyn Compton, both of whom had been frightened by this bizarre visitor, reconnoitred to see what evidence of his visitation he'd left behind. On the toilet seat in the bathroom was a cryptic note: "Allen Cohen is not to be in my prescense. My signature does not and will not involve Allen Cohen."

The note was signed "Sir Francis Bacon."

V

SHAKESPEARE'S MANGLED WILL

THERE is a tale invented long ago by some imaginative writer—and repeated with uncritical zeal by each fresh generation of biographers since Halliwell-Phillipps published his great *Outlines of the Life of Shakespeare* (1881)—that Shakespeare's will was drawn up for him on January 25, 1616, by Francis Collins, the poet's attorney. The story goes on to say that two months later, after the marriage (February 10, 1616) of Shakespeare's daughter to the local seducer Thomas Quiney, the poet summoned Collins to revise the will. The dramatist wished to change Judith's bequest to a marriage portion. This necessitated rewriting the first page. Collins or his scrivener (a clerk ubiquitous in the annals of Stratford) screwed up the date in rewriting the first page. He copied the date January 25 from the earlier draft of the will, instead of writing March 25, and then had to correct the blunder. This mistake, a trifling one, set the tone for the entire will.

If Collins did prepare the will, he did a wretched job and turned out a most imperfect document. Lawyers of today who defend Collins's mangled job should have their own wills butchered in the same manner. Assuming for a moment that Collins (or his scrivener) was culpable, he permitted the famous poet to blunder and flounder through three entangled pages of dictation. I can only explain the mass of errors, corrections and deletions by suggesting that Collins and his client indulged in a merry celebration before the attorney ever set quill to paper.

A few of the mistakes: Collins left a blank space for the name of Shakespeare's nephew, Thomas, when the poet couldn't recall it. A mere query to Mrs. Anne Hathaway Shakespeare would have sufficed to fill the gap. Collins wrote incorrectly the name of Shakespeare's close friend Hamnet Sadler, a prominent citizen whom the lawyer certainly knew. True, Sadler was occasionally called Hamlet Sadler, but Hamlet was not his given name and Collins should have known better. Collins allowed the poet to leave his granddaughter Elizabeth Hall all his plate except a silver-gilt bowl. Then, in another part of the will later on, he let him bequeath the same plate to his daughter Susanna and her husband, Dr. John Hall. In the first and second drafts of the will Collins permitted Shakespeare to bypass all mention of his lifelong companion, his wife, and then, as an afterthought, give her his second-best bed. To top off this wretched performance, Collins or his scrivener penned at the end of the will: "In witness whereof I have hereunto put my seale." Collins was certainly aware that the poet had no seal; on a previous occasion when a seal was required, Shakespeare had to borrow and use the seal of one Henry Lawrence. The result of this blunder by Collins or his scrivener was that the word seale had to be deleted and the word hand substituted. A final indignity from the lawyer or his clerk was the spelling of Shakespeare's name in two different ways in the body of the will.

In "Shakespeare's Will" *(Georgetown Law Journal)*, A. Wigfall Green insists that Collins or his scrivener did a pretty good job. However, as Green launches into a catalogue of some of the major blunders in the will his doubts seem to grow. Finally he cannot refrain from the comment that the "amanuensis" allegedly provided by Collins to prepare the will of the most famous man in Stratford, and one of the wealthiest, may have been "a trifle gauche and obtuse." Lawyers, as we all know, stick together, so it was a major concession for Green to admit that Collins's job was less than flawless. Green writes:

It will be noted that the name of one of the sons of Joan Hart [Shakespeare's sister] is omitted in the first line of page 1 [*sic,* page 2]. [Joseph Quincy] Adams calls this omission a pathetic touch, in that Shakespeare was unable to remember the name of one of his nephews. It is believed, however, to be the result of incompetency of the amanuensis. Shakespeare probably assumed that the scrivener knew the name of his three nephews, and thought it was unnecessary to dictate them; the scrivener probably did know the names of two, but failed to recall the Christian name of the third, for which reason he left a space to fill in later; or, as is, perhaps, more probable, Shakespeare dictated the Christian name, but the scrivener failed to catch it; rather than annoy Shakespeare, he left a space, intending to obtain the name from some other member of the family, but he probably forgot, or the will was executed immediately upon his finishing the last line of it; thus, he may have had no opportunity to obtain the name. The defect, it should be noted, is not a fatal one; the three sons of Joan Hart would have taken, had the Christian name of no one of them been mentioned specially. One suspects that the amanuensis was a trifle gauche and obtuse, because of numerous other similar errors of a clerical nature. For instance, on page 1, lines 27 and 28, in the mention of his sister, one may well imagine that Shakespeare or Collins said simply "Joan Hart." The clerk did not hear the name; upon being asked to repeat, Shakespeare or Collins pronounced the name as it is spelled, viz., "Jo-an," but the clerk spelled it "Johane." When the poet repeated the name next, the scrivener spelt it phonetically, according to the common spelling of the day, viz., "Jone," in spite of the inconsistency. Moreover, in line 12 of page 2, Shakespeare undoubtedly dictated the name, "Hamnet Sadler," as the name is subscribed on page 3. But "Hamnet" from the mouth of Shakespeare could mean only "Hamlet" to the scrivener; therefore, he wrote it so.

You would think that Green would pause for a moment and reflect that because of the extremely intimate nature of the will Shakespeare might have preferred to write it himself, rather than confide family secrets to an attorney.

In an indictment of the patchwork document Archibald Stalker wrote in "Is Shakespeare's Will a Forgery?" (*Quarterly Review*, 1940):

> Shakespeare's will . . . is as defective a document as ever went unchallenged in the courts of law and literature. It contains many deletions and insertions not authenticated by signature, initials, or final testing-clause. It shows change of mind and bequest also unauthenticated. It is apparently a second draft, but even after the second draft was completed Shakespeare had not made up his mind about his intentions. Its mangled condition signifies that Shakespeare was helpless, that neither he nor the lawyer consulted the poet's son-in-law, Dr. Hall, about the form of the document, and that Dr. Hall took no interest in it though he was to be an executor and was vitally interested in seeing that the will, being very much in his wife's favour and much to the disadvantage of Judith Shakespeare, her sister, should be valid. It appears that no other relative was in a position to demand from the lawyer a proper document, though four hours would have sufficed to produce one, and as Shakespeare lived about a month after the date of the will he certainly could have signed a proper one. According to the document the great poet was irrational and forgetful in details, besides being unjust to his wife and unfair to his younger daughter. Still more, the legal draftsman must have been incompetent.
>
> These are large assumptions. One defect after another, one oddity after another has been explained by suppositions, but the accumulation of defects and oddities, the charges of general helplessness, incompetence, carelessness and lack of intelligence on the part of every person about the household of a great man, including his lawyer and himself, ought not to be accepted without full enquiry. . . .

Stalker's purpose was to cast doubt upon the authenticity of Shakespeare's will. He has, instead, provided a pile of excellent reasons for believing that the will was not conceived and drafted by Collins, but by Shakespeare.

Professor B. Roland Lewis, in his *The Shakespeare Documents,* takes the accepted position that Collins or his scrivener wrote the will. Professor Lewis writes: "While this will is obviously not a 'fair copy'—a final and finished recopied draft free from errors, erasures, blots and other blemishes—it is as 'fair' as most wills of the period. Certainly, the will is not merely a first 'rough' draft. It is not a product of mutilation and slovenliness; in comparison with other Elizabethan wills, it is not [as Professor Joseph Quincy Adams stated] a 'crude, patched up thing.' A letter-perfect will before 1600 is a rarity. This script certainly was not the work of an illiterate person, in plan, in phrasing, or in handwriting."

I must disagree with Professor Lewis's implication that mangled wills are abundant at that period. I have never run into a probated (or proved) Jacobean will with so many deletions and corrections as Shakespeare's.

The will is written on three sheets of foolscap, each sheet by a different maker and each slightly different in size. The first sheet is 12 1/8 by 15 5/8 inches; the second is 12 1/2 by 15 3/4; and the third is 12 1/4 by 15 3/8 inches. If Collins or his clerk wrote the will, it seems curious that he or his clerk could not produce matching legal paper on which to write the will of his old friend. Nearly all wills of the period were penned on uniform paper of foolscap size, about 12 1/2 by 16 inches. It is most unusual to find a will on sheets of different sizes.

If Collins was, as Professor Lewis and other authorities say, responsible for this wretchedly scrawled will, why did he invite beneficiaries to sign as witnesses and then ask for four witnesses instead of the two required by law? Is it possible that Collins or his scrivener was not familiar with the legal requirements (two witnesses who were not beneficiaries) for a will?

In every way this will seems to me to reveal the mind of a man tortured by doubts and indecision and, worse, by acute lapses of memory. The interlinear corrections in the text of the will are penned in such a crabbed script that it is likely no scrivener or lawyer would approve them. Professor Joseph Quincy Adams explains the legal blunders by suggesting that "Collins was in an agitated frame of mind, and working under unfavorable conditions. . . ." *(A Life of William Shakespeare)*. But neither Adams nor any other biographer of Shakespeare has attempted to explain the incredibly bad handwriting, the tremulous script so hard to decipher that it would fetch a blush to the visage of that master of unreadable chirography, Horace Greeley.

All of the contradictions and irregularities that have been attributed to ineptitude on the part of Collins or his scrivener can be explained with no difficulty if you accept Shakespeare as the unaided writer of the will.

Probably Shakespeare, who as we know from his plays possessed an excellent knowledge of law, had before him a standard form to follow. His "small" Latin seemed adequate to launch the will. Here is one of the forms for a will from a handbook called *Simboleographie*, by William West (1605):

West: forme of a Will
In the name of God Amen . . . . I, R.L., of &c. sicke of bodie but of good and perfect memory (God be praised) doe make and ordaine this my last will and testament in maner and forme following, that is to say: First I commend my soule into the hands of God my maker, hoping assuredly through the only merites of Jesus Christ my Saviour, to be made partaker of life everlasting, And I commend my bodie to the earth wherof it is made.

Shakespeare's Will
In the name of god Amen I William Shackspeare of Stratford vpon Avon in the countie of warrwick gentleman, in perfect health & memorie god be praysed Doe make & Ordayne this my last will & testament in manner & forme followeing That ys to saye ffirst I Comend my Soule into the handes of god my Creator hoping & assuredlie beleeving through thonelie Merittes of Jesus Christe my Saviour to be made partaker of lyfe everlastinge And my bodye to the Earth whereof yt ys made

As you can see, Shakespeare followed the standard form pretty closely, merely purpling the legal jargon.

Nearly all legal forms then, as now, picked a sample date in January. When Shakespeare sat down to date his will March 25, 1616, he may have copied, by error, the month of January from the form. Nobody knows when Shakespeare wrote the first draft of page one, but it was possibly very late in 1615 and more likely in January 1616, perhaps in anticipation of his daughter Judith's marriage to Thomas Quiney.

Some biographers of Shakespeare explain that Collins was an expert at putting over in court wills that were a little irregular and very messy in appearance. I was unable to find any evidence to support this assertion. These biographers go on to state that most wills of the Elizabethan and Jacobean eras were not masterpieces of clarity and legibility. However, judging from the hundreds of seventeenth century wills that I've examined in nearly half a century as a manuscriptophile, I can state unequivocally that Shakespeare's will merits the nit-ridden calamus award for the most mangled testament. In my opinion it was not written by a practicing lawyer or his clerk, but was personally composed and penned by Shakespeare.

VI

BY ME WILLIAM SHAKSPEARE

THE last will and testament of William Shakespeare is one of the most provocative documents ever penned. It contains not a word that suggests poetry or drama; yet it holds the key to the character, ideals and aspirations of the world's greatest poet. It is pregnant with undiscovered secrets. Thus it merits a penetrating examination (*illus.* 71, 72, 73).

Nearly all Shakespearean scholars are divided into three will-writing camps: those who believe that the poet's attorney, Francis Collins, wrote the will; those who believe that Collins's scrivener (clerk or amanuensis) wrote the will; and those who aren't certain whether Collins or his scrivener wrote the will, but are positive it was one or the other.

There is a fourth camp—a very lonely one, as I appear to be its only living member —according to which Shakespeare himself penned the will. Most of the scholars in the first three camps would amiably recommend that any person holding the "Shakespeare holograph" view have his cerebral cortex scrutinized by a competent alienist. Shakespearean scholar B. Roland Lewis bluntly calls the idea of a holographic will "untenable." In the past century only four clear voices were raised in support of the holographic will theory, and one of those quickly and abashedly retracted her view and joined the Collins camp.

The first to claim the will was holographic was Colonel John Cordy Jeaffreson, now remembered mainly for his romantic biographies of Byron and Shelley. Jeaffreson was the British Maurois. Then came J. Pym Yeatman in 1901. He was followed by an eccentric Austrian graphologist, Magdalene Thumm-Kintzell, who contended also that Shakespeare wrote some of Bacon's essays. Finally, in 1936, the very colorful Countess Clara Longworth de Chambrun.

It now falls to my lot to disturb many years of unruffled silence. But before presenting my evidence, I'd like to discuss my predecessors in the holographic theory. Although their long-forgotten essays were unfamiliar to me when I began writing this book, I feel their work should be brought to your attention and in that way pay tribute to their foresight and scholarly acumen.

J. C. Jeaffreson published his findings in a three-column article in *The Athenaeum* (1882). For the most part, Colonel Jeaffreson was on target. He writes:

A careful study of two different fac-similes of Shakespeare's will and an examination of the original document at Somerset House have caused me to think . . . that, instead of being intended for the will itself, the writing was meant only for a sketch for the instruction of a competent draughtsman . . . and that it was written throughout by Shakespeare himself. . . .

The errors, the erasures, the insertions, the evidence of the rewriting of the first sheet, the diction, the penmanship, the structure, and the whole general character of the document proving beyond all doubt that, instead of being meant in the first instance for the will itself, it was only the rough draft and sketch *for* a will, and that it was not made by a lawyer. . . .

The rough draft for Shakespeare's will (which accidentally came to be the will itself) was not penned by a lawyer; it is inconceivable that Shakespeare asked a non-legal friend to make it for him; it follows that Shakespeare made it for himself. . . .

I have no hesitation in saying that the signatures support the opinion that the will is holograph. Of course there are differences between the writing of the signatures and the writing of the body of the document; but all the differences are such differences as one would expect to find between the free, strong handwriting of a man sitting at his desk in 'perfect health' and the feeble handwriting of the same man broken with fatal illness and propped with pillows in his bed. The *e*'s of the signatures differ from well-looped *e*'s of the body of the will, but they are all *made for the loop,* and obviously would have been well looped had the exhausted writer retained his old command of the pen. Moreover, once and again one comes in the body of the will on a slovenly *e,* that, wanting the clear loop, and in that respect resembling the *e*'s of the signatures, indicates that the free-hand writer of January [when pages 2 and 3 of the will were probably written] would in times of extreme physical weakness and urgent haste make his *e*'s precisely like the *e*'s of the dying testator. [Colonel Jeaffreson was not familiar with the secretary script and did not realize that the loop on the *e* was not required and that Shakespeare, like many other Elizabethans, wrote the *e* with or without the loop, according to whim.] The same remarks may be made in respect to the *y* of the third signature (in the word 'By') and the *y*'s of the earlier writing. . . .

The preceding excerpts from Colonel Jeaffreson's brief article make up most of the evidence he adduced for his belief that the will was holographic. In a subsequent issue of *The Athenaeum* (May 20, 1882) Dr. F. A. Leo, editor of the *Jahrbuch der Shakespeare-Gesellschaft,* opposed Colonel Jeaffreson's view: "Will Mr. John Cordy Jeaffreson kindly compare the letter *p* in the name Shakespeare, written by the poet himself on the three leaves of his will, with the same letter as it is found twice in the context of the will in the name Shakespeare?

"In the handwriting of Shakespeare, received as genuine, the letter *p* always has the same character . . .

"Should this not be sufficient evidence against the [common] identity of the writer and the signer of Shakespeare's will?"

Jeaffreson replied to Dr. Leo in the May 27, 1882, issue of *The Athenaeum*, pointing out that "Shakespeare was one of the many seventeenth century writers who did not uniformly and rigidly adhere in their signatures to letters of a particular and invariable fashion." Jeaffreson might also have noted that the authentic signature of Shakespeare on the counterpart of the deed of purchase to a gatehouse in Blackfriars (March 10, 1613) incorporates a *p* of the same pattern as the *p* in the signatures written in the text of the will.

Little attention was paid to Colonel Jeaffreson's article, perhaps because his evidence was brief and inconclusive. The arguments of J. Pym Yeatman eighty-two years ago in *Is William Shakespeare's Will Holographic?* (n.p., 1901) are more cogent; yet his assault on the ramparts of establishment scholarship was quickly and vigorously repulsed. Yeatman, like Jeaffreson, was not a handwriting expert but he noted some salient facts that should, I think, be clear to anyone who examines the writing in Shakespeare's will.

After a discussion of the diversity of Shakespeare's signatures and the resultant scholarly confusion, Yeatman comments on the handwriting in the will:

The writer of the signatures was the scribe who wrote the Will, and the only question left, if this be the case, is whether the scribe wrote the signatures for the Testator, or whether the Will is not in fact holographic. The first hypothesis may be rejected safely, and the second supplies the great want, in itself a most extraordinary circumstance, that in this draft there is a positive evidence of the Poet's handwriting.

There is a great difference which has to be accounted for between the writing of the signatures and that of the draft itself; but this is explained by the double date upon it, showing that some two months had elapsed since the preparation of the draft commenced and its execution as a Will —months during which the Will was written by instalments, and it is obvious from the contents that the Testator had lain on a bed of sickness; for although there are some few corrections— chiefly additions—to it, the old blunders of the writer had not been properly corrected, and so remain to the end. The Poet died on the 23rd of April, nearly a month after the execution of the Will—if the date of the month is accurate—but no attempt seems to have been made to alter it, or to retranscribe it—tolerable proof that the state of his mind did not permit him to reconsider it, and it was probably only in a fluttering of vital energy, which often occurs just before the end, that he was prevailed upon or desired to execute it, in its imperfect form, in order that an intestacy might not occur.

Yeatman makes a brief attack upon Sir Sidney Lee for assuming (as did Lee's predecessor Halliwell-Phillipps) that Shakespeare summoned Francis Collins to write the will. Yeatman continues: "Nothing can be clearer than that Francis Collyns did not write the draft, for we have the clearest evidence of his handwriting in his own signature, which he appends first to the Will. His hand is a small, crabbed, tailless, lawyer-like hand, quite unlike that of the Poet, or whoever wrote the draft, which is in a large, bold, free hand, remarkably so for that period, and just such a hand as we should expect the Poet to employ. . . ."

Yeatman is on the right path but he stumbles into a clump of primroses when he avers that "some of the corrections in the Will were made by Francis Collyns." After this unwarranted concession to the prevailing scholarly opinion, Yeatman sinks deeper into the Collins-wrote-the-corrections morass. Eventually, he rallies with an extraordinarily important discovery of which he fails to take any advantage: "The last [interlinear] addition, that of the bequest of the second best bed to his wife, is, however, very clearly in the Poet's feeblest hand, and exactly corresponds with the signature below it. It is more like his signature appended to the Will, but it is not unlike the handwriting of the draft; in fact it is the golden link between them, of the utmost value, in proof that one hand wrote them both. This correction was evidently the last made."

In her article "The Book Shakespeare Used—a Discovery" (*Scribner's Magazine*, 1936), the Countess Clara Longworth de Chambrun announced that she had turned up a copy of the second edition of Holinshed's *Chronicles* annotated by Shakespeare. She writes: "Not only does the possession of this volume give us material enough to form a solid basis of comparison with other texts, but I do not hesitate to declare that the Shakespeare will is written throughout by him, and that other documents hitherto unrecognized will soon be authoritatively established. . . ." The countess goes on to say that "the result of this study . . . confirms beyond doubt the authenticity of the signature affixed to Florio's translation of *Montaigne's Essays.* . . ." She adds that the annotated copy of Holinshed (which, with the Montaigne book, will be discussed in a later chapter) also put the stamp of authenticity upon a disputed document known as the *Northumberland Manuscript.* The countess concludes her remarkable essay by a summary: "So the discovery of Shakespeare's *Holinshed* and the comparison therein contained [establish that] the will . . . is written throughout in the same hand as the Holinshed marginalia, the [title page of the] Northumberland Manuscript and the duly attested signatures of William Shakespeare of Stratford-on-Avon in the County of Warwick, Gentleman!"

The immense significance of the discovery about Shakespeare's will by the Countess de Chambrun hardly arched an eyebrow in the soporific realm of academia of the Thirties. Nobody believed her. In fact, she didn't even believe herself. Two years later, in her book *Shakespeare Rediscovered,* she recanted. After hypothecating that Shakespeare's lawyer, Francis Collins, was suffering from arthritis when he penned the will (which explained his erratic penmanship), the countess declared that "there is no shadow of a doubt that Francis Collins held the pen when the poet's Will was consigned to paper and any critic who would continue to uphold a contrary opinion formerly expressed must divest himself of all literary probity." The countess concludes: "I can only say *mea culpa* when I remember that in the first flush of conviction that Shakespeare's Will was holographic I expressed that belief in an article written in *Scribner's.* . . ."

The claims for the authorship of Collins or his scrivener are at best tenuous. The handwriting in the will is, for the most part, an excellent example of the secretary, or running, hand employed by Shakespeare in his six known signatures. If Collins's scrivener wrote the will, most likely that is the script he would have used. But there are curious features about the chirography in the will, bizarre individual characteristics, that make it most unlikely that this is a clerical document.

[71] Shakespeare's Last Will and Testament, page 1

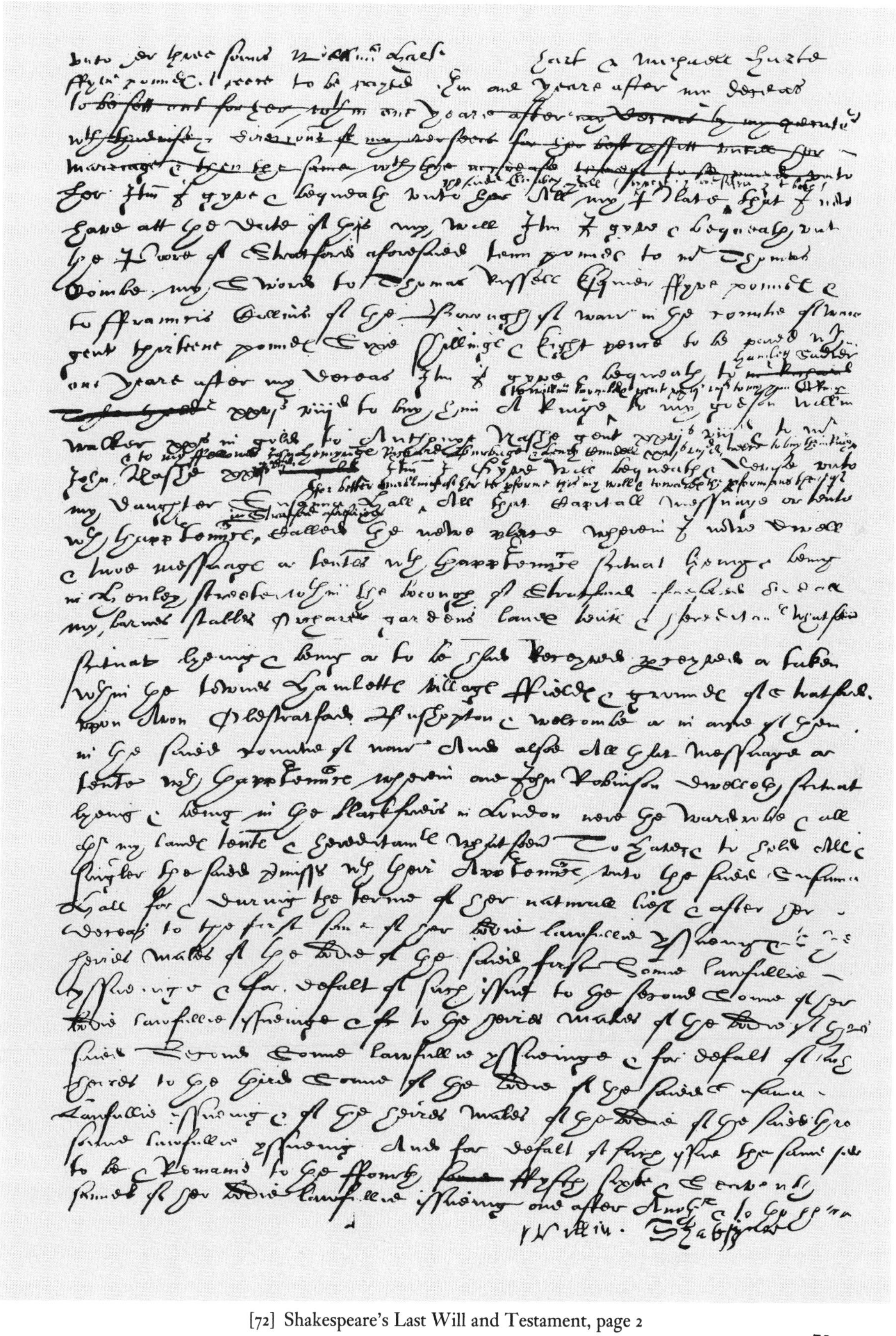

[72] Shakespeare's Last Will and Testament, page 2

[73] Shakespeare's Last Will and Testament, page 3

Illustration 74 shows three examples of Collins's signature, including the one scribbled [b] on the will. Collins died in 1617, the year after Shakespeare did, and his signature on the will appears feeble and tremulous by comparison with his bold, earlier signatures. Also illustrated is the handwriting in John Combe's will, said to be that of Collins's scrivener; neither Collins's script nor that of his scrivener bears any similarity to the handwriting in Shakespeare's will *(illus. 75, 78)*.

The script in Shakespeare's will varies enormously. A scrivener's job, on the other hand, was to write in legible script. He was not expected to vary his spelling and handwriting from line to line, to form his words differently according to penchant, and he was required to use punctuation when needed to clarify a thought. The penman of

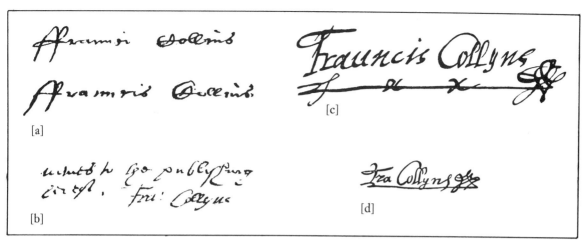

[74] Comparison of Handwriting of Francis Collins with That of Shakespeare's Will

[a] Francis Collins's name as it appears twice in Shakespeare's will, penned in the secretary hand of Shakespeare.

[b] Notation, "witnes to the publishing hereof," in Shakespeare's enfeebled hand, identical with the script in the interlinear additions to the will. The notation is signed by Francis Collins. Notice the difference between the way Collins writes his name and the way Shakespeare pens it in the will. The visual resemblance between Shakespeare's notation and Collins's signature is caused by the similarity in ink intensity. The feel of the two handwritings is entirely different. Collins's signature indicates that he could not have written the easy, flowing first draft of Shakespeare's will or the fragmented, broken, almost illegible interlinear additions. Collins's script is modern, with every letter (except the faded *a* in *Fra:* and the faded terminal *s*) very legible, whereas Shakespeare's five-word note is in the secretary script and difficult to decipher.

[c] Early signature of Francis Collins. Observe that the lawyer's script here, as on the will, is much easier to read than the "old-style" secretary hand used by Shakespeare. The poet employs the antiquated *ff* for *F* and the secretary *C* that looks like a dolled-up *O*. The minuscule letters are also different, especially the *y* in Collyns. Collins swings the tail of his *y* to the left, as in modern writing, and Shakespeare swings it to the right, as in the *By me* that precedes his signature at the end of the will. Collins uses the modern *r* and Shakespeare prefers the secretary *r* that resembles a *u* or *v*. Collins's terminal *s* is modern. Shakespeare employed the secretary terminal *s* that looks like an *o* with a tiny tongue of ink flickering upward from its top.

[d] Early signature of Francis Collins, showing his abbreviated given name, *Fra*, also used in his signature on the will.

the will used *i* and *y* interchangeably. The same word sometimes has a terminal *e*, sometimes not, as *said* and *saide*. He also seemed to be unaware that commas and periods were at his disposal.

The will was written in at least two installments. First the entire will of three pages, then a subsequent revision of page 1, running two lines over into page 2, and finally the interlinear bequests. The handwriting of page 1, penned later than that of pages 2 and 3, shows a disintegration of the script in the lower third of the page. The chirography is not as smooth or well organized and there is an uncontrolled formation of words. It is clear that the penman's health has deteriorated in the period between the writing of the first and second drafts.

[75] Comparison of Handwriting from John Combe's Will and Shakespeare's.

(Top) Four lines from manuscript of John Combe's will, attributed to Francis Collins's scrivener. Combe's bequest of £5 to Shakespeare is mentioned and Shakespeare's full name occurs as the first two words in the third line. I have examined a photocopy of the will, dated January 28, 1613 (now in the Public Record Office, London, Prob. 11/126, formerly in Somerset House, catalogued as 118 Wood or 118 Rudd). It bears no corrections of any kind and is a fair copy penned by a fluent amanuensis. The sheets are numbered at the bottom in a modern hand. It seems scarcely possible that this is the document other writers claim is in the same hand as Shakespeare's will. B. Roland Lewis (in volume 2 of *The Shakespeare Documents*) writes: "The will of the wealthy John Combe [who, by the way, was the godfather of Francis Collins's son. C.H.] was written by the same clerk who wrote the last will and testament of William Shakespeare. Combe's will, also, was drawn up by Francis Collins. Combe's will is preserved today at Somerset House [It was moved in 1962 to the Public Record Office. C.H.], catalogued as '118 Rudd.' It is written on nine folio pages, on one side of the sheet only, each page numbered at the bottom. Like Shakespeare's will it contains a number of deletions, alterations, and interlineations. Like Shakespeare's will it, too, is not a 'fair' copy. It has no punctuation, is not paragraphed, and has no signatures of witnesses. Like many of that day, the will calls for the testator's signature 'unto everye sheete herof'; but John Combe's signature appears at the bottom of the last sheet only."

If Professor Lewis is discussing the same document of which a photocopy now lies before me, then he was grossly misinformed, for the 118 Wood copy is definitely a fair copy, with no corrections or interlinear markings. It is certainly not in the same hand as Shakespeare's will.

(Bottom) Four lines from Shakespeare's will in which the poet's name appears (last word of the top line and first word of the second line). The handwriting in Shakespeare's will is completely different from that in John Combe's. Compare the writing of the name of William Shakespeare (first two words of line three) as it appears in Combe's will with the poet's name in his own will.

74

There is also carelessness and hesitation in the mode of expression. The penman begins a word, then expunges it and starts another. This could, of course, be the result of a dictating testator, bumbling around trying to get his ideas straight. But it is not probable that even a confused testator could cause a professional scrivener to abandon the uniformity of his script.

The handwriting of the interlinear changes and additions also suggests degeneration of health. If Shakespeare were dictating the will, the scrivener must have been either ill or inebriated, for the handwriting is at times so tremulous that it is nearly impossible to decipher. The beauty and power of the first draft of pages 2 and 3 have vanished. In their stead is a wayward path of shaky, broken script with many letters strangely fragmented. Surely in writing a will a clerk would have been more careful to place the words evenly between lines and write with special clarity because of the limited space. But there seems to have been little attempt at legibility, only a labored, uncertain effort to set down the ideas in as little space as possible. Shall we assume that Collins, or his scrivener, was a very ill man?

I think not. The variations in the handwriting are precisely those we have previously observed in the six known signatures of Shakespeare. Many of the individual letters of the alphabet used by the poet in his variant signatures crop up in the will. Letters one would expect to be most consistent—consonants like *p*, *b* and *y*—vary greatly. The capital letters are wild and uncertain. The name Shakespeare is written in the will three times, each time differently. At the top of page 1, in the upper left, it is set down as *T*[estator] *Wm Shackspeare*. In the first line of text it is spelled *Willm Shackspeare*, with a gracefully encircled tittle (supralineal device) over the *m* to indicate an omission of several letters. On page 3, the last word of line 7 and the first word of line 8, it is spelled *Willm Shackspere*, with a straight line over the *m* to indicate the omission of *ia*. The testator's name written three times by Collins or his scrivener and spelled a different way each time? In that case, it could have been the lawyer or his clerk who signed the six variant signatures of the poet!

Not only is the spelling of Shakespeare's name varied; the handwriting too is different in each of the signatures. Examine the two signatures at the very top of the first page of the will. On the far left, the *Wm Shackspeare* that follows the *T* is certainly in the same hand (it has the same feel) as the *Shackspeare* in line 1 of the body of the will, but the capital *S* is different. So are the *b*, *c*, *k*, *p*, *e*, *r*, and the terminal *e*. Is this the handwriting of a methodical, trained scrivener?

If we had nothing else to go on, we could accept the enormous variations in orthography and handwriting as potent evidence that this will is entirely in the hand of the testator, William Shakespeare.

Probably in early January the poet obtained three large sheets of foreign-made foolscap, not quite matching in size but doubtless the best available in Stratford. He wrote a complete draft of his will on three pages but did not immediately sign it. Some time later, most likely two months, on March 25, 1616 (the first day of the legal year), he rewrote the first page, or the first two-thirds of the first page, to include a marriage arrangement for his daughter Judith, who had been hastily wed under mysterious circumstances on February 10, 1616. Shakespeare put down January instead of March, but corrected the error. In rewriting the relevant section of the page, he crowded the lines together at the bottom and ran two lines over to the top of page 2, thus avoiding a rewrite of pages 2 and 3, already finished.

In the signature after the initial *T*, for Testator, at the top left of the first page, Shakespeare drew a line sharply down from the *Wm* to indicate that the word was an abbreviation of his first name. Under the signature the poet inscribed a huge *R*, probably for *Recognoscatur* [Let it be known]. Beneath the *R* and starting next to it is a swirl that resembles a Michigan cyclone. This swirl is nothing more than a pen-and-ink gesture of satisfaction. Many writers burst out with a similar flourish when they flog to completion a truculent manuscript. I venture to predict that if the original manuscript of *Hamlet* ever turns up, it will bear a similar exultant flourish on the last page.

The writing on the lower third of the first page of the will and in the first two lines of page 2 strikes me as very much deteriorated from the original script on pages 2 and 3 of the will and the script at the beginning of the first page of the will. It is the penmanship of an enfeebled man. And the crowding of words and lines at the bottom of page 1 produces an even less ebullient and more cramped script. The interlinear additions and corrections show a progressive disintegration of the handwriting. By the time Shakespeare makes the last interlinear correction, leaving his second-best bed to his wife (page 3), his hand trembles violently, resulting in a script so migratory that the words are almost impossible to decipher. The poet may have penned this final addition to his will only a few minutes before his death. In my opinion it was immediately after he wrote this line that the four witnesses gathered to watch the dying man struggle through his attestation of authorship: "By me William Shakspeare."

According to Sir Edmund K. Chambers, the ink of the interlinear insertions is different from that used in writing the body of the will. And Dr. Samuel A. Tannenbaum, a sharp observer, noted that the ink on the interlinear corrections is the same as the ink used by the witnesses: Julyn̄s Shawe, John Robinson, Hamnet Sadler and Robert Whatcott. This would indicate, as does the tremulous signature of Shakespeare, that the final changes were made very near the end of the poet's life. Shakespeare, as Malone pointed out two centuries ago, likely signed page 3 of the will first, then page 2, and finally page 1.

There has been a lot of comment on the difference in legibility between the words, *By me William* and the surname *Shakspeare*. I think the strength of the dying man just gave out. George Greenwood, in *Shakspere's Handwriting and the Northumberland Manuscript*, says: "I am convinced that these three words, 'By me William' were not written by the testator, but by some other person—probably the law-scrivener—on his behalf. If the testator could have written these three words so well, so firmly and distinctly, why should he have made such terrible scrawls of his surname and his two other Will signatures?"

The words *By me William* were certainly penned by the poet, in my opinion, for they match in feel and in size and lettering the first part of Shakespeare's surname, written moments before his hand became so tremulous he could not control the formation of the letters. Perhaps Sir George should have set a sharper eye on the words *By me William*, for he would have then detected a clearly visible tremor in the writing. This is especially obvious in the double *l* in *William:* the descending strokes are almost spastic. In the surname, *Shak* is shaky and the fragmented capital *S* seems almost to have eluded the testator's pen. The *peare* is readable only with great difficulty: the first *e* lies open at the top; the tremulous *r* is sharp instead of bowed up at the base, and the terminal *e*, like its predecessor, is badly formed and also open at the top.

Removing individual letters of the alphabet from the body of the will and placing them with the signatures in which very similar letters occur reveals how strikingly the eccentric penmanship in the will resembles the eccentric penmanship in the signatures. The examples in illustration 76 disclose what an entire volume of sesquipedalian verbiage could not reveal.

When I first detected that the interlinear additions to the will were in Shakespeare's hand, it was the feel of the writing that convinced me. Only later did I compare the individual words and letters. The first letter I looked for was the letter *e* in the *me* of the signature. I found, as I had anticipated, an identical *e* in the word *p[er]forme* in the interlinear sentence "for better enabling of her to perform*e* this my will . . ." Incidentally, elsewhere in the will the same *e* occurs frequently. The next letter I checked was the *m* in *me*. The letter occurs everywhere throughout the interlinear text and is the same as in the subscription to the will. I then checked the *y* in *By*. An identical *y* occurs on page 2, in the interlinear line beginning "& to m*y* fellowes . . ." I recollected that in this same line Burbage is mentioned, so I looked at the capital *B* in *B*urbage and found that it was formed in exactly the same way as the *B* in *By me*. The capital *B* starts with a stroke that looks like a check mark that converges to a point. The second part of the *B* looks almost like a figure 8 listing to the right.

The next part of the signature I examined was the *ha* in *Sha*kespeare; I found a similar formation in the name *Ha*mlett Sadler, a supralinear notation at the extreme right of page 2, about a third of the way down. Although the *h* in *Ha*mlett is not connected to the *a* with a lower loop, as in the signature, the identical loop that Shakespeare used in signing his surname may be found three times in the interlinear name of Jo*h*n Hem-*yn*ges, as well as elsewhere in the interlinear text.

In the abbreviated signature Will̄m at the very end of line 8 on the last page of the will, the *ill* and *m* are formed precisely like the same letters in the name *William* in the signature. The bar, or tittle, over the *m*, indicating an abbreviation, was so much a part of Shakespeare's usual signature that even when he signed his given name in full, as he did at the end of the will, he automatically put a bar above the *m*. The *a*'s in the signature at the end of the document are, as you will at once perceive, the same as the *a*'s in the interlinear text.

Some biographers of Shakespeare who believe the writer of the will to be Collins's scrivener also believe he wrote the names of the witnesses. But a careful examination of the signatures of the witnesses reveals that each is in a very different hand *(illus. 77)*. Take

[a] "By me William Shakspeare," signed to page 3 of the poet's will

[b] Composite signature on page 3 reconstructed with letters taken from the body of Shakespeare's will

[c] Signature of Shakespeare on page 2 of the will

[d] Composite signature on page 2 of the will, reconstructed with letters taken from the body of the will

[e] Signature of Shakespeare (badly eroded, as it appeared in 1863) on page 1 of the will

[f] Composite reconstructed signature on page 1 of the will with letters taken from the body of the will

[g] Original signature of Shakespeare from the Belott-Mountjoy deposition, June 12, 1612

[h] Reconstruction of Belott-Mountjoy signature of Shakespeare with letters taken from the body of the will

[i] Original signature of Shakespeare on a conveyance for a gatehouse in Blackfriars, March 10, 1613

[j] Reconstructed surname of Shakespeare in the gatehouse signature with letters taken from the body of the will

[k] Original signature of Shakespeare on a mortgage to the Blackfriars gatehouse, March 11, 1613

[l] Mortgage signature reconstructed with letters taken from the body of the will

[76] The Six Authentic Signatures of Shakespeare and Reconstruction of Each Using Letters from Words in Body of Shakespeare's Will

The "k" in three of the reconstructions was taken from the interlinear writing in the will and increased 30% in size to conform with Shakespeare's usual script. The symbol for *per* is a composite of two different pen strokes found in the body of the will.

the capital *J* in *Julyn̄s* (first witness), for example, and compare it with the capital *J* in *John* (second witness) and you will see how different is the writing. Notice how Jo*h*n (second witness) writes his *h* and compare this letter to the *h* in Robert W*h*atcott (fourth and last witness). Or look at the terminal *t* in Rober*t* (fourth and last witness) and compare it with the terminal *t* in Hamne*t* (third witness). I could continue with these tedious comparisons, but I think that the cases I've cited suffice to show that each of the witnesses signed. The misleading visual similarity of their scripts can be attributed to the fact that all of them used a dark ink.

In defense of the scholars who have for two centuries insisted that Shakespeare's will was not penned by the dramatist, I must confess that if I had never seen any of Shakespeare's signatures except the six previously known examples, and had tried to determine from them whether or not Shakespeare's will was holographic, I should certainly have concluded that it was not. There is little in the other signatures of Shakespeare, aside from the "By me William Shakspeare" on the will, to lead us to the conclusion that the tumultuously flowing script of the will is in the same handwriting as the wild scrawls that the poet had previously affixed to legal documents. However, writing now after the fact, I can discern a number of interesting similarities in the letters of his name in the signatures and the letters of certain words in the will. I have also tried to reconstruct Shakespeare's three earlier signatures by the use of letters or combinations of letters drawn out of the body of the will *(illus. 76)*. Notice that the *S* in *Shaksper* on the Blackfriars conveyance (1613) is almost the same as the *S* used in the will. Look at the lower belly of the capital *S* in *Shackspere*, the first word in line 9 of page 3 of the will *(illus. 73)*, and note its remarkable similarity to the Blackfriars conveyance *S*. Compare the *h* in the Blackfriars *Shaksper* with the *h* used on pages 2 and 3 of the will *(illus. 72, 73)*. They are virtually identical.

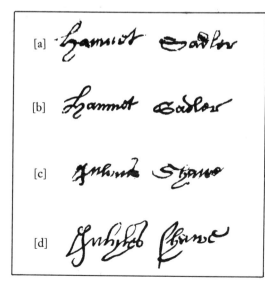

[77] Signatures of two of the witnesses to Shakespeare's will. Some authorities believe that the signatures of the witnesses were all signed by the same person, but this is certainly not the case.

[a] Signature of Hamnet Sadler as a witness to Shakespeare's will
[b] Signature of Hamnet Sadler from an undated document
[c] Signature of Julyn̄s Shawe as a witness to Shakespeare's will
[d] Signature of Julyn̄s Shawe on a document dated 1597. Shawe's signature has changed somewhat in nineteen years, but his capital *J* and distinctive *h* in Shawe are easily recognizable.

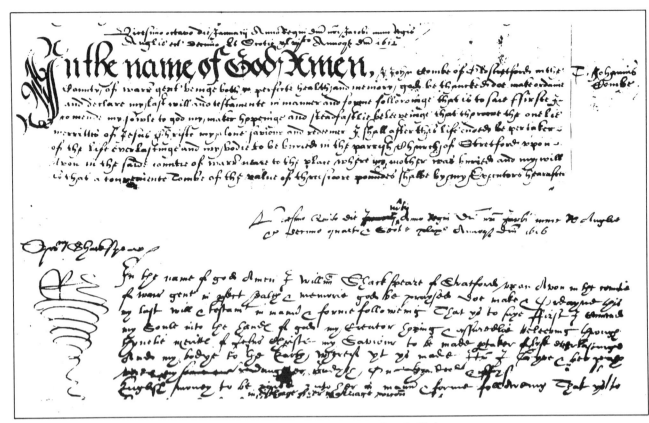

[78] Will of John Combe Compared with Shakespeare's

(Top) The Latin exordium and first eight lines of John Combe's will possibly penned by Francis Collins's clerk. *(Bottom)* The Latin exordium and first eight lines of Shakespeare's will, written in the poet's hand.

The feel of the handwritings is entirely different, the scripts totally unalike. The scrivener who penned Combe's will wrote out the word *and,* with a *d* very different from Shakespeare's; the poet, in writing his will, used an ampersand instead of *and.* The key word *the* in the two scripts is also completely different. The only similarity in the handwritings is that both were done in the secretary hand.

The prevailing academic opinion about these two documents is expressed by Marchette Chute, fellow of the Royal Society of Arts, in her *Shakespeare of London:* "The will [of Shakespeare] is a rough draft, full of corrections, and it has been suggested it was left in that state because Shakespeare was so ill there was no time to make a fair copy. But the lawyer in the case was Francis Collins of Worcester, and Collins was not in the habit of always making a fair copy of

the wills he drew for his clients. He was an experienced lawyer who knew exactly what would stand in court, and the nine-page will he made for John Combe, two years earlier, is also full of deletions and corrections. . . ." This identical old wives' tale, unanimously voiced by Shakespearean scholars, has been uncritically copied by one Shakespeare expert from another Shakespeare expert and so on from the time the first scholar invented it. I have carefully studied a photocopy of the nine-page will of John Combe. It is in the hand of a professional scrivener, fastidiously penned. It contains no spelling irregularities and no corrections or deletions. The statement of Chute (and other scholars) that Collins "was not in the habit of always making a fair copy of the wills he drew for his clients" is an assertion of such importance that the source of it, or the reason for it, should be documented. I venture to say, however, this statement also was cribbed from a Shakespeare scholar who got it from another scholar who got it from another scholar who got it from another scholar who made it up.

80

It remains to fix conclusively the authenticity of Shakespeare's handwriting in the will by a comparison with the three holographic pages by Writer D in *The Booke of Sir Thomas More* (written about 1593) long suspected to be in the hand of the youthful Shakespeare, but never definitely established as his script. If you are curious about the comparison, you have my permission to skip ahead and take a peek at the illustrations in Chapter IX.

TRANSCRIPT OF THE

WILL OF WILLIAM SHAKESPEARE, MARCH 25, 1616

Vicesimo quinto die [Januarij] Martii, anno regni domini nostri Jacobi, nunc regis Angliæ, &c., decimo quarto, et Scotiæ xlix°, annoque Domini 1616.

— T. Wm. SHACKSPEARE

In the name of God, Amen! I William Shackspeare, of Stratford upon Avon in the countie of Warr., gent., in perfect health and memorie, God be praysed, doe make and ordayne this my last will and testament in manner and forme followeing, that ys to saye, First, I comend my soule into the handes of God my Creator, hoping and assuredlie beleeving, through thonelie merittes, of Jesus Christe my Saviour, to be made partaker of lyfe everlastinge, and my bodye to the earth whereof yt ys made. Item, I gyve and bequeath unto my [sonne and] daughter Judyth one hundred and fyftie poundes of lawfull English money, to be paied unto her in the manner and forme foloweng, that ys to saye, one hundred poundes <u>in discharge of her marriage porcion</u> within one yeare after my deceas, with consideracion after the rate of twoe shillinges in the pound for soe long tyme as the same shalbe unpaied unto her after my deceas, and the fyftie poundes residwe thereof upon her surrendring <u>of</u>, or gyving of such sufficient securitie as the overseers of this my will shall like of, to surrender or graunte all her estate and right that shall discend or come unto her after my deceas, or <u>that shee</u> nowe hath, of, in, or to, one copiehold tenemente, with thappurtenaunces, lyeing and being in Stratford upon Avon aforesaid in the saied countye of Warr., being parcell or holden of the mannour of Rowington, unto my daughter Susanna Hall and her heires for ever. Item, I gyveand bequeath unto my saied daughter Judith one hundred and fyftie poundes more, if shee or anie issue of her bodie be lyvinge att thend of three yeares next ensueing the daie of the date of this my will, during which tyme my executors are to paie her consideracion from my deceas according to the rate aforesaied; and if she dye within the saied tearme without issue of her bodye, then my will ys, and I doe gyve and bequeath one hundred poundes thereof to my neece Elizabeth Hall, and the fiftie poundes to be sett fourth by my executours during the lief of my sister Johane Harte, and the use and proffitt thereof cominge shalbe payed to my saied sister Jone, and after her deceas the saied lli. shall remaine amongst the children of my saied sister, equallie to be divided amongst them; but if my saied daughter Judith be lyving att thend of the saied three yeares, or anie yssue of her bodye, then my will ys, and soe I devise and bequeath the saied hundred and fyftie poundes to be sett out by <u>my executours and overseers</u> for the best benefitt of her and her issue, and <u>the stock</u> not <u>to be</u> paied unto her soe long as she shalbe marryed and covert baron [by my executours and overseers] but my will ys, that she shall have the consideracion yearelie paied unto her during her lief, and, after her deceas, the saied stock and consideracion to bee paied to her children, if she have anie, and if not, to her executours or assignes, she lyving the saied terme after my deceas. Provided that yf suche husbond as she shall att thend of the saied three years be marryed unto, or att anie after [*sic*] doe sufficientlie assure unto her and thissue of her bodie landes awnswereable to the porcion by this my will gyven unto her, and to be adjudged soe by my executours and overseers, then my will ys, that the said clli. shalbe paied to such husbond as shall make such assurance, to his owne use. Item, I gyve and bequeath unto my saied sister Jone xxli, and all my wearing apparrell, to be paied and delivered within one yeare after my deceas; and I doe will and devise unto her the house with thappurtenaunces in Stratford, wherein she dwelleth, for her naturall lief, under the yearlie rent of xijd. Item, I gyve and bequeath unto her three sonnes, William Harte, . . . Hart, and Michaell Harte, fyve pounds a peece, to be paied within one yeare after my deceas [to be sett out for her within one yeare after my deceas by my executours, with thadvise and direccions of my overseers, for her best profitt, untill her mariage, and then the same with the increase thereof to be paied unto her]. Item, I gyve and bequeath unto [her] the saied Elizabeth Hall, all my plate, except my brod silver and gilt bole, that I now have att the date of this my will. Item, I gyve and bequeath unto the poore of Stratford aforesaied tenn poundes; to Mr. Thomas Combe my sword; to Thomas Russell esquier fyve poundes; and to Frauncis Collins, of the borough of Warr. in the countie of Warr. gentleman, thirteene poundes, sixe shillinges, and eight pence, to be paied within one yeare after my deceas. Item, I gyve and bequeath to [Mr. Richard Tyler the elder] Hamlett Sadler xxvjs viijd to buy him a ringe; to William Raynoldes gent., xxvjs viijd to buy him a ringe; to my godson William Walker xxs in gold; to Anthonye Nashe gent., xxvjs viijd; and to Mr. John Nashe xxvjs viijd [in gold]; and to my fellowes John Hemynges, Richard Burbage, and Henry Cundell, xxvjs viijd a peece to buy them ringes. Item, I gyve, will, bequeath, and devise, unto my daughter Susanna Hall, for better enabling of her to performe this my will, and toward the performans thereof, all that capitall messuage or tenemente with thappurtenaunces, in Stratford aforesaied, called the New Place, wherein I nowe dwell, and two messuages or tenementes with thappurtenaunces, scituat, lyeing, and being in Henley street, within the borough of Stratford aforesaied; and all my barnes, stables, orchardes, gardens, landes, tenementes, and hereditamentes, whatsoever, scituat, lyeing, and being, or to be had, receyved, perceyved, or taken, within the townes, hamletes, villages, fieldes, and groundes, of Stratford upon Avon, Oldstratford, Bushpton, and Welcombe, or in anie of them in the saied countie of Warr. And alsoe all that messuage or tenemente with thappurtenaunces, wherein one John Robinson dwelleth, scituat, lyeing and being, in the Blackfriers in London, nere the Wardrobe; and all my other landes, tenementes, and hereditamentes whatsoever, To have and to hold all and singuler the saied premisses, with theire appurtenaunces, unto the saied Susanna Hall, for and during the terme of her naturall lief, and after her deceas, to the first sonne of her bodie lawfullie yssueinge; and for defalt of such issue, to the second sonne of her bodie, lawfullie issueinge, and [of] to the heires males of the bodie of the saied second sonne lawfullie yssueinge; and for defalt of such heires, to the third sonne of the bodie of the saied Susanna lawfullie yssueing, and of the heires males of the bodie of the saied third sonne lawfullie yssueing; and for defalt of such issue, the same soe to be and remaine to the Fourth [sonne], Fyfth, sixte, and seaventh sonnes of her bodie lawfullie issueing, one after another, and to the heires males of the bodies of the saied fourth, fifth, sixte, and seaventh sonnes lawfullie yssueing, in such manner as yt ys before lymitted to be and remaine to the first, second, and third sonns of her bodie, and to theire heires males; and for defalt of such issue, the said premisses to be and remaine to my sayed neece Hall, and the heires males of her bodie lawfullie yssueinge; and for defalt of such issue, to my daughter Judith, and the heires males her bodie lawfullie issueinge; and for defalt of such issue, to the right heires of me the saied William Shakspeare for ever. <u>Item, I gyve unto my wief my second best bed with the furniture.</u> Item, I gyve and bequeath to my saied daughter Judith my broad silver gilt bole. All the rest of my goodes, chattels, leases, plate, jewels, and household stuffe whatsoever, after my dettes and legasies paied, and my funerall expenses dischardged, I give, devise, and bequeath to my sonne in lawe, John Hall gent., and my daughter Susanna, his wief, whom I ordaine and make executours of this my last will and testament. And I doe intreat and appoint <u>the saied</u> Thomas Russell esquier and Frauncis Collins gent. to be overseers hereof, and doe revoke all former wills, and publishe this to be my last will and testament. In witness whereof I have hereunto put my [seale] <u>hand</u>, the daie and yeare first abovewritten.

By me WILLIAM SHAKSPEARE.

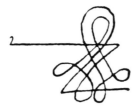

VII

THREE DRAMATIC BEQUESTS

Of Shakespeare's bequests in his will, all of them set forth in a dispassionate, perfunctory and businesslike manner, there are only three that strike me as provocative. All three are interlinear, probably added at the last moment when Shakespeare realized he was soon to confront the Dark Man. The first, "& to my fellows John Hemynges, Richard Burbage, and Henry Cundell, xxvjs viijd a peece to buy them ringes" is most suggestive. In *A Life of Shakespeare* Hesketh Pearson hints that Shakespeare may have asked Heminges and Condell to edit his plays. This is also my belief. It was not out of mere sentiment that Shakespeare left money for a mourning or memorial ring to each of these "fellowes," the only surviving members of Shakespeare's original company. If sentiment were his only motive, why did he leave out his old friend Ben Jonson and a dozen other writers, actors and noble benefactors?

At the time of Shakespeare's death, Jonson had been at work for four years on a collected edition of his own plays, the first volume of which appeared in 1616. No doubt Shakespeare was well aware of Jonson's project, the first of its kind ever attempted by a dramatist. It strikes me as odd that Shakespeare, a man of dynamic genius who had virtually retired in 1612, would sit twiddling his thumbs or puffing his pipe under a mulberry tree and not seek some challenging outlet for his formidable intellectual energies—say, a competitive effort with Jonson. True, there were apparently some part-time occupations, which I will discuss later. And no doubt he was called upon from time to time to overhaul the dramas of younger playwrights for the King's Men. In 1613 he had helped John Fletcher with his play, *The Two Noble Kinsmen*, as the touch of his genius in it tells us, and the fact that his name appears as co-author on the title page of the published version. But Shakespeare's restless genius would surely require a grander vehicle to keep him from the temptations of Satan. My belief is that he was at work on a collected edition of his plays and poems. When he first drafted his will he was obviously not aware of the imminence of death. But then his sickness struck and suddenly became dangerously acute. Shakespeare may have summoned his three old friends to request that they complete the work he'd just started. John Heminges and Henry Condell were uniquely qualified to gather and publish Shakespeare's collected writings. They exercised control of the copyrights to many of his manuscripts and prompt books. They were also the custodians of those manuscripts of Shakespeare's to which the King's Men owned the rights. They knew which dramas Shakespeare had written, which he had collaborated on, and which were falsely attributed to him. Heminges was manager of the King's Men and all three members of the ring-bequested trio had acted in the poet's plays. Indeed, Burbage had scored his first success nearly twenty years earlier in *Richard III,* and was the star of *Hamlet, King Lear* and *Othello.* No doubt he knew much of the dialogue in the plays from memory, knew it the way Shakespeare might wish it to be recorded.

If Shakespeare did consult with these three actors, and they did agree to press forward with the task of collecting his plays and poems for publication, a mourning ring for each was a logical and appropriate memento of Shakespeare's affection and gratitude. It would also answer the question, brought up time after time, about the disposal of Shakespeare's manuscripts and library, both strangely overlooked in the will. If my supposition is correct, Shakespeare, either before his death or by verbal instructions left with his executor, Dr. John Hall, turned over to Heminges, Condell and Burbage not only all his draft manuscripts but all of his pertinent library, such as any pirated quarto editions of his plays and editions of his poems, many very possibly bearing his manuscript corrections.

The trio of actors was reduced to a duo by Burbage's untimely death in 1619. Had Burbage lived, he might conceivably have reviewed the text with punctilious care and cut down by a fine measure the number of errors in the 1623 First Folio. In their Preface to the First Folio, addressed to "the Great Variety of Readers," Heminges and Condell plainly indicate that they took some of their text right from Shakespeare's original manuscripts. "His [Shakespeare's] mind and hand went together; and what he thought, he uttered with that easiness that wee have scarse received from him a blot in his papers." Earlier in this illuminating Preface, Heminges and Condell hint strongly that Shake-

[79] Signatures of John Heminges and Richard Burbage

85

[80] Shakespeare's last writing: "It[e]m I gyve unto
my wief my second best bed w[i]th the furniture"

speare himself may have started the work on the collected writings: "It had bene a thing, we confesse, worthie to have bene wished, that the author himselfe had liv'd to set forth and overseen his owne writings; but since it hath bin ordain'd otherwise, and he by death departed from that right, we pray you do not envie his friends the office of their care and paine to have collected and publish'd them. . . ." Note the phrase "had liv'd to have set forth and overseen his owne writings." If Shakespeare had not contemplated or begun the task, would not this phrase read: "had set forth and overseen his owne writings"?

Since original manuscripts, other than those that served as prompt books, were not esteemed or collected in Shakespeare's time, very possibly Heminges and Condell or their literary assistants and proofreaders discarded as worthless Shakespeare's prompt manu-scripts as soon as accurate (as accurate as they could make them) texts were in print.

The second interlinear bequest that I find provocative is one that literary historians have hashed over thousands of times: "Item I gyve unto my wief my second best bed with the furniture." The handwriting of this bequest weaves up and down and is otherwise one of the most wretched scripts that ever I beheld (*illus. 80*). So spastic and meandering is this line that it took a century for scholars to decipher it. It was doubtless the last full line ever penned by Shakespeare.

My opinion is that Ann Hathaway Shakespeare expected to get the second-best bed (the best bed would go with New Place, Shakespeare's mansion, to the poet's daughter Susanna Hall) but as Shakespeare lay dying, perhaps drifting into semiconsciousness, his daughter Judith (whom, I am convinced, the poet intensely disliked) did not wait to hear the death rattle but claimed the second-best bed for her new home. Only six weeks earlier she'd married a ne'er-do-well seducer, probably in defiance of her father's wishes, and she no doubt longed for and desperately needed a fine bed. Possibly, if there were a dispute, it could have been settled only by pillowing the dying man in the darkened chamber, holding a flickering candle over his shoulder and forcing him to scratch into the will his last bequest. I am pretty sure that, as most Shakespearean scholars contend, the second-best bed was the one that Shakespeare and Ann shared. The best bed was probably a huge, elaborate, heavily carved and canopied monstrosity exclusively for the use of important or noble guests.

The third dramatic bequest illuminates Shakespeare's personal character. It is really nothing more than a deletion and substitution; yet it goes far to establish the inflexible morality of the poet. It is to Mark Eccles's excellent book *Shakespeare in Warwickshire* that I am indebted for this data. On page 2 of his will, at the last moment and in enfeebled script, Shakespeare deleted the name of his old friend Richard Tyler as recipient of "26 shillings 8d to buy him a Ringe" and substituted the name of Hamnet Sadler, an intimate friend after whom Shakespeare had named his only son. The probable reason for the deletion, Mark Eccles points out, is that Tyler had got involved in some peculation with the funds raised for the victims of a destructive fire in Stratford. Tyler was charged with being "unreasonably slack." To Shakespeare, a man of impeccable morals and very possibly (although I cringe from uttering it!) a pillar of staid respectability in his community, this could likely have been sufficient cause to purge his old friend from the will.

There was little in Shakespeare of the liberal. Even in his youth he must have turned a wry glance on the raucous impiety of his friends Christopher Marlowe and Thomas Kyd, both of whom were accused of heresy. The final evidence of Shakespeare's stiff morality is, I think, the quatrain on his gravestone, likely his own doggerel, against bone-removers. I personally would be flattered if anyone made a wassail bowl of my skull or drumsticks of my thighbones. But to a devout, staunchly respectable man like Shakespeare such a compliment would be sacrilegious.

VIII

WAS SHAKESPEARE MURDERED?

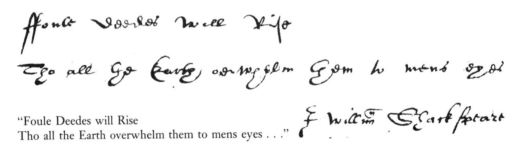

"Foule Deedes will Rise
Tho all the Earth overwhelm them to mens eyes . . ."

(Composite formed from words and letters in Shakespeare's holographic will)

IT was Monday, March 25, 1616, in the quiet hamlet of Stratford-upon-Avon. The river flowed gently, as always, and the townsfolk bustled about their mundane tasks, as always. What most of them did on this particular day would be forgotten in a few days or weeks.

But in Stratford's handsome New Place, a huge brick and timber mansion that belonged to the retired poet and actor Will Shakespeare, trouble was afoot. A fearsome event was soon to take place that would wait 367 years to yield up its dark secret.

The master of the house was in a pique. As a result, he was about to rewrite his will, at least the first part of it. By Stratford's standards Shakespeare was a rich man. He had a great deal of property to leave his heirs. Although he was eager to pass his estate on to a male heir, there was none. His only son, Hamnet, had died twenty years earlier, and his married daughter Susanna had produced no boys. But the lack of an heir was not

Shakespeare's most pressing problem. The big problem was his daughter Judith, married only six weeks. Shakespeare had already penned the first draft of his will, probably in January 1616, but had not yet signed it. He had provided liberally for Judith, who, he supposed, would then be wed within a few days. Shakespeare was not fond of his younger daughter, twin of his dead son, Hamnet, but he had left her all his silver, a most valuable bequest. He was to leave his wife nothing except a second-best bed, perhaps partly because he knew that his daughter Susanna would always care for her and partly, in the opinion of my wife, Diane, because he felt that whatever Ann Hathaway Shakespeare inherited from him would be wheedled, begged or stolen away from her anyway by Judith.

The marriage of Judith had been postponed—probably forbidden—by Shakespeare because he had learned some very disturbing news about his prospective son-in-law, Thomas Quiney. However, Judith and Quiney were married on February 10, 1616, very likely in secret, without Shakespeare's permission.

Biographers have ignored or glossed over the probable impact on Shakespeare of his discovery that Quiney was much worse than just the village ne'er-do-well. To the moralistic poet the sudden news that Quiney had made another woman, Margaret Wheeler, pregnant before proposing to his daughter Judith must have been devastating. Almost certainly Shakespeare acted in the only way possible: he canceled the wedding and forbade the marriage. In his article "Shakespeare's Family in Stratford Records" (*The Times Literary Supplement*, May 21, 1964), historian and archivist Hugh A. Hanley offers a plausible reason for the cancellation: "While the negotiations for the marriage were going on in January, Shakespeare may have remained in ignorance of Quiney's entanglement with Margaret Wheeler. He had probably himself initiated the negotiations in order to make provision for Judith . . . The news that the young man had got himself into trouble with another woman and that an illegitimate child was on the way would have come as a blow to Shakespeare's pride and provided a reason for suspending the negotiations. Quiney, now possibly under pressure from Margaret Wheeler's relatives and anxious not to lose the chance of an advantageous marriage, had a strong motive for bringing about a *fait accompli*. Taking advantage of Shakespeare's absence (there is a tradition that the poet contracted his fatal illness in London) and with the connivance of Judith, who was anxious not to let slip what might be a last opportunity of marriage, he obtained a licence . . . to enable the ceremony to go forward without delay. . . ."

My own opinion is that Shakespeare was horrified at the news of Margaret's pregnancy. Likely he poured upon young Thomas a cascade of recriminations and threats. I have earlier mentioned that Shakespeare was a deeply religious, judgmental man. There was no room for a bounder in Shakespeare's family, so he likely put a quietus to the marriage. How could he do otherwise? Even though he wished to get rid of his daughter, the thought of her marriage to a seducer who had abandoned his victim must have stiffened every moralistic hackle in Shakespeare's body. Hugh Hanley is possibly right that Judith and Tom were furtively wed while Shakespeare was absent from Stratford.

For Tom Quiney the situation must have been catastrophic. Probably Margaret and her parents were pressuring him to break off his engagement with Judith and marry the pregnant woman. If so, when he stalled them, or refused altogether, Margaret likely threatened to make him support the soon-to-be-born illegitimate child. Quiney probably cringed at the idea of a public disgrace, the pointed finger of contumely so much a part of life in small provincial towns like Stratford, with its population of fewer than two thousand. Moreover Quiney's financial condition appears to have been precarious. Right after his engagement to Judith, Tom, who had been operating a tavern called Atwood's, on High Street, traded establishments with his brother-in-law and got a larger tavern, The Cage, in a better area. Cash was almost certainly tight with young Quiney and he probably counted heavily on a marriage dowry or at least a loan from his future father-in-law to pay whatever additional sum he owed on the swap.

On her part, Judith, the younger of Shakespeare's two daughters, was eager to marry Quiney. No doubt she had tried and failed to get her father to sanction the marriage. Susanna was pleasant, witty, and kind. She was married to Shakespeare's close friend, the famous Dr. John Hall, who some years later would decline a knighthood. Susanna was the perfect consort for the celebrated doctor and an ideal companion for her father. I had not intended to inflict upon you this less-than-tripping epitaph incised upon Susanna's gravestone in the Holy Trinity Church at Stratford, but I now perceive that it has some bearing on Shakespeare's decisions in writing his will:

> Witty above her sex, but that's not all,
> Wise to salvation was good Mistress Hall,
> Something of Shakespere was in that, but this
> Wholly of him with whom she's now in bliss.
> Then, passenger, hast ne'er a tear
>   To weep, with her that wept with all;
> That wept, yet set herself to cheer
>   Them up with comforts cordial.
> Her love shall live, her mercy spread
> When thou hast ne'er a tear to shed.

Does not this sound like a eulogy of Lear's loving daughter Cordelia?

And now, as I turn to Judith, Shakespeare's Goneril (the fictional daughter of Lear who sought to destroy her father and who poisoned her sister Regan), I shall ask you to put up with a bit of hypothecation mingled with some hard—very hard—facts as I depict the relationship between Judith and her father. I wish I could purloin a little of the rampant imaginations of James Orchard Halliwell-Phillipps and Sir Sidney Lee, but those erudite biographers of Shakespeare taxed their fantasies to the point where there's nothing left for me to steal.

Judith was the twin of Hamnet, Shakespeare's only son. The twins were baptized on February 2, 1585. It must have been a glorious moment in Shakespeare's life, for he was eager to establish a dynasty and coveted a male heir. Of Hamnet we know nothing except that he was buried on August 11, 1596, probably three days after his death, aged exactly

[81] In this romantic engraving of Shakespeare's home life, the thirty-two-year-old poet is declaiming from *Hamlet.* An anachronism, since *Hamlet* was probably not written until 1601 or 1602 and Shakespeare's son *Hamnet* died in August 1596; here, the eleven-year-old youth stands at the right of his father, holding a whip. The poet's favorite daughter, Susanna, leans affectionately on his knee. Judith, also eleven and the twin of his son, rests upon his shoulder, and his wife, Anne Hathaway, sews and listens raptly. There is a lute on the floor—perhaps the poet has just played and sung one of his own songs to the family. The implausibility of this scene lies not in the fact that it was created from the artist's imagination, but rather in our well-founded supposition that Shakespeare was not a "family man." That he loved his son and daughter Susanna we cannot doubt. But he lived all or most of his active working life in London, away from his family. His visits to them in Stratford must have been infrequent before his semiretirement there, sometime between 1610 and 1612. Romantic as it is, it may be as accurate as most of the portraits that are accepted by scholarly historians. No portrait from life of Shakespeare is known to exist.

eleven years and 190 days. Hamnet's death must have been devastating for the poet. I shall presume that Hamnet had got most of his father's attention and affection, and Judith the leftover love. She was probably intensely jealous of her brother. It would be interesting, perhaps morbidly so, to know the cause of Hamnet's death—and what role, if any, his twin sister played in it.

Although Shakespeare wrote like a god, he was a mortal like you and me and no doubt with the same petty, often unworthy emotions. I believe that whenever Shakespeare had a squabble with Judith he said to himself: "Why didn't *she* die instead of Hamnet?" Judith grew up as a poor substitute for the boy Shakespeare had lost. She was illiterate, unable to write even her name. I doubt if Shakespeare gave any thought at all to her education. She was certainly not clever, probably not even comely. And she must have resented her father's rejection. As time passed, Judith became one of the best known spinsters in the village, living in the same mansion with her wealthy father but probably not enjoying his confidence or his love. Most likely there were frequent clashes between them. (Dare I "pull a Sidney Lee" and suggest that in *King Lear* [1607] Shakespeare had in mind his daughter Judith when he created Goneril and his daughter Susanna when he created Cordelia?)

By the time she was thirty-one Judith had probably just about resigned all hope of snagging a husband. Into this unhappy situation stepped or, rather, leaped a twenty-seven-year-old adventurer, a Stratford vintner and tobacconist, Thomas Quiney. Both Shakespeare and Judith had almost certainly known Tom since he was born. He was the son of Shakespeare's old friend, Richard Quiney, fourteen years in his grave. Young Quiney was well educated and could read and write some French and Latin. His flair for the artistic may be discerned in his handwriting, especially in the baroque signature submerged in a swirl of paraphs *(illus. 82)*. Thomas's business as vintner and tobacconist was struggling for survival. No doubt young Quiney was a convivial chap, with many friends and like as not his pick of the pretty young Stratford lasses.

Why, then, did Thomas court and marry an illiterate spinster four years his senior?

In answer I am going to give you a rundown on the facts we know about Thomas Quiney. He was baptized on February 26, 1589. He became a wine merchant in Stratford and, in 1611, leased a small house next door to his mother for use as a tavern. On February 10, 1616, he and Judith Shakespeare were married. Tom was twenty-seven, Judith thirty-one. They were ill-starred lovers (if, in fact, they were lovers at all). The pair had not obtained a special license from the Bishop of Worcester, required because they were wed during the prohibitive Lenten season (January 28 to April 7), apparently in secret, and in a great hurry. After the couple failed to answer two summonses to explain their failure to get a proper license, Thomas was excommunicated from the Church of England. Perhaps Judith was, also.

Shakespeare almost without doubt was mightily disgraced by their conduct and its results. But he had another reason for being upset when he sat down to rewrite his will. Tom Quiney had failed to come up with his share of the marriage settlement—£100 (some say £150) in land. In his *Shakespeare* (1949), Ivor Brown observes that Shakespeare "strongly disliked omissions and unpunctualities of this kind." I would put it more strongly: young Thomas was a welsher and Shakespeare despised welshers.

Most biographers voice the opinion that Thomas was known as a lush but I have not picked up any hard evidence to substantiate this assertion. In *Shakespeare of Stratford*, C. F. Tucker Brooke calls Quiney "apparently a shiftless person." And A. L. Rowse, in *Shakespeare the Elizabethan*, says that Quiney was "a vintner, he drank" and (in *William Shakespeare, a Biography)* that he "turned out a tippler."

Quiney, we know from records of the time, was fined a shilling for swearing and a like amount for permitting tippling in his house. The trifling sum of his fine indicates

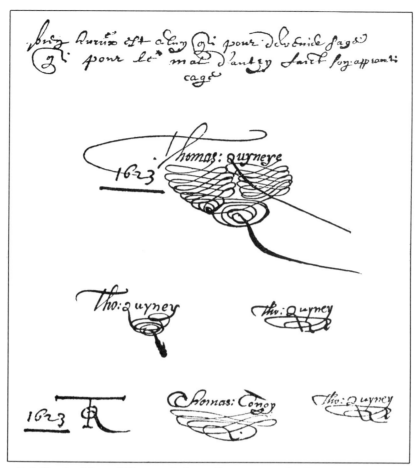

[82] Handwriting of Thomas Quiney. Signatures, and a French motto Quiney slightly misquoted: *"Bien heureux est celui qui pour devenir sage/Qui pour le mal d'autrui fait son apprentissage"* ("Happy is he who, to become wise, serves his apprenticeship from other men's troubles").

that he was treated as a person of low degree and small consequence. On another occasion Quiney was charged with selling unwholesome and adulterated wine. In *William Shakespeare. His Family and Friends,* Charles Isaac Elton points out that Quiney's excuse for defrauding his customers was that he had trusted Francis Creswick, a Bristol wine supplier who had hustled him with some bad wine. Elton continues: "One may suspect, however that he [Quiney] had become too expert in the mystery of making artificial wines and restoring pricked and musty vintages. There were plenty of tavern-keepers who could make claret or alicant out of cider and mulberries, and malmsey or a pint of brown bastard with thin white wine and a few raisins of the sun."

A few years after Shakespeare died, Tom Quiney got into serious financial trouble and tried to sell The Cage, where he lived with Judith and his two surviving sons (both of whom died in 1639; his first son, Shakespeare Quiney, had died in infancy). Dr. John Hall and several other kinsmen of Shakespeare thwarted Quiney's plans by seizing the property to manage in trust for Judith. Tom may have intended to take the proceeds, abandon his wife and two sons, and run off to London. Later, after their children died, Quiney did desert his wife and go to London. It is not known when or where he died.

Shakespeare and young Tom Quiney had something in common, something that fetched out the nobility and manliness in Shakespeare and the cowardice and villainy in Quiney: they had both got an unwed mistress pregnant. Likely both men had promised marriage at some time prior to the seduction, but when Shakespeare learned that Ann Hathaway was with child—Ann was eight or nine years older than he—the poet did the gentlemanly thing and married her. Whether he loved her is debatable; I think he did not. But he did what any man of honor would; the wedding took place on November 27, 1582. Their first child, Susanna, was baptized six months later, on May 26, 1583.

Thomas Quiney had got Margaret Wheeler big with child. That she was pregnant and that Thomas was the father was abundantly clear to them both at the time Thomas married Judith Shakespeare. The unfortunate woman who had given Quiney her love died in childbirth with her infant on or about March 12, 1616. She and her baby were buried on March 15, 1616. At this point Shakespeare realized, if he had not earlier, that Quiney was a worthless bounder. I do not conceive it possible that Shakespeare could look upon this human worm without curling his lips in contempt. Quiney deserved a horsewhipping for starters, but I think it quite likely, as I shall explain later, that he deserved much more than just a flogging.

As Shakespeare prepared to rewrite his will, the tension between him and Quiney must have been fearsome. A fresh disgrace had come to the poet from his new son-in-law. On Tuesday, March 26, 1616, Quiney was slated to appear before the ecclesiastical court (known as the "bawdy court") held by the vicar of Stratford for a hearing and sentence on a charge of carnal copulation. Further, the legality of the marriage of Judith and Quiney was still up in the air because of Quiney's excommunication. It was possible that the marriage might be declared invalid and the grandson Shakespeare longed for could be branded a bastard. Thomas was to enter a plea of guilty at the bawdy court and receive a sentence to perform public penance, a further disgrace to Shakespeare's name and reputation. However, this sentence was later set aside and a fine of one shilling imposed. One dead mistress, one dead infant. Fine: a sixpence each.

At New Place there must have been an atmosphere of seething anger, maybe hatred, as Shakespeare sat down to revamp his will. Very likely he and his daughter, perhaps joined by Quiney, have had a terrible row about the new terms in the testament, according to which Judith will just about be cut out and the small amount of money left to her will be subject to such harsh terms that she might never get it all. Quiney will not only be cut out, but he won't have a prayer of getting his hands on any of the wealthy poet's property. In short the new will represents an utter disaster to both Judith and Tom Quiney. But Shakespeare is probably adamant, for, in all likelihood, he has now divined the character of this duo and his righteous indignation has come to a boil.

As he starts to write the new will, Shakespeare is evidently distraught and accidentally puts down January instead of March in the Latin exordium. He corrects this mistake and gets the legal and regnal (year of the king's reign) right. Shakespeare describes himself as "in perfect health & memorie god be praysed." There is no reason to question this description. The poet's script is firm and bold, alive with swirls and curlicues, much like it was two decades earlier. As Shakespeare comes to the first bequest, he inadvertently starts to write *sonne in L*[aw] and has to slash out the words that designate the fortune-hunter. Nowhere in the will does he mention the name of Quiney. His Cordelia, Susanna Hall, he alludes to with her full, married name but his newly wed daughter is simply "Judith." He will cut his bequests to Judith down to an insulting minimum and the money he gives her is so tied up in *ifs* and *maybes* that she probably will never get it all. The valuable silver, with which Quiney may have planned to pay his debts, the poet leaves instead, with a deft touch of the quill, to his granddaughter Elizabeth Hall.

The final testament of the poet will be complete as soon as he revises page 1, with a little trickle of two lines over onto the second page. The will can then be handed over to the playwright's lawyer, Francis Collins, or tucked away in a drawer against the time when the poet's soul will be commended into the hand of God.

But almost from the very moment he starts to write, Shakespeare's great memory seems flawed. His script remains bold, clear, powerful even as he passes the midpage mark of the large folio sheet, but then he begins to make mistakes, serious ones. His memory begins to blank out. He writes "my neece Elizabeth Hall" in alluding to his beloved little granddaughter. (Professor Pierce Butler, in his *Materials for the Life of Shakespeare* [1930], says that "niece" was a synonym for "granddaughter" in Shakespeare's day, but I do not recall seeing this usage elsewhere.) This apparent blunder foretells the cerebral collapse that will overtake him in a few minutes.

Shakespeare dips his quill and forgets to wipe off the excess ink. The blots and smudges grow more frequent. Three-fourths of the way down the page his writing begins to fragment. He seems uncertain of what he wants to say. He puts heavier and heavier pressure on the pen. His disturbed state of mind gets more acute with every line he writes, as if he were writing in anger or in pain. His words are heavy with ink and tiny blots ooze like spore from his quill. The text that was so beautiful at the start is now a mangled, smeary, written-over mess. As the cataclysmic moment nears, Shakespeare is confused and indecisive, perhaps in physical agony; he repeatedly crosses out and re-writes. Finally he collapses in what appears to be the middle of a sentence (*illus. 83*).

When next Shakespeare takes up his pen, after a week or perhaps three, his script is smaller, entirely without amenities. It shakes and meanders, slithers and smears. The lines are not straight and the letters are often unclear. It is the hand of a debilitated man who has suffered a serious stroke.

The new script, entirely different from the bold hand with which Shakespeare began his will, starts on line 12 (counting up from the bottom of the page) with the words "but my will ys that she shall have the consideration." Examine these words and compare them with the script only five or six lines above. You will, I think, agree that a fearsome change

[83] Shakespeare suffers a near-fatal stroke. This remarkable portion of Shakespeare's holographic will (the bottom half of page 1) shows the rapid disintegration of his hand (lines 1–10) and the utter collapse of his script and ideas (lines 11–13). From line 13 to the bottom of the page appears the script of the poet after his debilitating stroke, possibly caused by arsenic poisoning.

[84] Shakespeare's handwriting before and after his collapse. In each example the words on top were written before the stroke; the same words appear beneath and were written after his attack.

[a] It [e]m I gyve & bequeath   [f] Willm
[b] my will   [g] bodye/bodie
[c] be   [h] Stratford
[d] after my deceas[e]   [i] Harte
[e] I   [j] Poundes/poundes

has overtaken the poet in the period that lies between the writing of the two sets of lines. You will also notice that the text during which Shakespeare had his stroke deals with his daughter Judith. Count up fourteen lines from the right side of the bottom of the page. Shakespeare begins line 15 from the bottom by discussing Judith's possible children. The text during which his collapse occurred (start reading at the left margin) is: "anie yssue of her bodye then my will is and soe I devise and bequeath the saied hundred and fyftie poundes to be sett by my executors and overseers for the best benefitt of her and her issue and the stock not to be paied unto her soe long as she shalbe marryed and covert baron by my executours and overseers. . . ."

Shakespeare's memory is further affected. He cannot recall the given name of his young nephew, Thomas Hart, so he leaves a blank space at the top of page 2, in the overflow of the rewritten first page. The name of his old friend, Hamnet Sadler, he records as *Hamlet* (perhaps a nickname, but not Sadler's legal given name).

If you wish to see with devastating clarity the drastic and sudden change in Shakespeare's script, please turn page 1 of the will (*illus. 71*, Chapter VI) upside down and look at the writing. The lower fourth of the page appears to be penned by a different person. And so it was, after a fashion. The will was begun by a man who probably had every expectation of living for another ten years. The bottom portion likely came tremulously from the quill of a man who very probably lay at the threshold of death.

[84]

Although it seemed clear to me as I studied the gradual deterioration and sudden collapse of the writing on the first page that Shakespeare had suffered a stroke, I felt I needed an expert medical opinion. I consulted Dr. Michael Baden and explained my belief that Shakespeare had suffered a cerebral hemorrhage as a result of intense anxiety over his domestic problems.

"That's what we call a hypertensive hemorrhage," said Dr. Baden. "Such a stroke is possible, but very improbable."

As Dr. Baden examined the handwriting, I told him again the tale about how Shakespeare supposedly died of a fever contracted after a "merry meeting" with his fellow poets Ben Jonson and Michael Drayton. (In view of his family problems, Shakespeare had good reason to go on a binge.) I added that the story was apocryphal and was not recorded until about half a century after Shakespeare's death.

"The story may well be true," said Dr. Baden. "Of course the consumption of alcohol, even a large quantity, would not cause a fever or death. Most people who die after a drinking bout die as the result of an injury suffered while intoxicated. A fall, perhaps. Shakespeare may have fallen or stumbled into some object and sustained a subdural skull fracture. At the time it might have seemed of little importance."

I asked if there could be a time lapse between the injury and the formation of a blood clot in the brain.

"Yes, indeed," Dr. Baden said. "The victim may go to bed and wake up with a headache and a little cut on the head. Hours later the blood clot may occur. Meanwhile, the injured person could function normally.

"A blood clot would quickly affect the handwriting and motor movements. Eventually the patient would go to bed, contract pneumonia and die with a high fever. If Shakespeare did injure himself after drinking, the injury did not affect the dominant lobe of his brain, as he was still able to use his pen, even though his memory was impaired.

"I think it quite possible that the story about Shakespeare dying after a drinking bout may be true. It would explain the handwriting, the partial recovery and the eventual death."

[85] Was Shakespeare murdered in this old mansion? This huge residence, built about 1475 by Sir Hugh Clopton, a Stratfordite who was Lord Mayor of London in 1492, had ten fireplaces, two gardens and two orchards. With its enormous frontage of sixty feet and depth of seventy feet, the mansion was known to the Stratford villagers as "the Great House." Shakespeare bought it for sixty pounds when it was a decaying ruin with ghost-haunted memories. In the 1560s William Bott, a friend of Shakespeare's father, bought the place. It was noised around Stratford that Bott poisoned his daughter with arsenic that he'd hidden under a green carpet. The house of death, still a valuable bit of real estate, inspired a second poisoning. Soon after Shakespeare bought New Place in 1597 from William Underhill, the seller's son, Fulke, after an assurance that he was slated to inherit all his father's property, used "the inheritance powder" to kill his father. Fulke was caught and hanged at Warwick but the title of New Place was in jeopardy for a while until Shakespeare could establish that he had not bought the old mansion from the murderer. Shakespeare renovated it, very likely in the hope that it would provide a peaceful retreat for his old age. But he was apparently destined to share the fate of the two others associated with this mansion of murder. He died mysteriously in the mansion on April 23, 1616.

The former chief medical examiner paused for a moment, and then went on: "There is another possibility I should mention, probably not relevant in this case. I've seen many suicide notes written by persons who ended their lives by taking poison. Their notes follow the exact pattern of the first page of Shakespeare's will. The writer starts out clearly and coherently, and gradually his handwriting becomes more and more disjointed and blotted and his memory begins to erode. Eventually, if he is unable to finish the suicide note, he stops abruptly, probably in the middle of a sentence. This suggests to me that Shakespeare may have been poisoned.

"But this isn't a very tenable theory," he added, "because there wasn't anyone who wanted to knock off Shakespeare." Dr. Baden caught the startled look in my eye and leaned forward intently. "Or was there?"

"Yes, there was," I said.

I explained that Thomas Quiney had probably married Judith Shakespeare for her money and, if Shakespeare rewrote his will, Quiney stood to lose everything.

"In the Elizabethan era," said Dr. Baden, "it was easy to commit murder without getting caught. The weapon was arsenic. There was no test for detecting it in the seventeenth century. Colorless, odorless, tasteless. You could put it in wine, milk or food. The victim would never suspect. You could kill with one big dose or take your time and let your victim appear to die of natural causes. In the latter case, progressive arsenic poisoning, the victim has an initial attack and on his partial recovery suffers from memory

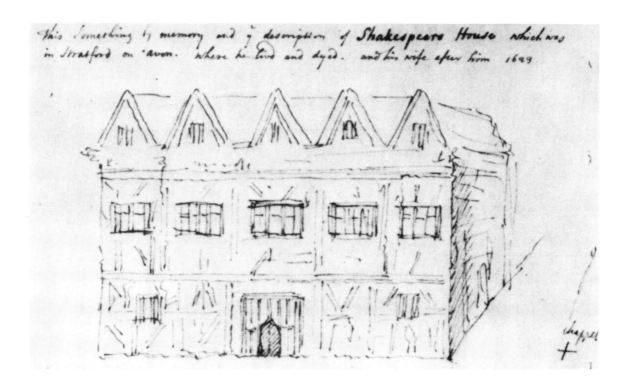

lapse and poor motor response. If Shakespeare had been administered a nonlethal dose, the first reaction would have come upon him gradually, as indicated by the writing in the will. Afterward, when he partially recovered and returned to his task, his script would be tremulous and he would have to struggle to remember things."

I said that Quiney certainly had a powerful motive for killing Shakespeare. "A successful murder would ensure his future wealth and prosperity. He was a man without business scruples and he had lots of opportunities. He may have had breakfast with Shakespeare on the morning of March 25, 1616, to discuss his plea at the bawdy court. I have a hunch that he had a willing accessory, Shakespeare's daughter Judith."

"Murder is a definite possibility if not a probability," said Dr. Baden. "Quiney could have given Shakespeare a glass of wine with arsenic in it, something to cheer him up or knock out the hangover after his night on the town with Jonson and Drayton. Or Judith could have put a little arsenic, furnished by Quiney, into her father's food every day until death occurred, seemingly from natural causes. A massive dose might have aroused suspicion. Murder by arsenic, if properly done, was foolproof in Shakespeare's day. It was such a common practice to 'put away' rich relatives with arsenic that the poison was known as 'inheritance powder.'

"And if Shakespeare were murdered with a series of doses, he would eventually die with a high fever."

I asked if Quiney would have any problem getting a lethal supply of arsenic.

"None at all. Since he was a vintner he had to use arsenic to keep rats, mice and other vermin out of his storeroom. This required the constant use of arsenic. He also had the vintage or medicinal wines in which to put the arsenic after he'd selected his victim.

"Arsenic poisoning is nearly always an 'inside job,' done by one family member to another, someone the victim trusts and who has access to his food or drink."

After discussing Shakespeare's death with Dr. Baden I consulted my well-thumbed copy of Osler's *Practice of Medicine.* I wanted a lot more information about arsenic. I discovered that the poison does not have an instant effect, like cyanide, for instance,

[86] Martin Droeshout's portrait of Shakespeare from the First Folio (1623), probably copied from an earlier drawing or painting, shows the poet in middle age.

which kills in less than a minute. After arsenic poisoning, there is usually about an hour before the victim begins to feel the stomach pains. If Shakespeare had received the poison during breakfast or lunch, he would have had time to write about half a page before the full impact of the poison.

From other sources I learned that arsenic was used by the Borgias. When Sir Thomas Overbury was imprisoned in the *Tower of London* (1613) his jailers murdered him by putting into his food great spiders and cantharides (crushed dung beetles or Spanish flies) mixed with arsenic.

In my quest for murder evidence, I barreled ferociously through heap after heap of books about Shakespeare. Eventually I ran into something that excited my interest in J. Hain Friswell's *Life Portraits of Shakespeare* (1864). Friswell noted, as I myself recollected after a bit of memory jogging, that the features of Shakespeare in the bust at the Holy Trinity Church in Stratford are elliptical and puffed up *(illus. 87)*. The sculptor may have utilized a life mask or plaster death mask taken by Dr. John Hall, Shakespeare's son-in-law. Friswell writes: "The head is oval, and is very fleshy, the jaw being heavy and massive, and the cheek round and full . . . The nostrils are raised and drawn up, a fact often quoted as proof that the sculptor worked from a cast taken after death."

Most of the portraits of Shakespeare, as all scholars know, show the poet with rather slender features *(illus. 86)*. While the authenticity of the various portraits can be disputed, the point remains that there is a marked difference between the bust in Stratford, said to be based on a death mask, and the earlier pictures of the dramatist. Friswell's phrase "very fleshy," combined with my own recollection of the rotundity of the face in the bust, led me to telephone my amiable friend Dr. Baden and annoy him with a further question:

"When a person dies of arsenic poisoning, is there any noticeable effect upon the features after death?"

"If the arsenic was administered over a period of time, the face will exhibit fluid retention and might be very puffy. This is the result of kidney failure, which occurs in

[87] Shakespeare bust in Holy Trinity Church, Stratford. The face may have been based on a death mask made by Shakespeare's son-in-law, Dr. John Hall.

[88A]

[88B]

[89]

Three convivial poets. [88A] Michael Drayton (1563–1631), a Warwickshire poet, believed to be a close friend of the dramatist's. [88B] Ben Jonson, Shakespeare's rival and friend. [89] William Shakespeare, a portrait from the 1640 edition of his *Poems*.

arsenic poisoning. I should mention, though, that such puffiness could also result from heart failure or a skull fracture."

I asked: "What effect would cholera or typhoid fever have on the features?"

"The face would be drawn, rather than puffed up."

Dr. Baden finished the conversation by telling me that he had talked with several specialists in cerebral diseases about the first page of Shakespeare's will and they concurred that the poet had suffered a stroke while writing it.

After this helpful chat with Dr. Baden, my mind turned back to Quiney's mistress, Margaret Wheeler, and her infant child. Her death, and the death of her baby, were certainly great blessings to Quiney. Margaret had stood between him and possible worldly success and esteem. In the tiny hamlet of Stratford she would have been, for the rest of his life, a constant reminder of his unsavory past. Quiney's already precarious financial condition would have been aggravated were he forced to contribute to her support or the support of his illegitimate child. I had a strong hunch that Quiney had done Margaret in.

Meanwhile, I pressed my search for more information about arsenic as a murder weapon. According to Vincent J. Brookes, a police medical officer, arsenic is sometimes used to induce abortion. In his book, *Poisons* (1975), Brookes confirms Dr. Baden's remark: "The poisoner may either give a large dose or administer smaller doses to simulate a natural illness." Raymond T. Bond, in his *Handbook for Poisoners* (1951), has furnished a capsule description of what happens to the victim: "Symptoms of arsenic poisoning appear within an hour—a burning in the throat, stomach pains, cramps, pallor, shallow breathing, thready fast pulse, coma, convulsions and collapse."

[90] Tavern sign of the Mermaid, a pub supposedly frequented by Shakespeare, Jonson, Raleigh and other poets, located on Broad Street in Cheapside, London. This representation of the sign was made in 1640, twenty-four years after Shakespeare's death, but it is probably the very same design that drew the great poet and his friends inside.

It is said that after a "merry meeting" with Drayton and Jonson, Shakespeare contracted a fever from which he died. According to Dr. Michael Baden, death by fever after a drinking bout is not possible. As depicted in these old portraits, the trio look as though they had been roistering all evening. If they actually did have such a merry meeting, it was probably in London at the Mermaid, where Jonson had founded his famed literary club in 1603; it seems unlikely that Jonson would travel to Stratford just to go on a spree with Shakespeare and Drayton.

The similarity of Bond's description to a difficult labor interested me. Since I suspected Quiney of murdering Margaret Wheeler, I discussed the subject with Dr. John K. Lattimer, probably the world's foremost urologist and author of many writings about presidential assassinations. I asked Dr. Lattimer if the symptoms of arsenic poisoning did not strike him as mimicking the symptoms of a difficult labor. He concurred and said that a "murder by arsenic could easily be mistaken for death during childbirth."

I also wondered what Dr. John Hall's reaction would be if his close friend and father-in-law exhibited all the symptoms of arsenic poisoning. I found out by a more detailed perusal of Osler's book. Osler explains that the symptoms of arsenic poisoning are a burning pain in the stomach, vomiting and intense thirst. Under the section in his book devoted to cholera, Osler points out that the symptoms of cholera are almost identical with those of arsenic poisoning. Cholera also affects motor movements, recovery is slow and death may result from heart failure. In Shakespeare's day cholera was a very common disease in England and especially in Stratford, notorious for its swampy, unsanitary conditions. David Garrick, the celebrated Shakespearean actor, in 1769 called Stratford "the most dirty, unseemly, ill-pav'd, wretched looking town in all Britain." And James O. Halliwell-Phillipps, in *An Historical Account of New Place, Stratford-upon-Avon* (1864), echoed the opinion of Garrick with an indictment of Stratford's "dung hills, pigsties, fetid ditches, bad roads."

As soon as Shakespeare was stricken Dr. Hall was probably called to his bedside and, in all likelihood, treated him for cholera. And this, too, would explain why Shakespeare was buried two days after his death instead of the usual three. Dr. Hall wished to avoid any possibility of contagion.

I had one final question for Dr. Baden: "Is there any way, at this late date, to tell whether Shakespeare was murdered?"

"If his remains were exhumed," replied Dr. Baden, "we could still detect if he had sustained a skull fracture. And, more important, if he died from arsenic poisoning, and the poison had been administered over a period of a few weeks in small doses, the arsenic would be right in his bones."

I sensed that Dr. Baden would very much like to perform an autopsy on the remains of Shakespeare. I, too, would like to look upon the long-mute evidence that lies hidden in his coffin in Holy Trinity Church.

Strange, is it not, to reflect that Shakespeare, like his famous rival with the mighty line, Christopher Marlowe, may have died a murder victim?

IX

THE PLAYWRIGHT AT WORK

IN the British Museum there is an ancient, badly damaged manuscript that goes under the modest appellation *MS. Harley 7368*. It is one of the most precious literary manuscripts in English, for it includes three foolscap pages, plus three lines at the top of another page, in the youthful handwriting of William Shakespeare. The lines from Shakespeare's quill are a part of *The Booke of Sir Thomas Moore,* a prompt book (manuscript of the play used to cue actors and musicians during performances) written in 1593 or thereabouts. Some scholars place the date as much as a decade later, but the handwriting seems to me to belong to the young poet. The play bears pages and revisions in five different hands. From the time the manuscript was first edited, by Alexander Dyce in 1844, *The Booke of Sir Thomas Moore* (usual spelling is More) has intrigued many of the most inquisitive Elizabethan scholars. The least inquisitive was Dyce, who launched the celebrated prompt book with nothing more than a laconic remark that the author was unknown. In 1871, Richard Simpson published his hunch that Shakespeare was the author of two folios, 8 and 9, both dealing with the insurrection of the London apprentices. His hunch was right. He also correctly surmised that the folios were in the poet's own hand. Simpson further attributed half a dozen other folio sheets to Shakespeare. His belief was the first grenade lobbed into a scholarly coterie on the authorship of the three folios ascribed to Writer D, an unknown author now identified by most experts as Shakespeare.

While the world of scholarship has for eighty-two years been unanimous in its view that Shakespeare's will was penned by lawyer Francis Collins or his scrivener, there was no such affable concurrence about the play manuscript. Phials of vitriol were flung wildly about in academic circles from the moment Edward Maunde Thompson published his monograph *Shakespeare's Handwriting* in 1916. With nothing but six signatures, all of them, as we know, wretchedly written, Sir Edward searched avidly for clues. Nobody ever finagled and finessed the letters of the secretary script with more skill than Sir Edward as he compared and measured and charted his way to a triumphant finale.

Some twenty-five years ago, I read a rebuttal to Thompson, *The Booke of Sir Thomas Moore* (1927) by Samuel A. Tannenbaum. I was very nearly positive at the time, as Tannenbaum was, that the three folios of Writer D were not in the hand of Shakespeare. Sir Edward, being more perceptive than I, however, was able to establish with reasonable certainty that Shakespeare had authored the three pages.

There's a mighty odd thing about Thompson's achievement. It was mainly the presence of the spurred *a*, that *a* with a little curved hook leading into it, that started Thompson on his effort to fix Shakespeare as the writer. Thompson regarded the spurred *a* as uncommon in Elizabethan scripts. Actually, it is not a great rarity. The fact that the spurred *a* occurs in the Belott-Mountjoy signature of Shakespeare and also in the three foolscap sheets by Writer D is a mere coincidence that I would have dismissed as of little consequence *(illus. 95, 96)*. Thompson's success, which he richly merited, was really the result of serendipity. It reminds me of an O. Henry story, *The Green Door*. A young man is strolling down Broadway in New York when a stranger thrusts a card into his hand bearing a mysterious, penned message: "The Green Door." The young man, his curiosity aroused, enters a large building behind the stranger, ascends a rickety stairway, and discovers a green door on the second floor. There he is just in time to rescue a pretty, young girl who, in hunger and desperation, has turned on the gas to end her life. He takes her to dinner and they fall in love. Then the young man learns that all the doors on the second floor are painted green and that "The Green Door" is the name of a play being performed across the street. So it was with Sir Edward. He took a clue that wasn't much of a clue and parlayed it into one of the most important Shakespearean discoveries of modern times.

After reviewing the identical evidence that led Thompson to the belief that Writer D was Shakespeare, Dr. Tannenbaum reported: "On the basis of Shakespeare's extant seven signatures [Tannenbaum included in his tally the disputed signature of Shakespeare in a copy of Montaigne] the test of handwriting is at present against the assumption that he wrote those three pages. . . . If these three pages are Shakespeare's he must have acquired not only a new calligraphic alphabet but also new writing habits between 1593 and 1603, the earliest possible date for his signature in his copy of Montaigne's *Essays*,—which is improbable almost to the degree of impossibility." However, Dr. Tannenbaum did concede that the "essential and specific differences between Shakespeare's acknowledged autographs and the three pages in *Moore* are not of a nature to prove that he could not possibly have been the author and the writer of the revision in the insurrection scene, inasmuch as we know that the handwriting of fluent Elizabethan penmen often offered specific differences in different documents and sometimes even in the same document."

More positive than Dr. Tannenbaum is Gerald H. Rendall, a proponent of Edward de Vere's authorship of the plays and the sonnets. In *Shake-speare: Handwriting and Spelling*, Rendall derides the views of Sir Edward Thompson (continued on page 111):

[91] Palimpsest vellum cover of *The Booke of Sir Thomas Moore* (More is usual spelling), a late sixteenth century prompt book that contains three pages in Shakespeare's hand and a few additional lines on a fourth page.

```
all         marry god forbid that                                    FOL. 9ᵃ

moo         nay certainly yoᵘ ar
            for to the king god hath his offyce lent            221
            of dread of Iustyce, power and Comaund
            hath bid him rule, and willd⸍yoᵘ to obay
            and to add ampler maĩe. to this
        he [god] hath not [le] only lent the king his figure
            his throne [his] sword, but gyven him his òwne name
            calls him a god on earth, what do yoᵘ then
            rysing gainst him that god himsealf enstalls
            but ryse gainst god, what do yoᵘ to yoʳ sowles
            in doing this o desperat [ar] as you are.          230
            wash your foule mynds wᵗ teares and those same hands
            that yoᵘ lyke rebells lyft against the peace
            lift vp for peace, and your vnreuerent knees
            [that] make them your feet to kneele to be forgyven
            [is safer warrs, then euer yoᵘ can make]
            [whose discipline is ryot ; why euen yoʳ [warrs] hurly] [in in to yoʳ obedienc.]
            [cannot ꝓceed but by obedienc] TELL ME BUT THIS what rebell captaine
            as mutynes ar incident, by his name
            can still the rout who will obay [th] a traytor
            or howe can well that ꝓclamation sounde           240
            when ther is no adicion but a rebell
            to quallyfy a rebell, youle put downe straingers
            kill them cutt their throts possesse their howses
            and leade the maĩe of lawe in liom
            to slipp him lyke a hound ; [saying] [alas alas] say nowe the king
            as he is clement, yf thoffendor moorne
            shoold so much com to short of your great trespas
            as but to banysh yoᵘ, whether woold yoᵘ go.
            what Country by the nature of yoʳ error
            shoold gyve you harber go yoᵘ to ffraunc or flanders   250
            to any Iarman ꝓvince, [to] spane or portigall
            nay any where [why yoᵘ] that not adheres to Ingland
            why yoᵘ must needs be straingers. woold yoᵘ be pleasd
            to find a nation of such barbarous temper
            that breaking out in hiddious violence
            woold not afoord yoᵘ, an abode on earth
            whett their detested knyves against yoʳ throtes
            spurne yoᵘ lyke doggs, and lyke as yf that god
            owed not nor made not yoᵘ, nor that the elaments
            wer not all appropriat to [ther] yoʳ Comforts.         260
            but Charterd vnto them, what woold yoᵘ thinck
            to be thus vsd, this is the straingers case

all         and this your momtanish inhumanyty
            fayth a saies trewe letts vs do as we may be doon by

[all] LINCO weele be ruld by yoᵘ master moor yf youle stand our
            freind to ꝓcure our ꝑdon

moor        Submyt yoᵘ to theise noble gentlemen
            entreate their mediation to the kinge
            gyve vp yoʳ sealf to forme obay the maiestrate
            and thers no doubt, but mercy may be found. yf yoᵘ so seek it   270
```

[92] Folio 9, a page in the hand of Writer D (Shakespeare) from *The Booke of Sir Thomas Moore*. The two other Shakespeare folios are too badly damaged to be reproduced.

[93] Transcription of Folio 9 in Shakespeare's hand from *The Booke of Sir Thomas Moore*. The entire manuscript was edited and reproduced by W. W. Greg (*Malone Society Reprints*, 1911).

[94] Lower portion of Folio 13b of *The Booke of Sir Thomas Moore*. The first three lines are in Shakespeare's hand; the balance of the writing is probably Thomas Dekker's.

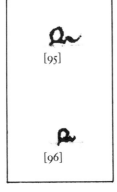

[95]

[96]

[95] The spurred *a* from the surname in Shakespeare's signature on the Belott-Mountjoy deposition.

[96] The spurred *a* as it appeared in the word *that* (line 105) in *The Booke of Sir Thomas Moore*. Sir Edward M. Thompson described the writing of the spurred *a*: ". . . the pen, descending in a deep curve from the overhead arch, is carried to the left into the horizontal spur and then to the right *horizontally* until it ascends to form the second minim."

Neither on the side of script nor authorship has the proposed identification been able to withstand the ordeals of criticism. As regards handwriting, the plain truth is that Hand D of 'the Addition' [as it is usually called] and the Shakespearean signatures are not reconcilable. To bring them into accord Sir E. M. Thompson had first to inflict upon the penman writer's cramp, and then reduce him to the spasmodic efforts of a dying man. But even these extreme measures will not avail to close a gap that remains irreducible. The Addition is in the hand of a trained and practised scrivener or copyist, the signatures are those of one to whom writing is a laborious and unaccustomed effort. The identification was at the outset vigorously combated by Sir G[eorge] Greenwood, most of whose contentions were well founded. . . .

In *Shakespere's Handwriting* (1920), Greenwood concludes his attack on Sir Edward with the remark: "I have arrived at the conviction that his 'conclusions,' so far from being 'just,' are but the baseless fabric of a dream."

The Baconians, as usual, got in their licks. In a book packed with charts and graphs —*Manuscript Said to Be Handwriting of William Shakespeare Identified as the Penmanship of Another Person* (1924)—Edwin J. Des Moineaux contends that the three contested pages were written by Francis Bacon. He concludes: "We believe that the identity of the writer [Francis Bacon] of the script reproduced [from the Sir Thomas More play] . . . is so apparent that further dissection and lengthy comment would be superfluous."

Van Dam, an expert on Shakespeare's plays, writes in *The Text of Shakespeare's Hamlet*: "It is obvious the three pages *must* have been written by a scribe."

The subject of the three pages by Shakespeare, evidently composed to infuse some vitality into the play, is a scene in which the Londoners rise against aliens living in the city. The insurrection was put down by Sir Thomas More, then sheriff.

There is other evidence for Shakespeare's authorship besides the paleographic proofs of Thompson. Professor R. W. Chambers made a detailed study of the tone, composition, and language in the three pages and discovered that they revealed many of Shakespeare's techniques. In "The Expression of Ideas, Particularly Political Ideas—in the Three Pages, and in Shakespeare" (*Shakespeare's Hand in the Play of Sir Thomas More*, edited by Alfred W. Pollard, 1923), Chambers compares the political ideas in the 147 lines of Writer D, especially the crowd scene, with Shakespeare's crowd scenes in other plays, mainly *Coriolanus* and *Julius Caesar*. Chambers notes that in the three pages there is "a uniquely passionate conception of the necessity of respect for law and order; a sympathetic understanding of the workings of uneducated minds and the logic of crowds; and a conviction that the most excited crowd can be swayed by oratory of the proper kind." He concludes that the understanding and sympathy of the author with the crowd points inevitably to the creative genius of Shakespeare. Chambers's analysis is a triumph of scholarship.

Professor J. Dover Wilson reinforced the opinion that three leaves were in Shakespeare's hand by showing how the script itself helped to explain the misprints in the Folio and the quartos. (I discuss Wilson's views in detail in Chapter XVI.) I have included here examples of the identical features, and they are numerous, in Shakespeare's handwriting

1	
2	
3	
4	
5	
6	
7	
8	
9	
10	
11	
12	
13	
14	
15	
16	
17	
18	
19	
20	
21	
22	
23	
24	
25	
26	

[97] The Feel of Shakespeare's Handwriting. A composite of Shakespeare's beautiful script in which the lines speed on lithesome nib:

> Come and trip it, as you will,
> On Shakespeare's light, fantastic quill

So Milton might have put it—presuming, of course, that he wasn't distressed by a sudden switch from trochaic trimeter to iambic tetrameter!

From this composite, you can get the feel, or overall impression, of Shakespeare's impetuous, torrential script. The feel is much more important than the examination of individual letters and words in judging authenticity. In the more than two decades that separate the components of this example, there appears hardly any change in the feel of the poet's penmanship, despite the purpose of the writing: in one case, a joyous, free creative passage; in the other, a will, the writing of which was undoubtedly a sad occasion. Lines 1–4 are from the holographic will; lines 5–8 from the legible page (of three) in *The Booke of Sir Thomas Moore*; lines 9–12, from the will; 13–15, from the play prompt book; 16–21, the will; and 22–26, the play prompt book.

112

26
25
24
23
22
21
20
19
18
17
16
15
14
13
12
11
10
9
8
7
6
5
4
3
2
1

[98] The Upside-down Feel of Shakespeare's Handwriting. If the "feel of Shakespeare's handwriting" composite is examined upside-down, so that the words are totally obfuscated and only the pen strokes and over-all impression of the writing is apparent, it is extremely difficult to tell the difference between Shakespeare's writing in the play *Sir Thomas Moore* prompt book (about 1593) and the poet's writing in his will (March 1616). The slight variations in the formation of a few letters, characteristic of any person's script when examples are separated by several decades, disappear when the composite is viewed upside down. The intensity of the script is the same, despite the near quarter century that separates the two documents. The lines are approximately the same distance apart; the space between words is almost the same; the slant and pressure of the quill strokes are nearly identical. The curvaceous swinging loops under Shakespeare's *h*'s, *y*'s and ampersands are identically formed and reveal the same fluid spread at the base of every loop. Judging this composite only by its upside-down feel, the two manuscripts might have been penned a few days apart.

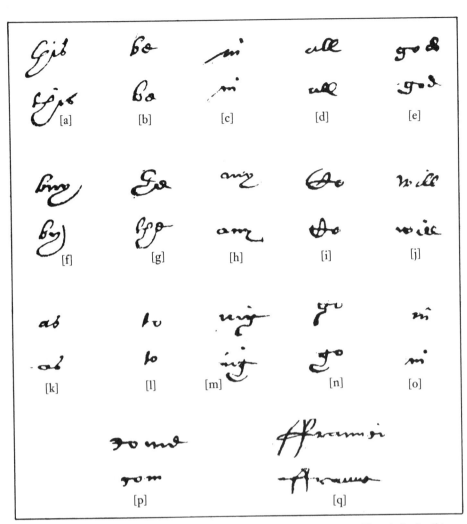

[99] Words and portions of words matched from Shakespeare's will and the legible page (of three) from *The Booke of Sir Thomas Moore*. Shakespeare's writing changed very little between 1593 and 1616. The top word in each set is from the will; the bottom, corresponding word is from the play.

[a] this	[i] Co
[b] be	[j] will
[c] in *(notice the position of the dot)*	[k] as
	[l] to
[d] all	[m] ing
[e] god	[n] go
[f] buy/by	[o] in (variant)
[g] the	[p] come/com
[h] any	[q] Frauncis/Fraunce

in the will and in the three folios from *The Booke of Sir Thomas Moore (illus. 99)*. There are, however, two minor differences in the writing. Shakespeare uses the spurred *a* frequently in the play, rarely in the will; probably he jettisoned the extra hook on the letter because it impeded the swiftness of his writing. He also got rid of a jaunty little squiggle in the *f* in *of*. Aside from these small changes, the script of the poet scarcely altered an ink blot in nearly a quarter of a century.

The manuscript pages of the prompt book that were penned by Shakespeare reveal a beautiful script that cascades across the page. The voluptuous bellies of his lower loops swing seductively from the *y*'s and *h*'s. His *f*'s are graceful and tall, like buggy whips. And the viper tongues that flicker from the terminal *s*'s give an exotic look to his penmanship.

That Shakespeare's quill raced tumultuously across the page cannot be doubted. His mind admitted of no impediments; his ideas often outran his pen, and he left bizarre abbreviations in his wake. Shakespeare cared nothing for the amenities of punctuation. The play was the thing. He rarely had to grope to set his lines on paper. And, as Heminges and Condell noted, he blotted out few words. There are only three lines crossed out in the *Moore* manuscript, deleted by some meddling clerk or bookkeeper.

X

GENTLEMAN LAWYER

SHAKESPEARE was fascinated by the law and its formal processes. He relished the pomp and solemn drama of the courts, the sharp exchange of wits under pressure. His plays, especially the earlier ones, often reveal an astute knowledge of the law's delicate machinery.

Few men of wealth and position would elect to compose and write their own wills as did Shakespeare. Yet, in its original state, the poet's will is lucid and cohesive, comprehensible in every detail. It cleaves tightly to the form prescribed by law. Only after his stroke did Shakespeare lose his grip on the entangled provisions. But it was his memory, not his legal knowledge, that failed him.

John, Lord Campbell, chief justice of the queen's bench and lord chancellor of England, wrote in 1859: "Among Shakespeare's writings, I think that attention should be paid to his WILL, for, upon a careful perusal, it will be found to have been in all probability composed by himself. It seems much too simple, terse, and condensed, to have been the composition of a Stratford attorney, who was to be paid by the number of lines which it contained. But a testator, without professional experience, could hardly have used language so appropriate as we find in this will, to express his meaning. . . ." Lord Campbell, who is replying in his book *Shakespeare's Legal Acquirements Considered* to some remarks by the notorious forger John Payne Collier, praises Shakespeare's legal background, noting that the poet has "a deep technical knowledge of the law" and an easy familiarity with "some of the most abstruse proceedings in English jurisprudence." With regard to Shakespeare's "judicial phrases and forensic allusions," Lord Campbell observes: "I am amazed, not only by their number, but by the accuracy and propriety with which they are uniformly introduced."

John Pym Yeatman, in *Is William Shakespeare's Will Holographic?* (1901), writes: "The curious thing is that the person who drafted this Will was evidently a skilled lawyer, for his phraseology and use of legal terms is accurate; he has only muddled them together."

In "Shakespeare's Will" (*Georgetown Law Journal*, March 1932), A. Wigfall Green is convinced that the will was drawn up by an inexperienced clerk of Collins's. His arguments tend, I think, to support the view that Shakespeare penned the will without consulting an attorney.

It would . . . appear that many of the apparent defects . . . are not real defects when considered in the light of the law of the day; it is, furthermore, evident that the will is a thoroughly formal instrument, showing adequate legal knowledge. It is manifestly incorrect to say that a will observing all the recognized testamentary forms, including elaborate dating, direction for payment of debts, the usual formal exordium, the creation of a highly involved trust, and withal signature on each page could have been mistaken for mere memoranda for the later making of a will, granting, of course, that the mere physical writing of the will is slovenly; nor is it probable that an attorney and a scrivener would produce a mere draft when they were called in to draw a will, it being uncustomary to retain an attorney for the preparation of memoranda. Even so, a perfect copy was in no respect necessary, even assuming that there was time for the engrossing thereof. Numerous wills of the day were drawn in a similar manner. Certainly the question of expense for making a fair copy was not involved, as the legal charge for the copy of a will was, in the early seventeenth century, one penny for ten lines.

Before leaving the subject of Shakespeare's will, I'd like to offer one more expert piece of testimony from Franklin Fiske Heard, a distinguished attorney whose article "Shakespeare as a Lawyer" appeared in *The Green Bag* (1883).

In all probability, Shakespeare's will was written by himself. It is expressed in terms at once apt and concise. The intention of the testator is abundantly manifest. On perusal, one is ready to exclaim with the Host in 'The Merry Wives of Windsor,'—'Thou art clerkly, thou art clerkly.'

Without professional education and experience, the technical knowledge of the law could not have been so appropriately used. In the interpolated clause making a bequest to his wife of personal property he omits the technical word 'devise,' which he used in disposing of his reality, and says 'I give,' &c. . . .

The first scholar to contend that Shakespeare's knowledge of the law was too profound to have been acquired by osmosis was Edmund Malone (1741–1812), critic and editor of Shakespeare. Malone it was who exposed the Shakespeare forgeries by William Henry Ireland at a time when the British Museum was ecstatic over them and James Boswell was kneeling to kiss the bogus pages. And Malone was the first to unmask the falsity of the Chatterton-Rowley fakes that had suckered in the know-it-all Horace Walpole. A barrister himself, Malone was awed by Shakespeare's enormous legal knowledge. He expressed the opinion (1796) that Shakespeare had spent some years of his youth in an attorney's office.

I would be remiss if I did not mention the belief held by most contemporary scholars that Shakespeare's great memory and genius for absorbing useful facts enabled him to pick up and weld together odds and ends of legal knowledge from his many friends, some of them no doubt law students and attorneys. This point of view is adroitly expressed by Dunbar Plunket Barton in *Links between Shakespeare and the Law* (1929): "[Shakespeare] lived in a litigious age, was brought up in a litigious atmosphere, dabbled personally in the buying of land, and became interested or involved in suits or disputes about such matters as mortgages and commons (privately owned land used by the community). He had at his elbow a library containing chronicles that were stored with points of crown, criminal and constitutional law. He had many opportunities of mingling with lawyers. All the dramatists of that age cultivated the art of picking up scraps of legal lore and turning them to dramatic account." Here, in fairness to Sir Dunbar's position, let me point out that Shakespeare's close friend and *soi-disant* cousin Thomas Greene was in London studying at the Middle Temple during the last years of the sixteenth century. The poet may have helped Greene in his studies and thus picked up a vast fund of legal knowledge. And, as I will later discuss in detail, Shakespeare was probably associated with Francis Bacon, one of England's greatest legal minds.

Before I go further, I'd like to cite a few additional expert opinions on Shakespeare's knowledge of law. In "Shakespeare and the Law: Was the Bard Admitted to the Bar?" (*Cleveland Bar Journal*, March 1965), Donald F. Lybarger, a judge in the Court of Common Pleas, Cleveland, Ohio, declares: "Much as we lawyers might like to claim the world's greatest dramatist, we can hardly do so in the absence of one scintilla of external proof to that effect. Neither is the evidence within the plays clear and convincing in establishing that connection."

If Shakespeare did study law, it was between 1579 and 1585. Almost nothing is known about him during this period. Benjamin F. Washer, in "William Shakespeare, Attorney at Law" (*The Green Bag*, June 1898), asks: "Does it appear to one as probable or plausible that a man whose early training and subsequent occupation was with court or counsel should write thirty-seven dramas, not one of which is founded on a legal plot or story?"

In the second part of his critical essay on Shakespeare as a lawyer (*The Green Bag*, August 1898), Washer provides a list of sixty-three real property terms used in Shakespeare's plays and the frequency of their occurrence. Most often employed are *heir* (107 times), *estate* (57), *bond* (48); and least often, at a single time each, are *certificate*, *commons*, *capable*, *demise*, *eject*, *entry*, *executor*, *fee* (to attorney), *fee*, *farm*, *precedent*, *praemunire*, *remainder*, *sufferance* and *tenture*.

George W. Keeton, in *Shakespeare's Legal and Political Background* (1967), takes an awkward position on the fence: "Shakespeare's legal knowledge differed little from that of other writers of his time, but his observation was closer and more accurate. . . . The legal and political ideas which he incidentally expresses were part of the intellectual equipment of all educated men of this time, and his touch was sensitive. Beyond this, the author would not wish to go."

One of the arguments of the Baconians is that the "Bumpkin of Stratford" could not have possessed the vast and intricate legal information exhibited in the plays. Ergo, the dramas were penned by a *magnus advocatus*, viz, Francis Bacon, Lord Verulam (Q.E.D.).

This specious argument, promulgated in Latinized phraseology, beguiled Edward James Castle, one of Her Majesty's Counsel, into the camp of the Baconians. However, in 1897 Castle published a book, *Shakespeare, Bacon, Jonson & Greene*, during the research for which he "came to the conclusion that Shakespeare was the sole author of . . . Venus and Adonis and Lucrece, the Sonnets and the Plays, and that there was no evidence that Bacon had anything to do with them, or had any necessity for imagining that he had."

Richard Grant White, distinguished author and lawyer, comments: "No dramatist of his time, not even Beaumont, who was a younger son of a judge of the Common Pleas, and who, after studying in the Inns of Court, abandoned law for the drama, used legal phrases with Shakespeare's readiness and exactness . . . legal phrases flow from his pen as part of his vocabulary and parcel of his thought." Another lawyer who testified to Shakespeare's legal attainments was J. B. Mackenzie, in "Was Shakespeare Bound to an Attorney?" *(The Green Bag,* February 1902): "What experience other than a more or less extended period of tribulation spent in the murky den of an attorney could, it may be asked, have enabled the user to acquire such command of the prolixities of conveyancing. . . . [Shakespeare] had an accepted distinction in the character of estates, a rational perception of which could hardly have been gained at random."

Lord Campbell was also of the opinion that Shakespeare was engaged for some years in the office of a conveyancer: "Were an issue tried before me as Chief Justice at the Warwick assises, 'whether William Shakespeare, late of Stratford-upon-Avon, gentleman, ever was a clerk in an attorney's office in Stratford-upon-Avon aforesaid,' I should hold that there is evidence to go to the jury in support of the affirmative, but I should add that the evidence is very far from being conclusive."

There is now new and, I feel, convincing evidence that Shakespeare did in fact once serve as a lawyer's clerk.

In the year 1614, proceedings were instigated by William Combe, heir and son of Shakespeare's old friend John Combe, who had died earlier that year, to enclose the common fields at Welcombe. Shakespeare owned land at Welcombe and was a farmer of part of the tithes. Thomas Greene, Shakespeare's cousin and Stratford town clerk, was also a landowner at Welcombe. In spite of bitter opposition from the local townspeople William Combe proceeded with his plans. His men dug ditches around the commons and the irate townsfolk filled them up. Meanwhile, Shakespeare moved quickly to protect his own interests. According to Mark Eccles, in *Shakespeare in Warwickshire,* a subsequent agreement between Shakespeare and William Replingham, an attorney acting for Arthur Mainwaring (or Mannering), steward of the Lord Chancellor who was lord of the royal manor of Stratford, was handled for the poet by his lawyer, Thomas Lucas, of Stratford, who also safeguarded the interests of Thomas Greene. In evidence is a document entirely in the hand of Shakespeare, signed by Thomas Lucas as witness, that I believe shows clearly that Shakespeare handled this property case on his own account and acted as his own attorney, and may also have been Greene's. Recollect, if you will, that both Lord Campbell and J. B. Mackenzie emphasized Shakespeare's expertise in "the prolixities of conveyancing." The document *(illus. 100)* is identified on the verso as "Coppy of the

[100] The Welcombe Enclosure Agreement, between Shakespeare and Replingham, October 28, 1614. Entirely in the handwriting of Shakespeare, with the poet's signature five times in the text.

[101] Endorsement on verso of Shakespeare-Replingham agreement. This document is mistakenly identified as a "Coppy."

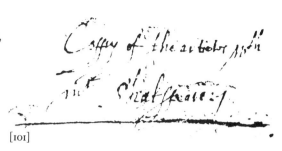

[101]

articles with Mr. Shakspeare" *(illus. 101).* This docket, in an unidentified script, would appear to be incorrect, for the agreement is not only penned by Shakespeare (and thus can hardly be regarded as a clerical copy); it also bears the original signatures of four witnesses. Witnesses do not sign clerical copies. Thomas Lucas signed as one of the witnesses. His handwriting is very different from that in the body of the document.

The contract, dated in Latin October 28, 1614, reads as follows:

Vicesimo octavo die Octobris, anno Domini 1614. Articles of agreement indented made betweene William Shackespeare, of Stretford in the county of Warwicke, gent., on the one partye, and William Replingham, of Greete Harborowe in the Countie of Warwicke, gent., on the other partie, the daye and yeare abovesaid.—Item, the said William Replingham, for him, his heires, executours and assignes, doth covenaunte and agree to and with the said William Shackespeare, his heires and assignes, that he, the said William Replingham, his heires or assignes, shall, upon reasonable request, satisfie, content and make recompence unto him, the said William Shackespeare or his assignes, for all such losse, detriment and hinderance as he, the said William Shackespeare, his heires and assignes, and one Thomas Greene, gent., shall or maye be thought, in the viewe and judgement of foure indifferent persons, to be indifferentlie elected by the said William and William, and their heires, and in default of the said William Replingham, by the said William Shackespeare or his heires onely, to survey and judge the same to sustayne or incurre for or in respecte of the increasinge of the yearelie value of the tythes they the said William Shackespeare and Thomas doe joyntlie or severallie hold and enjoy in the said fieldes, or anie of them, by reason of anie inclosure or decaye of tyllage there ment and intended by the said William Replingham; and that the said William Replingham and his heires shall procure such sufficient securitie unto the said William Shackespeare, and his heires, for the performance of theis covenauntes, as shal bee devised by learned counsell. In witnes whereof the parties abovsaid to theis presentes interchangeablie their handes and seales have put, the daye and yeare first above wrytten.

Sealed and delivered in the presence of us,

Tho. Lucas.
Jo. Rogers.
Anthonie Nasshe.
Mich. Olney.

[102] Comparison of key words in last will and testament of Shakespeare with identical words in the Shakespeare-Replingham agreement. Beneath each word from the will is the same word as it appears in the agreement.

[a] put	[f] & (ampersand)	[k] to	[p] for
[b] by	[g] first	[l] Thomas	[q] in (variant)
[c] the	[h] gent[leman]	[m] all	[r] unto
[d] above	[i] in	[n] That	[s] Willm Shackspeare
[e] Daie/Daye	[j] of	[o] Doe (do)	

You will note from the terms of the agreement that Shakespeare has obtained from Replingham a promise to compensate him for all loss by "inclosure or decaye of tyllage." It was a necessary concession by Replingham, since sheep pastures would yield less in tithes than fields of grain and hay.

Six years earlier, in the summer of 1608, Shakespeare had entered a claim in the Stratford court of record (small claims court) against John Addenbrooke for six pounds, plus twenty-four shillings damage. For what reason we do not know. Shakespeare apparently presented his own case before the court with such skill that, although the action dragged on from August 17, 1608, until June 7, 1609, the panel of twenty-four jurors found in his favor. The court then issued a summons for the defendant, but he failed to appear. Whereupon Addenbrooke's security, Thomas Horneby, a blacksmith, was ordered to make good on the judgment. Whether he shelled out the sum awarded by the court to Shakespeare is not known.

There survive several interesting documents concerning the case in Shakespeare's own hand. The poet kept meticulous records of the jurors and their verdict. No doubt Shakespeare personally interrogated them before accepting their services. His list of the panel of jurors selected is illustrated in this chapter *(illus. 101, 102)*. Seventeen of the names are in his handwriting, as is his own name at the top. A second list, again headed by a note incorporating his signature, contains *all* the jurors' names written by Shakespeare, with the verdict of costs and damages in his favor.

While this book was in the midst of a huge polish-up at the publisher's, I developed a sudden, inexplicable obsession that I'd overlooked a Shakespeare document, one I suspected lay right under my sightless gaze. For nearly two days this obsession gnawed at me. I became a haunted man. When my wife commented on my preoccupation, I said: "I've got a feeling that somewhere among my books and papers there's another signature of Shakespeare's. It's teasing me, mocking me, beckoning to me. I don't have any idea where it is, but I'm going to find it."

That evening I retired about 10:30, very early for me. With me to bed went my obsession. At 12:45 A.M., on March 13, I woke up, slid out of bed and walked into my living room. It was very cold. Outside a late-winter snowstorm was whistling. I sat down and decided to work my way slowly, cover to cover, through Schoenbaum's *William Shakespeare: a Documentary Life*. After more than three hours of intensive study, I had discovered nothing fresh. I went back to bed and rotated until dawn, my head full of disjointed thoughts.

By nine o'clock I had reconnoiterd some other volumes and come upon nothing new. I decided to pick away at random pages in Schoenbaum's book. Sometimes dumb luck is more effective than science, for, in less than an hour, I had the satisfaction of remarking quietly to my wife: "I've found another document signed by Shakespeare."

What I had been searching for was in the middle of page 241, an illustration of Judith Shakespeare's mark. I'd looked at this mark dozens of times before in Schoenbaum's book and in other books on Shakespeare. I knew it so well that I could easily draw it from

[103] Shakespeare's signature on the Quiney-Mountford Deed, December 4, 1612. The words *signu*(m) and *Judeth Shackespeare* written by Shakespeare on the deed for a house and property sold by Adrian and Elizabeth Quiney to William Mountford for £131, December 4, 1612. Elizabeth's son Thomas married Shakespeare's daughter Judith about three years later. Clearly, Judith was illiterate. She placed her signum, or mark, as a witness in the space provided by her father. The spelling "Judeth" is characteristic of Shakespeare's inconsistent orthography. In his will he spells her name "Judith" and "Judyth."

[104] A second signature of Shakespeare on the Quiney-Mountford deed. As in the previous signature, the words *signu*(m) and Judeth were penned by the dramatist. Under the clerk's writing, "Sealed & Deliv(er)ed in the p(re)sence (of)" appear as witnesses the signatures of Thomas Greene, Shakespeare's cousin, Greene's wife, Lettice, Edm: Rawlins and Judith Shakespeare. The elaborate paraph with which Rawlins concludes his signature extends far below his name, and Shakespeare was obliged to pen his surname around the paraph, so that the *Sh* and *ackespeare* are slightly separated and even the poet's *k* has a terminal squiggle from Rawlins's flourish impaling it.

[105] Clerk's handwriting in Quiney-Mountford deed

124

memory. What I hadn't previously observed were three words on either side of Judith's mark, all three in Shakespeare's handwriting: *signū (signum) Judeth Shackespeare.* Between the dramatist's writing of her given name and surname Judith had affixed her mark or, rather, her *signum,* for Judith's "signature" is a curious design, more than a mere "X."

The earlier part of the document that Judith signed as a witness was not illustrated by Professor Schoenbaum. Dated December 4, 1612, the transaction recorded the sale of a house and land by Elizabeth and Adrian Quiney to William Mountford, a wheelwright, for £131.

I'd always been a little puzzled as to why this important contract had been witnessed by an illiterate woman. The explanation now appeared clear to me: Shakespeare had apparently served as attorney for the Quineys, his close friends.

I wrote at once to Levi Fox, director of the Shakespeare Birthplace Trust, in Stratford, requesting a Xerox copy of a portion of the deed with the signatures of the witnesses. With his usual affable cooperation, Dr. Fox mailed me not only the copy I'd requested but a duplicate of another signature of Judith Shakespeare's on the same document, also prepared for her signum by her father.

Quite possibly the document was dictated by the poet and drawn up by a law clerk at Shakespeare's residence, New Place. Present also during the transaction was Shake-

[106] Surname of Shakespeare's signature from the Quiney-Mountford deed

[107] Another surname of Shakespeare's signature from Quiney-Mountford deed

[108] Surname of Shakespeare's signature from text of Shakespeare-Replingham agreement, October 28, 1614. This signature is almost identical with the signatures on the Quiney-Mountford deed of some twenty-three months earlier.

[109] Surname of Shakespeare's signature in text of poet's holographic will, about January 1616. The feel and appearance of the signature are the same as in the three preceding examples. As you will see from an examination of the script in the will or the words in the glossary, Shakespeare often used variant "*p*"'s and "*e*"'s in the same document.

[110] *Sh* from surname of Shakespeare in signature on the conveyance for a gatehouse in Blackfriars, London, March 10, 1613. One of six signatures long recognized as authentic by Shakespearean scholars.

speare's cousin, Thomas Greene, who was the first to affix his name as a witness. His wife, Lettice Greene, signed at his right. Then Edm. [Edmund] Rawlins. It was logical for the poet to summon his daughter Judith to act as an additional witness. Certainly, if Shakespeare was the lawyer representing the Quineys and negotiating the sale, he would not have wished to witness the document he had prepared.

I discussed my hypothesis about the unusual combination of signatures with my attorney, Jack Albert, who concurred that it was a valid one: that if Shakespeare had drawn up the deed he would have chosen not to act as a witness; nor would he have acted as a witness if he'd been an agent in negotiating the sale.

That Shakespeare was a close friend of Elizabeth Quiney's seems almost certain. The only surviving letter written to Shakespeare (likely never dispatched) is from Richard Quiney, Elizabeth's deceased husband, who addressed the poet as "my loving good friend and countryman." Elizabeth's son Thomas was to marry Judith Shakespeare in 1616.

Thomas Greene, the first witness, was educated at Middle Temple and became town clerk in 1603. Sidney Lee, in his *A Life of William Shakespeare,* writes of him: "Thomas Greene, 'alias Shakespeare' . . . claimed to be the poet's cousin. His grandmother seems to have been a Shakespeare. He often acted as the poet's legal adviser." I am inclined to question this last assertion, for although Greene and Shakespeare were involved together in several legal cases, there is no evidence that Greene gave any counsel to the poet.

Thomas Greene was known to be a tenant of New Place in 1609. In the late spring of 1611, Greene purchased a house. Whether he and his wife, Lettice, lived in the house or used it as investment property does not seem to be known. But in my opinion, it is quite likely that after 1609 Greene and his wife remained in New Place, renting rooms from Shakespeare. Evidently Greene was very close to Shakespeare, for when the poet died Greene sold his house and moved away from Stratford.

Except for the principals in this sale of a messuage, the only person who may not have been a resident of New Place was Rawlins, possibly an associate of William Mountford's, the wheelwright.

That Shakespeare might have drawn up this complicated deed and/or negotiated the sale of the property on behalf of Elizabeth Quiney recalls the opinion of legal authorities who have studied his dramas that the poet was an expert in the law of conveyance. And it also suggests the possibility that Shakespeare may, after his retirement to Stratford, have worked part-time as a legal consultant.

XI

"DOCTOR" OF HERALDRY

SHAKESPEARE aspired to be a gentleman. To achieve this distinction he required a coat of arms, the ultimate symbol of good breeding. An escutcheon would prove that he was not just a strolling player. There was nothing unusual about Shakespeare's aspirations for a family crest. To acquire a coat of arms was the goal of every successful middle-class businessman in the age of Queen Bess. But it was not until 1596 that Shakespeare was rich enough to pay the necessary pounds for the award. By this time, too, he had the support of many powerful men, including his generous patron, the Earl of Southampton. Sponsoring him also were the Earl of Essex, an influential force in the College of Heralds, and William Camden, historian and expert in heraldry. As for the requisite heroic ancestors, part of every application for a coat of arms, such worthies could be given substance and a name through his own imagination.

For many years I'd known about and often looked at photographs of the three rough-draft awards of a coat of arms to Shakespeare's father, John, but I'd never paid much attention to them. One summer day in 1983, I was perusing a pile of old volumes in the third-floor reading room of the lion-guarded New York Public Library while awaiting the arrival of some books I'd requested. In B. Roland Lewis's *The Shakespeare Documents*, I came upon a page illustrating one of the coat of arms documents. It had been penned in a galloping script that looked very much like Shakespeare's. I looked again and saw that it was Shakespeare's. I was enormously delighted with this accidental discovery, but I was puzzled about why Shakespeare had written such a technical document. I had to know, instantly. I bounded like a springbok out of the west reading room, through the corridor and the east reading room, and skidded to a halt in the genealogical room. At the desk was a pleasant, elderly man, about half as old as I am, who seemed to be awaiting me.

I said, "I wonder if you can save me a few hours of unwanted companionship with Guillim's *Heraldry* by answering a simple question?"

"Why not? What's the question?"

"If I lived in England in the departing decade of the sixteenth century and wanted to get a coat of arms, how would I do it?"

"You'd buy it."

"Just how would I buy it?"

"Well, you'd have to fulfill certain minimum requirements, of course. You would then present your application, written up in a prescribed form, to the College of Heralds at Derby House in London."

"Would I have to write the whole thing or would the herald write it?"

"You'd write it. You'd have to list all the reasons why you were entitled to a coat of arms. You would set the application up so it would be easy for the herald to prepare the official award in the event it was approved. The College of Heralds would then decide on your case. If you knew a lot of important people, you'd probably get the award. Or, better still, if you had plenty of money and were willing to grease a few palms you'd be certain to get it."

[111] Autograph letter signed by William Camden (1551–Nov. 9, 1623). Antiquarian, author of *Britannia* (history of British Isles, published 1586, in Latin), Camden was Clarenceux king of arms in the College of Heralds (1597–1623) and believed to have been a friend and supporter of Shakespeare.

The way the librarian described the process, it seemed probable to me that Shakespeare needed to know something about heraldry. I ran an immediate check on the poet's knowledge of the subject. The first thing I discovered was that there was a tremendous interest in heraldry in Shakespeare's day and London was full of "doctors of heraldry" who, for a fee, would assist the amateur. Apparently Shakespeare had consulted such an expert. Samuel A. Tannenbaum, himself an expert in heraldry, as well as in Elizabethan bibliography, writes in *The Shakspere Coat-of-Arms* that the first draft of Shakespeare's application "bears all the traces of having been written by one inexperienced in drawing up heraldic drafts." He points out that the description "is further elucidated by a pen-sketch of the shield and crest, without the helmet and mantle, however, in the upper left hand margin of the draft. It is worthy of note that in this rough sketch the colors of the falcon, the spear, the spear-point and the wreath are not indicated, and the motto (which is not mentioned in the body of either draft) *Non Sans Droict* appears twice above the crest, each time incorrectly." With his usual bad luck, Dr. Tannenbaum assembles a great heap of cogent evidence that Shakespeare himself wrote the drafts, then fails to perceive its significance. He concludes his pamphlet with the wistful comment: "It is pleasant to speculate—and the speculation is not wholly insupported by evidence—that the great William himself, the world's idol, had a hand in the drafting of this document. Some corroboration of this conjecture is found in the recently discovered proof that the poet was an expert in matters pertaining to heraldry, and was employed by the nobility to devise patterns of arms for them."

On October 20, 1596, the poet who wished to become a gentleman drafted—as was required by the College of Heraldry—an application for a coat of arms in the name of his father. John Shakespeare qualified for the award, since he had once held the office of "justice of the Peace, Bailiff, officer and chief of the town of Stratford upon Avon." The post of bailiff (a chief magistrate similar to a mayor) was one of the "divers offices of dignity" that made its owner eligible to apply for admission to the ranks of the gentry.

In his *Shakespeare Documents: Cartae Shakespeareanae* (1904), D. H. Lambert says of Shakespeare's grant of arms: "This exists in the form of two Drafts at the Herald's College made out by [Sir William] Dethick." The handwriting of Dethick, a bastard combination of secretary and italic, bears no similarity to Shakespeare's. One good test, aside from the different feel of the writing, is that Dethick's script is a vast deal easier to decipher than Shakespeare's. Stephen Tucker, editor of *The Assignment of Arms to Shakespeare and Arden* (1884), whose transcriptions of Shakespeare's three draft grants of arms are reproduced in this chapter *(illus. 113, 115, 117)* also contends that the documents were penned by Dethick.

The reason many modern biographers of Shakespeare accept the view that Dethick prepared and penned the draft applications for John Shakespeare is that they have never compared Sir William Dethick's almost modern script with Shakespeare's totally different secretary hand *(illus. 118)*. Compare the word *Willm* as Shakespeare wrote it with the *Willm* in Dethick's signature. All the letters are different, especially the *W.* Notice

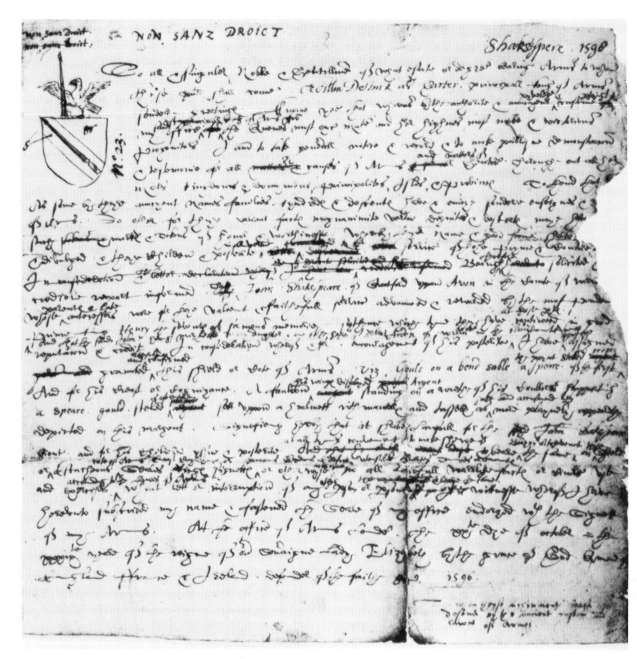

[112] Rough draft of Shakespeare's first application for Grant of Arms for his father, John Shakespeare. This draft and the two that follow, all in Shakespeare's handwriting, have been attributed by some experts to Sir William Dethick—although there is no similarity between Dethick's legible script and the poet's almost unreadable "speed writing" in these drafts (see illus. 118).

[113] Transcription of first application rough draft for Grant of Arms

ROUGH DRAFT ~~OF~~

Grant of Arms to John Shakespeare, 1596.

(No. I.)

———

NON SANZ DROICT.

Shakespere 1596.

To all & singuler Noble & Gentillme' of what estate or degree bearing Arms to whom these p'ntes shall come Will'm Dethick al's Garter. principall king of Arms sendethe greetinges. Knowe Yee that whereas by the authorite & auncyent ^p'veiege & cus-^ ~~p'teyning to said of principall king of Arms fro^~ tome ~~of~~ ^my^ ^office^ ^for^ the Quenes most exc' Ma^te^ and her highnes most noble & victorious progenitors. I am to take gen'rall notice & woord & to make publique demonstracon & testemonie for all ~~matters &~~ causes of Arms ^and matters of^ ~~& for all~~ Gentrie Thoroughe out all her Mates Kingdoms & Domynions, Principalites, Isles, & Provinces. To thend that Wh(ere) As some by theyre auncyent Names families kyndredes & descentes have & enioye sonderie enseignes & C(ottes) of Arms. So other for theyre valiant factes magnanimite vertue dignites & descertes may have . . . . . suche ~~tokens &~~ markes & Tokens of honor & Worthinesse. Whereby theyr Name & good fame shalbe . . . . & divulged & theyre Children & Posterite ^in all vertue^ ~~encouraged~~ ^better^ ~~to the better~~ ~~descerued~~ service of theyre Prynce & Contrie

~~In consideration & better declaration~~ ^the^ ~~wherof I have ben~~ ^Being herevnto soliceted and by report^ ^crediblye informed.^

Beinge ^therefore^ ~~herevnto~~ solicited & (by) credible report informed. That John Shakespeare of Stratford vppon Avon in the Counte of Warw(ike) whose ^parents & late^ ante-cessors were for they(r)e valieant & faithefull service advaunced & rewarded by the most Pruden(t) Prince king Henry the seventh of famous memorie sythence whiche tyme they have contin'eed ^at those p'tes^ in good reputac'on & credit ^And that the said John having maryed^ ~~the Mary~~ ^Mary^ daughter & one of the heyres of Robert Arden of Wilm^cote^ in the said Counte gent. ^In consideration^ wherof & for encouragement of his posterite I have ^therfore^ assigned ~~geven and~~ graunted ^and^ ^by these p'ntes^ ^confirmed^ this shield or Cote of Arms. Viz. Gould on a bend sable a speare of the first ^the poynt steeled^ ~~argent~~ ^proper^ And for his Creast or Cognizance A faulcon ^his winges displayed^ ~~proper~~ Argent ^argent^ standing on a wrethe of his Coullors supporting a Speare gould steled ^as aforesaid^ ~~argent~~ ^proper^ sett vppon a healmett wth mantelles and tasselles ~~as~~ ^hathe ben accustomed and^ more playnely appearethe depicted on this margent. Signefieng hereby that it shalbe lawfull for the sayd John Shakespeare Gent. and for his Children yssue & posterite ^at all tymes convenient to make shewe of^ ~~And that he or they maye vse &~~ beare the same ^Blazon (or) Atchevement^ ^theyre^ on ^Shield(es) or^ Escucheons ^cote of Arms Creast Cognizance or^ ~~Seales Ringes signettes~~ ^penons Guydons Edefices Vtensiles lyveries Tombes or Monum'tes^ ^at all tymes^ or other wyse ^in all lawfull Warrlyke factes or Ciuile vse and exercises^ ^according to the Lawes of Arms^ ^other^ ~~vse & beare the same~~ that * * w^th^out lett or interruption of any p'son or p'sons * * In Wittnesse Wherof I have herevnto subscribed my name & fastened the Seale of my office endorzed wth the Signett of my Arms. At the office of Arms Londo^n^ the xx^te^ daye of october = the xxxix^te^ yeare of the reigne of ou^r^ Sou^r^aigne Lady Elizabeth by the grace of God Quene of England ffrance & Ireland. defender of the faithe etc. 1596.

To whom theyse achivments must desend, by the auncient custom and lawes of Armes.

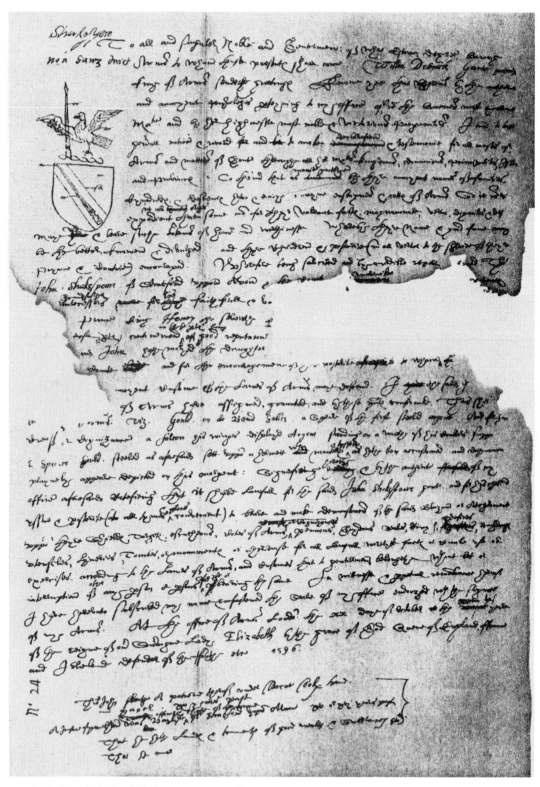

[114] Rough draft of Shakespeare's second application for Grant of Arms for John Shakespeare

[115] Transcription of second application rough draft for Grant of Arms

ROUGH DRAFT OF

Grant of Arms to John Shakespeare, 1596.

(No. II.)

—

Shakespere.

NON SANZ DROICT.

To all and singuler, Noble, and Gentilmen: of what Estate, degree, bearing Arms to whom these presentes shall come. Will'm Dethick Garter princip(al) king of Arms sendethe greetinges. Knowe yee that whereas by the authorit(ie) and auncyent pryveleges p'teyning to my office fro' the Quenes most excellent Ma^te and by her highnesse most noble & Victorious Progenitors. I am to take gen'all notice & woord ~~for~~ and ~~tee~~ to make ^declaration ~~demonstracion~~ & testemonie for all causes of Arms and matters of Gent. thoroughe all her Ma^tes Kingdoms, Dominions, Principalites, Isles, and Provinces. To the'nd that as ~~some me'~~ ^manie gentilme' by theyre auncyent names of families, Kyndredes, & Descentes have & enioye certeyne enseignes & cottes of Arms So it is ve(rie) expedient ^in all ~~tymes~~ Ages that some me' for theyr Valeant factes, magnanimite, vertn, dignites & des(certes) maye ~~have~~ ^vse & beare suche tokens of hono^r and worthinesse. Wherebye theyre Name & good fame maye be the better knowen & divulged and theyre Children & posterite (in all Vertu to the syrvice of theyre Prynce & Contrie) encouraged. Wherefore being solicited and by credible report (info)rmed. That John Shakespeare of Stratford vppon Avon in the Countie (of) Warwike . . . . parentes . . . . ^Grandfather antecessors ~~were~~ for ~~theyr~~ ^his faithfull & va(leant) . . . . Prince King Henry the seventhe of . . . . (t)hose p'tes) continewed ^in these p'tes being of good reputacon . . . . said John hathe maryed the daughter . . . . Counte ~~gent'~~ ^esquire and for the encouragement of his posterite ~~aforesaid~~ to whom ^suche . . . . auncyent custome of the Lawes of Arms maye descend. I ~~have~~ the said g(arter principal king) of Arms have assigned. graunted, and by these p'ntes confirmed: This shie(ld) of Arms. Viz. Gould on A Bend Sables a Speare of the first steeled argent. And for his Creast or Cognizance a falcon his winges displayed Argent ~~standing on a~~ wrethe of his Coullors suppo(rtinge) A Speare Gould steeled as aforesaid sett vppo' a helmett ~~and~~ ^w^th mantelles ^& tasselles as hathe ben accustomed and dothe more playnely appeare depicted on this margent: Signefieing herebye & by the authorite ~~aforesaid~~ of my office aforesaid Ratefieing that it shalbe lawfull for the said John Shakespeare gent. and for his cheldre' yssue & posterite (at all tymes ^& places convenient) to beare and make demonstraco' of the said Blazon or Atchevment vppo' theyre Shieldes, Targetes, escucheons, Cotes of Arms, ~~Creastes or Cognizances~~ Pennons, Guydons, Seales, Ringes, Edefices, Buyldinges, vtenseles, lyueries, Tombes, or monumentes or otherwise for all lawfull warrlyke factes or Ciuile vse or exercises: according to the lawes of Arms, and Customes that to gentillmen belongethe: w^thont let or interruption of any ^other p'son or p'sons ^for vse or bearing the same. In Wittnesse & p'petuall reme'brance hereof I have herevnto subscribed my name & fastened the Seale of my office endorzed wth the signett of my Arms. At the office of Arms Londo' the xx daye of October the ~~xxxix~~ ^xxxviij^th yeare of the reigne of ou^r Sou^raigne Lady Elizabeth by the grace of God Quene of England, ffrance and Irleland Defender of the ffaythe etc. 1596.

> This John . . . . A pa . . . . therof vnder Clarenc' Cook hand ⎫
> — paper. xx years past ⎪
> A Justice of Peace and was ^~~a~~ ^officer & cheffe of the towne Baylife ^ of Stratford vppo' Avon. xv or xvj ⎬
> years past ⎪
> That he hathe Landes & tenementes. of good wealth & substance. 500^li. ⎪
> That he mar. . . . . ⎭

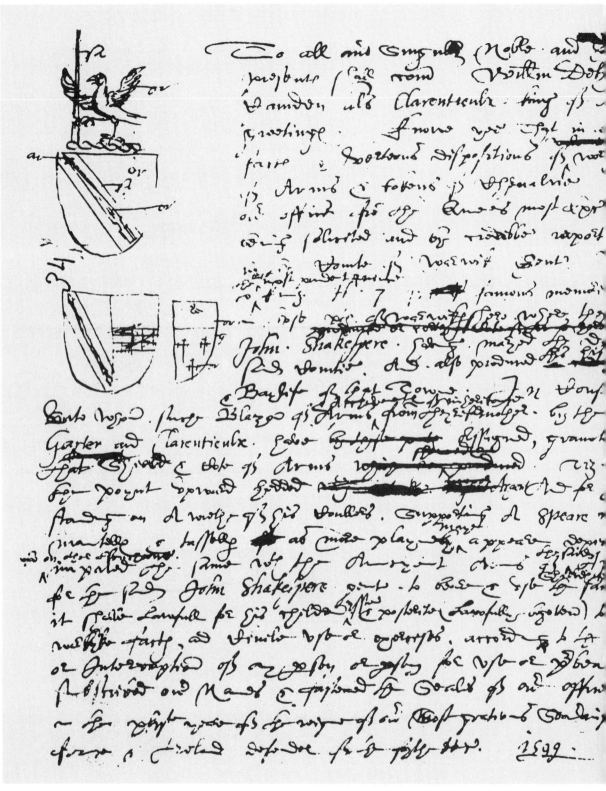

[116] Rough draft of Shakespeare's third application for Grant of Arms for John Shakespeare

Assignment of Arms for Arden, 1599.

To all and singuler Noble and Gentilmo' of ~~wha~~ all estates & degrees bearing Arms. To whom these presentes shall com' Will'm Dethick Garter-principall king of Arms of England and Will'm Camden al's Clarentieulx king of Arms for the Sowth, East and West p'tes of this Realme sendethe greetinges. Knowe yee. That in all Nations and Kingdoms the Record and remembrances of the valeant factes & verteous dispositions of ~~valeant or~~ worthie men have ben made knowe' and divulged by certeyne Shieldes of Arms & tokens of Chevalrie The grant & testemoinie wherof apperteynethe vnto vs by vertu of ou' office fro' the Quenes most Exc' Ma^te & her highenes most noble & Victorious Progenitors. Wherfore being solicited and by credible report informed. That John Shakespere nowe of Stratford vppo' Avon in the Counte of Warwik Gent'. Whose parent [great grandfather late] and Antecessor [was] for his faithefull & approved service to [the late most prudent Prince] King H. 7 of ~~most~~ famous memorie. Was advanced & Rewarded wth Landes & Tenementes geven to him in those p'tes of Warwikshere. Where they have continewed by [some] descentes in good reputaco' & credit [And for that] ~~produced a certeyne Cote of Arms heretofore Assigned vnto him. Whilest he was sometyme Baylefe of~~ The said John Shakespere having maryed the daughter & one of the heyrs of Robert Arden of Welling Cote in the said Countie. And also produced [this his Cote] ~~a certeyne~~ Auncient of Arms heretofore Assigned to him whilest he was [her ma'tes officer] & Baylefe of that Towne. In Consideration ~~Whereof.~~ [of the Premisses] And for the encouragement of his posterite vnto whom suche Blazon of Arms [& Atchevementes of inheritance] from theyre said mother by the auncyent Custome & Lawes of Arms maye [~~in this Realme~~ lawfullye] descend. We the said Garter and Clarentieulx. have ~~by these p'ntes~~ Assigned, graunted, & confirmed [& by these presentes exemplefied] vnto the said John Shakespere and to his posterite that Shield & Cote of Arms ~~which shewed & he~~ [~~Auncent~~] produced. Viz. in A field of Gould vppon A Bend Sables A Speare of the first the Poynt vpward hedded ~~wth Steele. Argent~~ [proper] Argent And for his Creast or Cognizance. A ffalcon wth his wynges displayed standing on A wrethe of his Coullors. Supporting A Speare ~~in pale~~ [Armed or] hedded & steeled ~~Argent~~ [sylver]. fyxed vppon A helmet wth mantelles & tasselles ~~of~~ as more playnely [maye] appeare depicted on this Margent. And ~~vnder the same~~ We have ~~farther~~ [likewise (v)ppo' on other Escucheone] impaled the same wth the Auncyent Arms of [the said] Arden of Willingcote ~~as aforesaid~~. Signefeing therebye That it [maye &] shalbe Lawefull for the said John Shakespere gent. to beare & vse the same [Shieldes of Arms] Single or impaled as aforesaid during his naturall Lyffe. And that it shalbe Lawfull for his children [yssue] & posterite (Lawfullye begotten) to beare vse & quarter [& shewe forthe] the same wth theyre dewe differences ~~for~~ [in] all Lawfull warlyke factes, and Ciuele vse or exercises, according to the Lawes of Arms & Custome that to Gent' belongethe. W^thout let or Interruption of any p'son or p'sons for vse or p' bearing the same. In Wytnesse & testemonye wherof We have subscribed ou' Names & fastened the Seales of ou' Offices. Yeven at the office of Arms London the . . . . in the xlij^te yeare of the reigne of ou' Most gratious Sou'aigne ~~Ladye~~ Elizabeth by the grace of God . . . . france & Ireland defender of the faythe etc. 1599.

[117] Transcription of third application rough draft for Grant of Arms

that in writing the *y* in *by* (line 3 of his note) Dethick hooks the lower loop to the left. Shakespeare, on the other hand, invariably hooks the lower loop of his *y* to the right, as in the word *my.* Look at the word *of* as Shakespeare penned it and compare it with the *of* written by Dethick in line 4 of his note. The words are totally unalike. In fact, neither in feel nor formation of letters and words is there any similarity between the scripts of Dethick and Shakespeare.

Shakespeare listed four reasons why his father was entitled to a coat of arms. First, the poet donned his imagination cap and created "antecessors" who had served valiantly

[118] Comparison of Shakespeare's handwriting with Sir William Dethick's. *(Top)* Shakespeare's script in the third and final application for a coat of arms. *(Bottom)* A handwritten signed note by Sir William Dethick. Notice that Shakespeare's secretary script sweeps torrentially across the page. Its feel is entirely different from Dethick's stately, rounded penmanship. Shakespeare writes so swiftly that the words are flat and streamlined, and the letters in some cases only partially formed. This "speed writing" is difficult to decipher and must have been a challenge even to Shakespeare's contemporaries. On the other hand, Dethick's signed note is in an almost modern script that is not hard to make out, once you get the knack of it. It reads: "I have sent you[r] verses prynted in Tubinge where that Lo[rd]

Spencer was entretayned w[i]th many Honors and Orations by the Rector and Learned of that universite: S[ir] Will[ia]m Dethick."

(Lower right) The name William Dethick penned by Shakespeare, in one of the 1596 applications to the College of Heralds, and beneath it Dethick's signature. There is not a similar letter in them. Some of the most startling differences are in the surname. Notice that Shakespeare's *e* resembles an *o*, whereas Dethick uses the Greek *e*. Dethick uses the modern *h* and Shakespeare writes the secretary *h*, with its lower loop swinging on to the next letter, *i*. The *ck* of both names is totally different and, as usual, Shakespeare's writing would be impossible to decipher for anyone not familiar with the secretary script.

137

under, and been rewarded by, the renowned monarch Henry VII. There are no records to verify the courageous acts of Shakespeare's great-grandfather; I regard the story as a pleasant invention of the poet's. (But, if you wish, you have my permission to believe that the bold ancestors really existed.)

Next, Shakespeare stated that John had married the daughter of one of the heirs of the distinguished Robert Arden, of Wilmcote. This was the truth and it must have gratified Shakespeare to tell it.

Third, Shakespeare claimed that Robert Cook, an official of the College of Heralds, had drawn up for his father a "pattern" [design sketch] of a proposed coat of arms twenty years earlier. Very likely, this was another fiction of the poet's. However, as there are many bardolaters who believe the story, I won't insist that it's not a gospel fact.

Last, Shakespeare created for his father, who was probably still in debt or no more than barely out of debt, a fortune of five hundred pounds with "lands and tenements in Stratford." In view of John's precarious financial situation, I have no doubt that the requisite palm greasing—probably forty or fifty pounds—at the College of Heralds was taken care of by his famous son.

I do not fault Shakespeare for these trifling exaggerations in his father's behalf. All applicants were expected to improvise a bit when necessary. And if anyone wishes to fault Shakespeare for merely following the custom, then let that person honestly answer this: Was there any man in England, or in Europe or in the whole world, more deserving of a coat of arms than Shakespeare? Or, for that matter, was there anyone more deserving of knighthood? (I am pretty much convinced that the poet and his friend Ben Jonson

[119] Two formal versions of Shakespeare's coat of arms. There are many variations, differing slightly in details, of this celebrated crest. The original formal award from the College of Heralds to John Shakespeare has never turned up.

would both have got a knighthood, too, if Essex and Southampton had succeeded in their effort to overthrow the political advisors of old Queen Bess.)

Shakespeare's first application for a coat of arms on behalf of his father is a thing of shreds and patches. Words and phrases are crossed out and rewritten. The text was so rapidly penned that some of the words are almost illegible. In the upper-left corner is the poet's pen-and-ink sketch of the proposed coat of arms. There is a shield with a spear surmounted by a falcon standing on his left leg and grasping a spear in his right foot. Possibly Shakespeare made the drawings and wrote the first two drafts at Derby House, office of the College of Arms in London, with occasional prompting or assistance by one of the heralds. The headlong speed of his script also suggests the possibility that Shakespeare may have penned the applications at the dictation of Dethick or Camden. The poet was apparently concerned only with setting down the necessary data as swiftly as possible.

Here is Shakespeare's description of his "shield or Cote of Arms": "Viz. Gould on a bend sable a speare of the first the poynt steeled proper And for his Creast or Cognizance A faulcon his winges displayed Argent standing on a wreth of his Coullors supporting a Speare gould steled as aforesaid sett uppon a healmett with mantelles and tasselles as hathe ben accustomed and more playnely appearethe depicted on this margent." Shakespeare forgot to draw in the helmet; or perhaps his art failed him.

Some color designations appear on the sketch: *or* (gold, or yellow); *ar* (*argent*—silver or white); and *sa* (*sable*—black). These are in Shakespeare's hand, and I see no reason to doubt that the sketch is from his agile quill. In fact, I feel quite sure that the shield was designed, as well as sketched, by Shakespeare, which if so, may explain why the award was questioned six years later because of its similarity to another crest. Of course, Shakespeare would not have had the extensive familiarity with coats of arms that a herald would possess and might have easily infringed by accident on another shield.

Dr. F. J. Furnivall, in "On Shakspere's Signatures" (*The Journal of the Society of Archivists and Autograph Collectors*, No. 1, June 1895), writes on Shakespeare's coat of arms: "The Elizabethan time was full of conceits and canting terms; and to all users of them the splitting of Shakspere's name in the verb 'shake'—shown by the fluttering bird in his coat-of-arms—and 'spear' was a matter of course. . . ." Referring to the way printers spelled Shakespeare's name, Furnivall continues: "I stick to Shakspere and leave Shakespeare to the second-handers—charming fellows, some of them, but too fond of type."

The sketch by Shakespeare reveals artistic skill. The motto, *Non sans droict* ("Not without cause"), is an excellent choice for Shakespeare, for he apparently was, as I've mentioned, a very moral man. I doubt if he ever entered the lists without a strong conviction that he was tilting in a righteous cause.

Two other drafts exist of the application for a coat of arms, both in Shakespeare's hand. In the second draft, also dated 1596 but with no month or day, the only changes are the substitution of *grandfather* for *antecessors* in the section on John Shakespeare's ancestry, and the substitution of *esquire* for *gent* in the description of his wife's father, Robert Arden. However, at the bottom of the draft Shakespeare has penned some rambling observations noting that John had been bailiff of Stratford and had earlier received a pattern for a coat of arms from the College of Heralds.

Apparently the College of Heralds granted the coat of arms on the basis of the poet's two draft applications. The original award, no doubt sumptuously got up on parchment with a colored family crest and an impressive seal, has long ago vanished. Thus there are some authorities who question that the award was ever consummated. In *Was Shakspere a Gentleman?* (1909), Dr. Tannenbaum writes: ". . . of the two rough drafts of the 1596 grant preserved at the College [of Heralds] neither is signed or sealed, and . . . no duly executed grant has yet been discovered. This is true also of the 1599 draft-grant. . . ." There is, nevertheless, quite a lot of evidence that the coat of arms was awarded. Shakespeare is alluded to as "gent[leman]" in documents of the period, and in the monument to Shakespeare in the Holy Trinity Church at Stratford his elaborate coat of arms surmounts his effigy.

Shakespeare was the first actor to be granted a coat of arms. Subsequently, six other members of his company joined the ranks of the armigerous. It is possible that Shakespeare aided them in preparing their applications and designing an appropriate coat of arms.

The third draft, dated 1599, with no month or day designated, was penned and submitted by Shakespeare with a request to impale the arms of the Ardens of Wilmcote, his mother's family, on the shield. He put the arms of the celebrated Warwickshire Ardens in the margin to indicate the manner of impalement, with the Arden arms next to it. But the Arden shield was never put on Shakespeare's arms. There may have been some objection from the College of Heralds, or perhaps the poet changed his mind. Lord Essex and consequently Essex's close friend, Southampton, were in disgrace with the queen in 1599 and Shakespeare may have lacked the necessary political pull to get the award. Mrs. C. C. Stopes, in *Shakespeare's Family* (1901), takes the pleasantly feminine view that Shakespeare's attempt to obtain a coat of arms for his father was really "in order to continue them to his mother."

Three years later, in 1602, John Shakespeare's award was challenged by Ralph Brooke, the York Herald, who drew up a list of twenty-three persons whom he charged with

[120] List of questioned awards of coats of arms. Although penned hurriedly and in a diminutive hand by Ralph Brooke, York Herald, the script is identical in feel to the italic writing employed by Brooke on more formal occasions.

obtaining coats of arms by more or less fraudulent means *(illus. 120, 121)*. Shakespeare's name was fourth on the list. Brooke, a cantankerous man who once called Jaggard "a blind printer," alleged that the arms of bailiff John Shakespeare were too much like those of "the old Lord Manley's." Although Shakespeare was in disfavor with Queen Elizabeth for writing *Richard II*, in which he depicts the overthrow of a British monarch, he had enough clout to get the charge squelched. Sir William Dethick and his associate, the renowned scholar William Camden, replied that the shield of John Shakespeare differed conspicuously from all similar coats of arms by the presence of a spear on the bend. In their answer, two copies of which have survived, they added that John Shakespeare had "borne magistracy and was justice of peace at Stratford-on-Avon; he maried the daughter and heire of Ardene, and was able to maintain that Estate." One of the straw-clutching Baconians, H. Kendra Baker, in "Shakespere's Coat-of-Arms" *(Baconiana,* April 1939), offers a bizarre explanation of how Shakespeare got out of the mess created by Brooke's accusation: Shakespeare and Bacon agreed that in consideration of one thousand pounds to the poet and the firm promise of a grant of arms, Shakespeare would go back to Stratford and "figure as the author of *Richard II* [actually, according to Baker, written by Bacon!] which had annoyed the queen by its seditious features."

The script of Shakespeare in the heraldry drafts is most interesting, with the fluid, easy character one might expect from a creative writer and its velocity is accelerated by continual verbal shortcuts and abbreviations. The poet, as usual, casts aside all pretense of punctuation or consistent spelling; he is constrained by no rules except the boundaries of his imagination. No doubt it is Shakespeare's undisciplined approach to the formal art of heraldry that inspired Dr. Tannenbaum's remark that the draft revealed the writer's inexperience in drawing up such documents.

Under the exigencies of Shakespeare's swift penmanship, almost every word is pared down or streamlined in some way or other. The long, sensuous pendant loops are sheared off. The tails of the *f*'s and long *s*'s are amputated. No room for amenities. *And* becomes *ad, ffraunce* is *frnce.* Many letters are flattened for speed.

I cannot escape the uneasy feeling that Shakespeare's inspired plays of the early seventeenth century—*Lear, Hamlet, Macbeth* and the others—may have been indited in a precipitous hand very much like this; if so, surely we should heap encomiums, not curses, on his compositors and printers. A statue in London or Stratford to William and Isaac Jaggard would not be amiss.

In his swiftly penned drafts Shakespeare slowed down only long enough to indite in a clear italic script, eloquent and precise, his family name and other important cognomens in the text.

In an age when creative spelling and little punctuation were amiably tolerated, Shakespeare abused the privileges. He was capable of writing an entire page without a single punctuation mark, not even a lonesome period. Yet the drafts, rife as they are with fanciful abbreviations and inconsistent spellings, show only two different spellings of the poet's surname—*Shakespeare* and *Shakespere.* In the two 1596 drafts the word *gentlemen*

Shakespear ye Player
by Garter

[121] This curious sketch of Shakespeare's coat of arms, entitled "Shakespear ye Player by Garter," is frequently reproduced in books about Shakespeare. The original is in the Folger Library. The sketch was presumably made in 1602, when Ralph Brooke challenged the award of the coat of arms to John Shakespeare on the grounds that the design was too similar to the arms of another family. Some writers aver that the sketch was a derisive one—"pejoratively intended," writes S. Schoenbaum—made by Ralph Brooke, but such a sketch would be senseless. The poet's right to ownership of a coat of arms was not in question. Nor was the right of his father, to whom the original award was made. Although Brooke's complaint against the Shakespeare award has not survived, the reply of Dethick and Camden in defense of the award indicates clearly that no allusion was made by Brooke to Shakespeare or his profession. The sketch, therefore, seems to be without purpose.

The sketch is part of a volume that comprises two separate manuscripts. Originally from the William Constable collection, it was bought in 1907 by Henry Clay Folger from Bernard Dobell. The sketch is drawn at the upper left of a page crowded with writing not relevant to Shakespeare and not in Brooke's fastidious script.

The printing under the sketch is certainly not, as some authors have claimed, in the hand of Ralph Brooke, the York Herald who questioned the originality of the design. As you can see for yourself, Brooke had a beautiful, refined italic script, totally unlike the labored printing on this sketch. Nor is the writing that of Sir William Dethick or William Camden. It does not, in fact, even resemble Elizabethan handwriting. The gratuitous use of the *ye*, with the *e* placed in an open thorn, seems like a clumsy attempt to simulate antiquity. The original purpose in splitting the top of the Anglo-Saxon thorn (th) and thereby turning it into a *y*, an open-topped letter, was to save space by writing *y* instead of *th* in *the* and *that*. Except for stonecutters and printers, its usage was pretty much out of fashion in Shakespeare's day. It had already become an affectation. (The examples of Elizabethan handwriting in Chapter 2 of this book show how rarely it was used.) Shakespeare didn't use it. Nor did Brooke, Dethick or Camden. All wrote out the word *the*. My opinion is that whoever penned "Shakespere ye Player by Garter" lived in the middle of the nineteenth century. His printing looks modern.

The sketch of the coat of arms is extremely crude and certainly not the work of anyone in the herald's office. The shield is lopsided and shakily outlined—probably the artist had never before tried to draw a shield. The spear is not long enough for the bend. There is a forlorn *o* in the field on the upper right of the bend. What its meaning is, I don't know. Possibly it's an aborted *or* (gold, or yellow). The falcon is badly drawn, his right leg is twice as long as his left. He has only one wing, and John Shakespeare's arms call for a falcon with his "wings displayed," or fluttering. The bird is brachycephalic, with a head as big as his thorax. His tail plumage extends grotesquely over the right side of the top of the shield; there is as much of him off the shield as on it. Also, the falcon should be perched on a helmet, as in the Shakespeare coat of arms, but this detail has been overlooked by the artist. In my opinion, whoever drew this coat of arms knew very little about art and nothing at all about heraldry. I regard this sketch as a forgery, possibly by that bastard of bardology, John Payne Collier. It is very different from the deftly sketched coats of arms that appear on the page with Brooke's list of questioned crests.

> *where longe sithence it pleased youe to grauntl vnto me,*
> *your Honorable alouance Vnder all youve hands, for the*
> *Office of Norrey kinge of armes, and vnderstandinge that*
> *twoe of youe haue latelye subscribed aseconde Bill, to one*
> *Paddy Lancaster heralt, apson, (were he well knowne*
> *vnto your Lop^s) not able to execute the same,*
>
> > *your Ho.^rs in all dutie bounde*
> > *Ra: Brooke: yorke: Heralt.*

[122] Handwritten Note signed by York Herald Ralph Brooke. Although the delicately beautiful script vaguely resembles the printing on the forged coat of arms, it shows a familiarity with the quill that is totally lacking in the "Shakespeare ye Player by Garter" inscription.

Professor S. Schoenbaum, in his *William Shakespeare: a Documentary Life*, states the prevailing scholarly opinion: ". . . beneath a rough sketch of the familiar arms, Brooke has written, 'Shakespeare ye Player by Garter.'" Schoenbaum alludes to Brooke's complaint as "a heraldic tempest in a teapot."

The feel of Brooke's script is entirely different from that of the caption in the forged coat of arms. The exquisite grace and skillful pen shading of Brooke's handwriting is absent from the crude fake. In the forged inscription, starting with the word *Shakespear*, a few of the obvious differences in the scripts can be noted. Entirely absent in the imitation are Brooke's graceful *b*, with its long stem; the beautifully formed *k* (see the word *kinge* in line 3 of Brooke's note); the handsome long *s*, with its graceful curve descending far below the line (see the word *pleased* in the middle of line 1 of Brooke's note); the *e*, with its second curve swinging high up, even to the point where it reaches the closed loop; and the beautiful *r*, often open from the base up, like a *v*. The word *Player* in the fake begins with an ornate *P* very similar to the type used a hundred years later in the eighteenth century. Notice that in the first word of line 5 of Brooke's note—*Paddy*—the York Herald uses an entirely different *P*. Compare the *l* in the forged word *Player* with Brooke's tastefully curved *l*, with its tiny hook at the top (line 1 of Brooke's note, the *l* in *longe* and in *pleased*). The *y* in *Player* is also very different from Brooke's. In line 4 of the York Herald's note, the word *youe* has a curvaceous, attractive *y*, totally different from the modern *y* in *Player*. Brooke's *b*, unlike the *b* in the word by in the forgery, has the same long, delicate stem as his *l*. Brooke uses two different *b*'s, but both are long-stemmed and beautiful, very unlike the modern *b* in the forgery. The *t* of Brooke also differs from that in the word *Garter* in the fake. The stem of Brooke's *t* has a forward slant, and the crossbar points upward; whereas in the forgery the stem is precisely vertical and the crossbar is precisely horizontal.

Ralph Brooke, the York Herald whose skill in art we may infer from his skill in penmanship, was born about 1560 and died on October 16, 1625. An implacable enemy of the historian William Camden, his associate in the College of Heralds, Brooke published a *Discovery of Errors* that he had uncovered in Camden's *Britannia*.

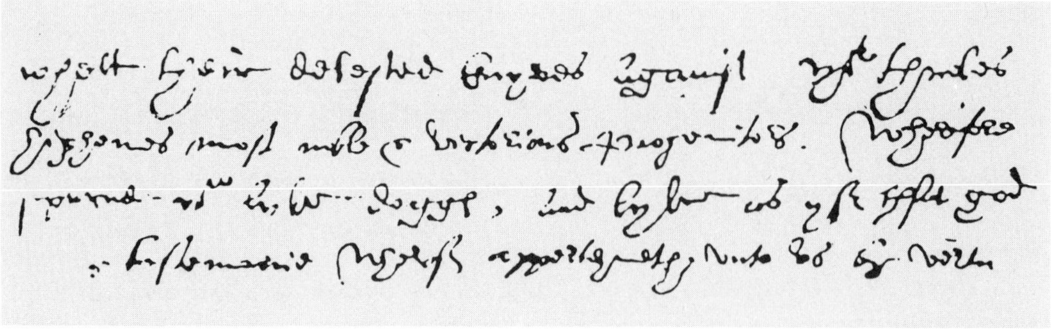

[123] The feel of Shakespeare's rapid, early script. The first line of this composite is from the legible manuscript page of *Sir Thomas Moore*. The second line is from the final application Shakespeare made for a coat of arms; the third from *Moore;* the fourth from the application.

is set down as *gentillmen* and *gentilmen*, *highness* is *highnes* and *highnesse*. And so on. A patient scholar could write a monograph on Shakespeare's wild orthography.

There is an entry, discovered in Belvoir Castle by Henry Maxwell-Lyte and W. H. Stevenson, in the accounts of Thomas Screvin, steward of the Earl of Rutland: "It[e]m Mty [March] to mr Shakspeare in gold about my Lordes Impreso xliiij s. To Rich Burbadge for paynting & making yt in gold xliiij."

The impresa, or emblem, created by this artistic duo for a fee of forty-four shillings each was designed for young Francis Manners, who had in 1612 succeeded to the title of Earl of Rutland. To commemorate this rise to eminence the earl was called upon to join in a great tournament arranged for March 24, 1613, to celebrate the accession of James I ten years before. It was the custom for each knight to enter the lists carrying a shield ornamented with a beautiful impresa painted in glorious colors on a cardboard-like shield. There was usually some hidden meaning in the figures on the shield and the spectators vied with one another in probing out the secret allusions.

Knowing as we now do that the poet was an expert in heraldry and possessed considerable artistic talent, we may consider it likely that he made the preliminary sketches and created the allegorical symbols for the earl's shield. Burbage, a skilled amateur painter noted for his portraits of actors *(illus. 127)* then implemented the finished work, probably

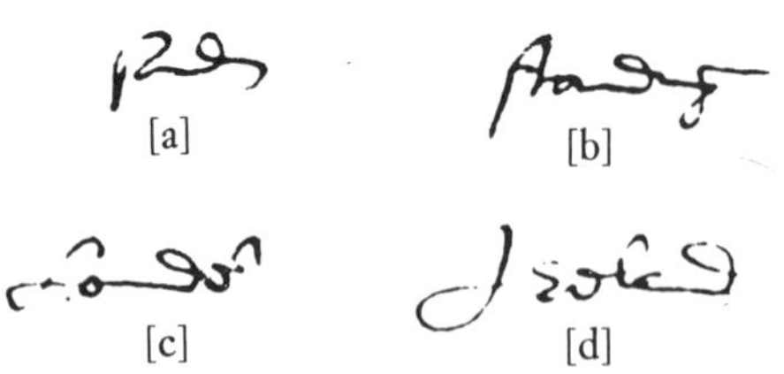

[124] Shakespeare's "Speed Writing"

[a] said
[b] standing
[c] London
[d] Ireland

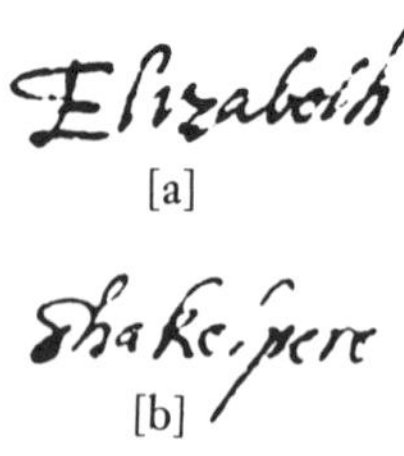

[125] Shakespeare's Meticulous Italic Script

[a] Elizabeth
[b] Shakespere

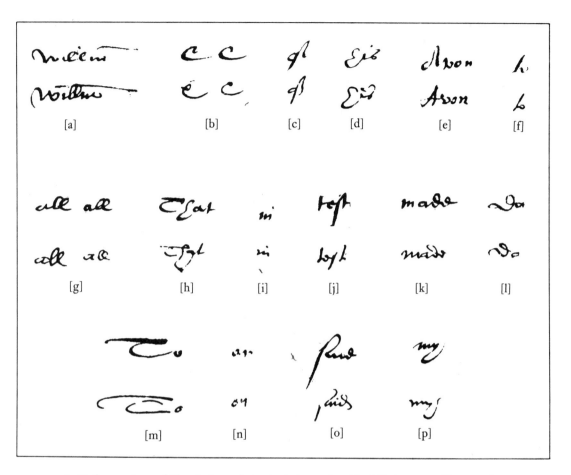

[126] Comparison of identical words in the holograph will of Shakespeare (first words given in each set) and in the applications for a coat of arms. Although about two decades separate these two examples of Shakespeare's handwriting, the similarity in many of the key words is remarkable. The will was carefully indited, but the manuscript applications for arms were penned sloppily and with great speed.

[a] Willm̅   [i] in
[b] & (ampersand) [j] test
[c] of   [k] made
[d] his   [l] Do
[e] Avon   [m] To
[f] to   [n] on
[g] all   [o] said
[h] That   [p] my

in lapis and gold. It is significant that in the record of payment Shakespeare's name comes first, perhaps indicating that he was regarded as the heraldry expert and Burbage merely as the artist who executed the poet's concept.

I've got a hunch that the "firm" of "Shakespeare and Burbage, Heraldry Experts, Coats of Arms and Armorial Shields to Order," did a roaring business in London. They had great connections with the knights and nobles of England, even with the royal family. King James knew and liked them both. And they also knew, we may surmise, scores of newly rich who wished to make the metamorphosis into gentlemen by acquiring a coat of arms. We can speculate that once retained for the job, "Doctor" Shakespeare would make out the required application to the College of Heralds, tugging the longbow a bit when necessary. He would then furnish Burbage with a heraldic sketch from which the actor would create a resplendent coat of arms.

[127] Richard Burbage as artist. *(Top)* Painting of the great actor (about 1567–1619), accepted by most scholars as a self-portrait. Its considerable technical adroitness indicates that Burbage, for whom Shakespeare wrote many lead roles, was also a skilled artist. The other portrait, similar in style, is of William Sly, a leading actor with Shakespeare's group. Burbage may also have painted a portrait of Shakespeare.

XII

FACTOTUM OF THE THEATER

THE pen-and-ink evidence of the great poet's artistry, his ability to sketch with skill, apparently survives in three forms. The first two are his daubery in cabalistic designs and heraldic emblems. The monograms Shakespeare created for two of the three known volumes from his library hint at some deep, inner significance. His initials can be read in all five of these strange designs, but I suspect the ink swirls contain more than just initials—possibly a secret message or Shakespeare's full name cunningly inwrought in the manner of an ancient *signum*. The designs are carefully executed and show a pleasing mathematical structure *(illus. 128)*. Shakespeare's imagination fused with his artistic talent to create a beguiling ornament that served the poet in place of a bookplate. (The monograms will be discussed in detail in the next chapter on Shakespeare's books.)

Far more talent was required to create the three original designs in the poet's applications, on behalf of his father, John, for a coat of arms. I've placed them side by side for easier judgment of their artistic worth *(illus. 129)*.

The rhythmic quality in the heraldic drawings suggests that Shakespeare was accustomed to turning a quick sketch. Yet although dashed off with great speed—like the rest of the documents—there is an instinctive balance and flow to the pattern, and Shakespeare put the accent on the proper things. The spear is a plain, wooden lance and the poet wasted no time with it; on the other hand, the wings of the falcon appear to be in motion, actually shaking the spear. The head and beak of the bird seem frozen in militant impassiveness. Only the spread tail is amiss. It looks more like an oldtime rattrap than a bird's stabilizer.

As already mentioned, Shakespeare probably supplemented his income by designing shields and coats of arms. This skill with the limning pen suggests that he may also have

[128] Two monograms by Shakespeare. Taken from two manuscript volumes once in the poet's library, these ornate sketches incorporate the poet's initials and show his bent for artistic design.

[129] Three sketches by Shakespeare for a coat of arms. These little drawings reveal Shakespeare's ability to make quick, effective and attractive sketches.

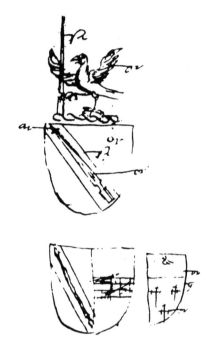

had a hand in designing stage props and costumes for the players in his acting company, the Chamberlain's Men (later the King's Men). The accounts of the famous theater manager Philip Henslowe, who died the same year as Shakespeare, give an excellent idea of the rich variety of stage props that a well-equipped acting troop had on hand. In 1598, for instance, Henslowe lists for the Admiral's Men a cage, three different tombs, stairs for Phaeton, the city of Rome, a tree of golden apples and so on. What a delight the poet would have taken in designing such artifacts! Years ago it was popularly believed that the stage used by Shakespeare was barren except for signs such as "the Forest of Arden" and the like. We now know that many productions were sumptuously done with costly and exciting props and costumes.

The only known picture of any of Shakespeare's plays being acted portrays a scene from *Titus Andronicus* (published in 1594), and is accompanied by a contemporary text that roughly illustrates the stage action *(illus. 130)*. Because this drawing is well known and has often been reproduced, I had examined it without the caution acquired in over fifty years of looking at old documents. The result was that it took me over three hours to evaluate the sketch and its text.

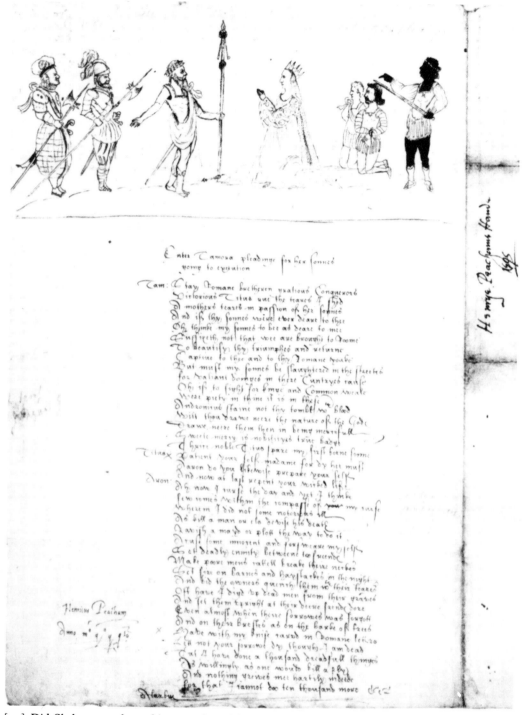

[130] Did Shakespeare draw this scene from *Titus Andronicus*? This unusual drawing, with its accompanying text, depicts the characters of *Titus Andronicus*, written by Shakespeare about 1592. Very possibly the drawing was created to explain and illustrate the basic costumes required to perform the drama. The text, written in a clerk's hand and somewhat different from the published version, roughly explains the drawing. Shakespeare, then in his late twenties, may have designed the costumes for the players. Because of the immense importance of this sketch, noted Shakespeare expert Professor J. Dover Wilson, once suggested "a symposium . . . designed to elucidate its complex problems."

I realized that the vertical, dated inscription in the right margin, as Joseph Quincy Adams years ago pointed out, is a forgery in a mid-nineteenth-century hand, probably (as Adams surmised) the work of that bane of bardology, John Payne Collier. Thus the date assigned by most scholars (1595, as written in the margin) becomes suspect. The signature of Henry Peacham at the lower left is obviously in a different hand from that of the manuscript and appears to have been written at a much later date. What puzzled me was the date under Peacham's signature. I couldn't translate it into Arabic numerals. The initials for the Roman numerals were clear enough—m^o q^o q q^{to}—yet every scholar seemed to read them differently. Since this date has been interpreted in so many ways, I invite you to take a look at it. Could the symbols be plainer?

Another thing about the date that struck me as peculiar (and I always look askance on anything "peculiar" in old manuscripts) is that it was set down in the initials of Roman numerals at a time when Arabic numerals were universally used to record the year; Roman numerals were frequently employed for the day of the month and for amounts of money, but not for the year. In view of this anachronism, I turned to the opinions of a few of the brilliant scholars who had worked on the manuscript and was astonished to find that, without exception, they recorded the date of the manuscript as 1594 or 1595, mainly on the strength of the marginal forgery.

The substitution of unreadable Roman numerals for Arabic numerals is precisely the sort of thing that Collier, whose scholarly abilities were, and are still, much exaggerated, would try to pull off. If Collier had lived half a century earlier the great scholar-sleuth Edmund Malone would have eviscerated him and stuffed him with his own malefactions. If he'd lived fifty years later John Carter and Graham Pollard would have published an "enquiry" that would have plopped him right into Newgate.

Professor J. Dover Wilson writes, in "Titus Andronicus on the Stage in 1595" (*Shakespeare Survey I*): "As for the date, whatever be the meaning of the third numerical symbol, which I follow Adams in reading 'g', though Chambers and the scribe of the [forged] endorsement take it for a '9' [an Arabic numeral in a Roman-numeral date?], the first two symbols prove that some year in the sixteenth century is intended, and I feel pretty confident that '1594' or '1595' is the correct translation, the more so as I hope to show grounds in a forthcoming edition of *Titus* for believing that the play did not come into existence before 1593."

In a postscript to *William Shakespeare: A Documentary Life*, Professor S. Schoenbaum suggests: "In the Longleat Manuscript [the *Titus Andronicus* page] the date Anno m^o q^o g q^{to} . . . may be expanded as 'anno millesimo quingentesimo quarto' (or quinto); hence 1594 or 1595." To accept Professor Schoenbaum's explanation for the date, we must assume that the writer of the date did not know the difference, or did not care about the difference, between a *q* and a *g*, for the third numeral is clearly *q* and bears no similarity to any form of Elizabethan *g*; that he was unaware that dates of the year were usually written in Arabic numerals; that he did not care whether the final symbol of the date was interpreted as *quarto* (four) or *quinto* (five); and that he furthermore was not versed in the proper way to write a date in Latin.

On my part, I was determined not to let the date beat me and I set to work to find out what the symbols meant. A short time later, I concluded what I should have perceived at a glance: it was a bogus date and had no meaning. This discovery made me extremely suspicious of the signature of Henry Peacham, regarded by scholars as the artist who drew the picture of the actors on the page. I discovered upon checking that there were two Henry Peachams. The elder (fl. 1577–1605) and the younger (1576?–1643?). Peacham the younger was also an artist, and Shakespearean experts have ascribed the text and drawing to him.

At this point I had invested over two hours in studying the page and had not yet uncovered the vital clue that could explain it. I now did what I should have done at the start: I gave the signature and date a very careful examination. It took me only a few seconds to discover the unusual capital *A* on *Anno* and tie it with the *A*'s in the manuscript excerpt from *Titus*. However, the capital *A* in Peacham's date was shaky and badly formed, an obvious attempt to imitate the fluent and beautiful A's in the manuscript. Look at the forged *A* in *Anno* through a magnifying glass and compare it with any of the *A*'s in the authentic manuscript text and you will perceive at once the great difference. The forged *A*, doubtless by Collier, shakes from here to Canarsie. The other letters in the counterfeit signature, except in a couple of cases where there is a similarity, were also childish attempts to copy the italic script in the manuscript. Obviously, John Payne Collier, who did this forgery, wished to convey the impression that both the

[131] *(Top)* Fabrication of Henry Peacham's signature, probably by John Payne Collier. *(Bottom)* Composite of Henry (Henricus) Peacham's name formed from letters in the *Titus Andronicus* excerpt. Not a single letter in the forged signature matches the authentic, Elizabethan italic script. The forgery appears to be in a mid-nineteenth century hand. It lacks the delicacy and beauty of the Elizabethan chirography. Even the *a*, which at first glance appears to be the same in the forged signature as in the authentic script, turns out to be entirely different when examined under a magnifying glass.

[132] *(Top)* The words *Anno* and *q*[uar]*to* in the forged date accompanying fabricated Peacham signature. That the forger intended to mimic Elizabethan script is revealed by his unusual *A* in *Anno*, a clear imitation of the *A* in the authentic manuscript. *(Bottom)* The same words reconstructed from the *Titus* manuscript. The forger was moderately successful in his shaky imitation of the quaint *A* but the rest, especially the signature of Peacham, fails to capture the feel of the original, sixteenth-century manuscript.

151

drawing and the text were done by Henry Peacham. But perhaps he couldn't decide which Peacham, the elder or the younger, so he simply penned a nonsensical date which —as can be seen from the vertical notation, also fabricated by Collier—only the forger himself could "decipher." The fake signature of Peacham's has an entirely different feel from the italic text *(illus. 131, 132)*. So contemptuous was Collier of his fellow scholars that he did not bother to imitate closely the handwriting of the document. Compare his incorrect *r* in *Henry* with the terminal *r*'s in *for her* in the first line of the text from *Titus,* and the way the clerk makes his capital *H* (first word in line 6 from the bottom of the page in the word *Have*) with the *H* in *Henry.*

At this point in my investigation I decided to check Professor J. Q. Adams's Introduction to the facsimile (1936) of the unique First Quarto (1594) edition of *Titus Andronicus.* Professor Adams alludes to the *Titus* drawing and its text as "a curious composite . . . apparently transcribed from a printed copy of the play." Adams adds: "Why the transcriber should have made such a curious textual composite (at some pains to himself) and have so strangely altered the story . . . is hard to understand."

Not unfamiliar with forgeries, Adams identifies Collier as the writer of some penciled notes of authentication on the *Titus* document and questions the genuineness of the vertical notation in the right margin. Further, he notes that the holograph manuscript of Henry Peacham the younger's *Emblemata Varia,* in the Folger Library, shows no similarity to "the secretary" (actually italic) hand of the *Titus* document. The signatures also vary. He concludes his analysis by noting that "the elaborate and detailed drawing at the top of the *Titus* document seems to be not in the style of, and very distinctly superior in technique to, the numerous drawings we have from Peacham's pen." After laying all the elaborate groundwork for identifying the signature of Peacham as a Collier forgery, Adams fails to do so.

With the two Collier forgeries eliminated, I now had before me an undated and unsigned manuscript page, with a drawing of the characters of *Titus Andronicus,* that did not appear to jibe with any known text. Professor Adams states that the forty lines of text under the drawing were "transcribed from either the 1611 Quarto or the 1623 Folio." He favored the Folio. According to Professor J. Dover Wilson, this assumption would necessitate the deduction "that the text with signature and date was added about a generation after the drawing was executed, assuming the scribe's [forger's] date refers to the latter [the drawing] and is correct." Wilson continues:

I do not wish to stress this point, though I think Adams is probably right in believing the Folio (1623) to be the source of the text. But I find it impossible to escape the conclusion that the text was at any rate added to the drawing by another man, even though the ink looks much alike in both, since that supposition goes far to clear up all the puzzles which have up to the present baffled students of the document. For assume with Chambers and Adams that drawing and text were produced by the same hand at the same time, and you are faced with the following unanswerable questions: (1) Why does the drawing seem to represent Tamora pleading for *two* sons, when in the play she has three sons and pleads for one only, her first-born Alarbus? (2) Why does the scribe alter the text to agree with the picture for the first half of Tamora's speech, and then revert to the original version in her last line? (3) Why does the name 'Alarbus', who is given nothing to say in the play, appear in the margin [as a speech prefix] at the end of the transcript? (4) What is Aaron supposed to be doing in the picture, and why does the scribe go to the trouble of copying out his bragging speech from Act V, Scene i, and of inventing, or partly inventing, a short speech for Titus to link it on to Tamora's from Act I? (5) Lastly, why does he describe the Gothic princes as 'going to execution' when what happens in the play is not an execution but a sacrifice to the manes [souls of the dead] of the Andronici?

Assume, on the other hand, that the drawing was executed by one man and the forty lines added some time after by another man who was attempting to provide an explanatory text for a picture he failed to understand, the foregoing questions will either not arise or find a ready answer.

The technical questions raised by Professor Wilson are augmented by still another problem that Wilson and others have attempted to solve by creating a poet-scribe, an inspired clerk who simply added two lines of blank verse to provide a transition. In the material quoted above, from *"Titus Andronicus* on the Stage in 1595," Professor Wilson alludes to a short speech for Titus, which he later explains as obviously "invented by the scribe":

> "Aaron do you likewise prepare your self
> And now at last repent your wicked life"

A lot of the other text is mixed up a bit, with parts of it a little different in wording and extracted from several different scenes in the play as printed in the First Folio of 1623.

Professor Wilson explains some of the characters in the sketch and wonders ". . . does that black profile belong to Burbage?" Wilson also ventures the opinion, well founded, I think, that characters of the lower classes in Shakespeare's plays wore "modern [Elizabethan] dress" and the exalted characters were in period attire.

Finally, he states that the sketch was "without doubt" done by an artist who "depicts, equally without doubt, what he actually saw at a performance of the play." Wilson winds up by saying that he hopes the reader won't think that he tried "to wring too much from the evidence." And he cites in his defense another case of "elaborate hypothetical structures," involving "a Dutchman's drawing of another Dutchman's sketch of what he remembered about the Swan Theater after a single visit." The well-known sketch of the Swan Theater by Johannes de Witt is pictured in every illustrated book about Shakespeare. I've always felt, as Wilson apparently did, that there is a slight aroma of *fromage hollandaise* about it. One of these days, if I have a few minutes to spare, I'll crank up my siege guns and see if it can withstand a little bombardment.

Professor Wilson thinks the players in the *Titus* scene represent the actors in Shakespeare's group, then known as the Chamberlain's company. I hold the same opinion. But there are other views. Martin Holmes, in *Shakespeare and His Players* (1972), advances the belief that the sketch illustrates a production by Henslowe's company.

In his essay, "The First Illustration to 'Shakespeare' " (*The Library*, June 1924), Edmund K. Chambers hints at, and rejects, another explanation of why the text does not accurately explain the drawing: "Are we . . . to infer that Peacham had before him an early version of the play and that this was afterward rearranged? It would be a hazardous conclusion. . . . " It was suggested to Chambers by a friend that the drawing and text were done by Peacham for a penmanship competition but Chambers, with good reason, I think, rejected this idea.

Let me go over the evidence that seems to me pertinent in the case of the drawing and text from *Titus Andronicus:*

1. Now that the forged additions by Collier are eliminated, including the bogus marginal date of 1595 and the nonsensical date in Latin abbreviations, we have before us an unsigned, undated document depicting a scene from *Titus,* a play as we now know it mainly written by Shakespeare probably sometime between 1589 and 1594. The page contains a garbled text from *Titus* that includes a patchwork line and two lines that do not appear in any published version of the play.

2. The drawing and the text are apparently not wedded, which suggests that they were done by different persons. But, since the ink is the same, according to scholars who have viewed the document, the drawing and the text were almost certainly executed at the same time, but possibly by different persons. Both the graceful italic penmanship and the antiquated spelling suggest that this is a document of the period, probably written very early in the 1590's. There would appear to be a contradiction in this idea, however, since Professor Adams avers that the text in the *Titus* excerpt is based upon the text of the play in the First Folio of 1623. At first supposition this would necessarily give the drawing's text a date after 1623 (which is precisely what Professor Wilson did), but the handwriting and the spelling belie such a later date. As I mentioned earlier, it is my belief that just before his death Shakespeare turned over to Burbage, Heminges and Condell his manuscripts, and that the Globe library of prompt books was available to them. We know, of course, that Heminges and Condell made use of such sources in preparing the First Folio. Thus these two editors may have used to prepare the 1623 Folio a text written several years before that of the 1594 edition, likely an original manuscript. In *The Facts About Shakespeare* Professors W. A. Neilson and A. H. Thorndike point out that the Folio text of *Titus Andronicus* "restores from some manuscript source a scene [scene ii, Act III] which had been dropped from the Quarto." The presumptive link between the *Titus* drawing's text and the First Folio does not, therefore, have any significance in establishing the date of the drawing.

3. Most scholars contend that the sketch and its text represent the recollections of a playgoer who thus recorded his visual impression, with some random text, after viewing the drama. Setting aside the obvious fact that this was a silly thing to do, why didn't the viewer get the facts right about the figures in the sketch and why did he feel obligated to add gratuitously one very garbled line and two new lines of blank verse not already in the play? The logical answer is that there was no playgoer at all. More likely, the scribe was copying another, much earlier text of *Titus,* in which the scenes and lines were placed very differently from the final published text. It is my opinion that Shakespeare had a fearsome struggle with this play. He probably started work on it in 1589 or 1590,

when he was only about twenty-five. He found it tough going, perhaps because it was too gory for his taste, yet he wished to write a popular and successful drama. I think he overhauled it two or three times, at least, before he was even moderately satisfied. Probably, too, he was working from versions created by other playwrights. It is certainly conceivable that the early text copied under the drawing by the scribe jibed closely with the sketch. If this text were written down in, or after, 1594, when the first Quarto of *Titus* was published, the scribe would likely have used the published version. But since the text is closer to the text of the Folio of 1623, it is my belief that the scribe's text definitely predates the first publication and was copied from an earlier manuscript or prompt book, very possibly the one used by Heminges and Condell in working up a text they thought Shakespeare might approve. There was obviously a speaking part for Alarbus in the text transcribed by the clerk, otherwise Alarbus's name would not appear as a speech prefix at the bottom of the page.

I would date the document between 1589 and 1594, probably about 1592. As the name of the play is not mentioned in this excerpt, and the passage contains two previously unknown lines that were later jettisoned, it is quite possible that the copyist used the 1592–1593 version when the play had one of its earlier titles—*Titus and Vespasian* or *Titus and Ondronicus.* Since no text of these earlier titles survives, there is of course, no absolute certainty that they allude to the same play, but it seems very likely it was the identical play being recast time after time by different playwrights or by Shakespeare.

4. Now, in this celebrated document, as all scholars are aware, the play's not the thing. The thing is the sketch with the costumed figures. This simple fact explains what I believe was the purpose of the drawing. *Titus* was very widely performed, in one shape or another, by various acting companies: the Earl of Sussex's Men on January 23, 1594, and the Earl of Derby's Servants and the company of the Earl of Pembroke. In this drawing, a scene from *Titus* that did not occur in the play as we know it, we have in my opinion a group of key characters *created to illustrate the costumes.* Some of the players are not in costume. Thus we have a sketch of the minimal costumes required to create the illusion of the play taking place in ancient Rome. It is my belief that this page was prepared as a costume guide for Shakespeare's company, or for one of the companies that performed *Titus* in the years before 1594.

5. The drawing is competently executed. The grouping is well balanced. The characters are excellently proportioned, but stiff. Each person has the same impassive features, the same frozen posture. The drawing seems to me to be the work of a painstaking amateur; a skilled professional artist would never, as it were, sketch himself into a corner. The halberd blade of the soldier on the far left is upside down, because the artist got himself into a spot where he couldn't fit it in any other way. You can judge of the danger and awkwardness of holding the halberd in this manner if you try carrying an ax with the blade up.

6. It can, I think, be surmised that Shakespeare was a factotum who had a finger, or more likely both hands and feet, in everything that took place on the stage. His job was not finished when he made the final, triumphant flourish with his quill after the last words

[133] Costumes of three famous characters in Shakespeare's plays, from a rare street broadside printed in the mid-eighteenth century. The costumes may be similar to those originally worn at some very early performances of the plays and perhaps based in part on designs by Shakespeare. *(Top left)* Edgar, a character in *King Lear*, as mad Tom O'Bedlam, a disguise he assumed during the play; *(top right)* "old Ton belly'd Jack" (Sir John Falstaff); and *(right)* Shylock in *The Merchant of Venice*.

[134] Posthumous caricature of Cambridge-educated Robert Greene (1558–1592), noted university wit and dramatist who lampooned Shakespeare as an "upstart crow" in his *Groatsworth of Wit* (1592). This portrait depicts Greene writing in his shroud. The Cambridge playwright was famous for his bristling red hair and fierce red beard. He died in great poverty, covered with vermin, his beard alive with lice. Although he ridiculed Shakespeare, Greene understood, perhaps better than most of his contemporaries, the transcendent genius of his rival from Stratford.

of the last act of a new play. He also, as scholars agree, selected for himself a minor role in most of his dramas. Almost certainly, too, he worked on the stage props, the scenery (if any, and usually there wasn't) and the costumes. Especially the latter. My opinion is that this drawing was either made by Shakespeare or was copied from a drawing made by him. It is hard to conceive that the dramatist, having peopled the stage with characters, would permit another person to dress them. He would probably insist upon designing and sketching the costumes and stage props necessary to complete the illusion created by his plays. The reason the sketch doesn't exactly fit with the text is that Shakespeare, or another artist, depicted in it only the necessary characters to exhibit his costumes. He left it to a clerk to fill in some appropriate text so the drawing would not be orphaned on the page.

I cannot claim to be the first to call Shakespeare a factotum, or the first to suggest that he worked on stage props. That honor goes to Robert Greene, known in his day as a University Wit who flirted briefly with success, then died in poverty. In his posthumous *Groatsworth of Wit* (1592), Greene attacked, with sarcasm and innuendo, the youthful Shakespeare: "There is an upstart crow beautified with our feathers, that with his *Tyger's heart wrapt in a Player's hide* [a direct quote of a line from Shakespeare's *Henry VI*, with the word *Player's* substituted for *woman's*] supposes he is as well able to bombast out a blank verse as the best of you, and being an absolute *Johannes Factotum* is, in his own conceit, the only Shake-scene in a country."

Most literary critics hold the view that Greene was alluding to Shakespeare's revamping of other author's dramas when he devised the word Shake-scene. But expropriating the ideas and plots of other writers was so common among Elizabethan dramatists that it hardly merits a criticism. So far as I know, except for John Payne Collier, no one has ever taken Greene literally when he called Shakespeare a *"Factotum."* Now, Greene was graduated from Cambridge with a master of arts degree. He also was awarded a degree by Oxford. He had a superb word sense and did not use words without a mind to their distinction. The word factotum means, if I err not, "a person employed to do all kinds of work" or "an employee who serves in a wide range of capacities." As for "Shake-scene," I presume if new scenes were to be manufactured, Shakespeare would be on hand to take part in the task. The poet certainly must have had a wide reputation for being extraordinarily talented and knowledgeable about every facet of writing and producing plays. His contemporaries, especially those who were jealous of him, like Greene, would be impressed (and depressed) by his ability to act and write poetry and turn out exciting plays that audiences liked, to design and build stage props, to create and sketch costumes and, very possibly, to compose incidental music for the recorder, drum, lute and trumpet. Further, I have a hunch that Shakespeare was the director or assistant director of every play he wrote. He knew the stage intimately. He knew precisely where the players

[135] Sir John Falstaff and the hostess of the Boar's Head tavern. This illustration, part of the frontispiece to Francis Kirkman's *The Wits, or Sport upon Sport* (1663), depicts the early costumes worn by these two Shakespearean characters. They may be modeled after costumes designed by the dramatist.

[136] Is this bearded man a self-portrait of William Shakespeare? If Shakespeare drew the *Titus Andronicus* sketch to illustrate the costumes recommended for use in performances of the play, as seems possible, he may have portrayed the fellow members of his acting company. And he himself nearly always took a minor role in his own plays. The kneeling bearded figure, one of the captive sons of Tamora, could be a self-portrait of the youthful actor—the resemblance to the poet is rather striking.

[137] The "Wooden O." Two views of the celebrated first Globe theater. *(Right)* A sketch from Visscher's *A View of London,* published in 1616 but depicting the Globe as it was a few years earlier. *(Bottom)* A drawing probably based on Visscher's view. The Globe, in which Shakespeare acted in his own and other plays and of which he was a shareholder, was alluded to by the dramatist in the Prologue to *Henry V* as the "wooden O."

On June 30, 1613, during a performance of *Henry VIII,* a cannon was fired on stage and some of the burning wadding hit the thatched roof and set fire to it. The theater burned to the ground. No one was injured, although one man, according to a letter of Sir Henry Wotton to his

nephew (July 2, 1613) "had his breeches set on fire, that would perhaps have broiled him, if he had not by the benefit of a provident wit put it out with bottle ale."

If, as many scholars claim, only one prompt book of each of Shakespeare's plays existed, they would very likely have been burned up in this fire. However, prompt books were probably prepared in multiple copies, all carefully guarded to prevent publication or unauthorized use by rival acting companies. Duplicate copies might have been in the hands of the Globe directors or the principal actors, including Shakespeare, who likely found occasion to update speeches or scenes in his plays, especially when they were revived for fresh performances.

should enter and exit, where they should stand, what inflections their voices should take, what gestures they should use. The reason Shakespeare always selected a minor role for himself, in my opinion, was not because he lacked skill as an actor but because he was very busy with all other aspects of production. We know that when Shakespeare acted in Jonson's *Every Man in His Humour* (1598), he likely played the lead role, for his name heads the list of "principall comoedians" in Jonson's collected plays (1616). When Greene called Shakespeare a *"Johannes Factotum"* he probably meant precisely that—that Shakespeare could and did do every type of work and creative task connected with the writing and producing of a play. Greene must have ground his mandibles in vexation to see this "upstart" hick who had blossomed from a Stratford cowpie overtake and surpass *him,* a Cambridge and Oxford man, in an exhibition of multifold genius never before known in England.

Let me conclude this chapter with a few comments inspired by Professor John Dover Wilson's guess that Aaron, the Moor, might be Burbage in blackface. I don't object to this hypothecation. But perhaps Wilson forgot that Burbage was inclined to corpulence. Shakespeare probably wrote *Hamlet* as a starring vehicle for Burbage and in it gave him a description as "fat and scant of breath." Of course Burbage may have been slender in the *Titus* days, a decade earlier, but he wound up as a natural Falstaff who needed no false upholstery. Now, since Professor Wilson has set the example and ventured a guess on the identity of one of the actors in the *Titus* drawing *(illus. 130, 136)* I feel encouraged to do the same thing myself. My eye falls upon the bearded kneeling figure, captive son of Tamora. Might it not be a self-portrait of Shakespeare, who, like Alfred Hitchcock, customarily took a minor role in his plays? His features are delineated in far more detail than those of his kneeling brother—the straight, finely shaped nose, the high forehead, the same heavy jaw, so apparent in the Stratford bust, the slender and delicate fingers. And he has an almost dreamy look, as if lost in reverie.

XIII

EX LIBRIS WILLIAM SHAKESPEARE

No bookman, Shakespeare! The great dramatist was not seduced by the rich luxury of uterine vellum or the sensual caress of polished calf. He was not turned on by a black river of Caxton's beautiful type flowing down a creamy white meadow of page. What Shakespeare asked from books, and what he got in abundance, was a now-and-then inspiration, a fresh idea, a few intimate facts that could be made into a living drama. Shakespeare used his little collection of books as a tool to rejuvenate and revitalize his wondrous imagination.

How can we surmise this? Because Shakespeare, as you will see shortly, apparently scribbled all over the pages that he found useful in his books and left untouched those chapters from which he could pluck no nourishing data. He obviously cared little for the appearance of his books (he wrote a recipe on the index page of one volume) and he never signed one, so far as I know, except when trying out a new quill. He seemed to care not a tuppence if his books wandered off into another man's library. Unlike his bibliomaniacal friend Ben Jonson, who wrote his name punctiliously in every volume he owned—and there were many of them—Shakespeare evidently looked to his modest array of books for service only. Once they had performed their duty, he turned them out. He even seemed to care abundantly little whether his own plays and poems got into print. His sonnets peregrinated in manuscript a long while before they ever fell into the hands of a publisher. In his will the poet bequeathed shillings and pence to his friends but he did not bother to mention his library, probably because it was small, undistinguished, and of trifling worth. I presume most of his reference books went to his son-in-law, Dr. Hall, as part of the furnishings of New Place.

Although I doubt if Shakespeare ever read purely for pleasure after he began to write,

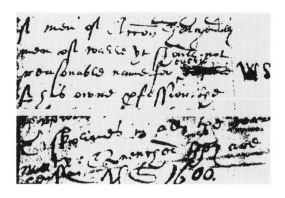

[138] Handwriting by Shakespeare in his own manuscript copy of Essex's *Apologie*. It is difficult to transcribe these fragments into modern English because portions of the words are smudged or missing. The last line, above the dated initials, can easily be read: "ma[jes]ty: Quenched they are . . ." This is apparently a quotation from a statement by Queen Elizabeth after the abject failure of Essex's rebellion. These excerpts contain two "W.S." initials in Shakespeare's hand.

his plays reveal a vast knowledge squeezed from his early studies of the classics. In his treatise *Shakespeare's Books. A Dissertation on Shakespeare's Reading and the Immediate Sources of His Works,* H. R. D. Anders makes a superb examination of the poet's reading. There was the Bible, of course, and the Arthurian legends and Robin Hood. There were volumes about exploration in America and Africa and the Indies, the Roman writers—Aesop, Vergil, Caesar, Cicero, Ovid (likely the source of *Venus and Adonis*), Plautus, Seneca, Livy, Pliny, Lucan, Josephus, and perhaps Juvenal and Horace. The Greek writers were represented—Homer, Heliodorus, Marianus, and most especially Thomas North's translation (1579) of Plutarch's *Lives,* from which Shakespeare drew his plots for *Julius Caesar, Timon of Athens, Antony and Cleopatra,* and *Coriolanus,* and there were Montaigne, Rabelais and Ronsard from France; the Italians, source of romantic tales—Boccaccio, Bandello, Giraldi Cinthio, Giovanni Florentino, Straparola-Barnabe Riche (one of the sources of *Twelfth Night*), Ariosto and Petrarch, and the Old English authors, Chaucer, John Gower, and the historian and printer William Caxton. Shakespeare's reading among his contemporaries was omnivorous: Arthur Brooke, Samuel Daniel, Edmund Spenser, Thomas Watson, Sir Philip Sidney, the old sonneteers like Wyatt and Surrey, John Lyly's *Euphues,* Thomas Lodge, Robert Greene, Sir Francis Bacon and books on demonology, such as those by James I and Reginald Scot. (Shakespeare believed in the devil but I think he could not have experimented, as I did. During my early years in college I tried many and many a time to summon up Satan by using the charts and charms in Scot's *Discoverie of Witchcraft,* but the Sinful One never showed. I suspect that Marlowe and Kyd tried the same thing, also without success.) The dramatic authors of his day Shakespeare read with particular care: Christopher Marlowe, Thomas Kyd, John Lyly, George Peele, George Whetstone, Samuel Rowley, George Gascoigne, Thomas Preston, Ben Jonson, Beaumont and Fletcher (Shakespeare collaborated with Fletcher) and Sir William Alexander.

Perhaps some of these books, annotated in the margins by Shakespeare, still survive, unrecognized on the rare-book shelves of libraries, private and public. They might bear the poet's annotations and pointing index fingers on the pages that interested him, but probably not his signature.

After an exhaustive quest, I have accounted for only three books from Shakespeare's library, two of them in manuscript. One of the manuscript volumes, known as the *Northumberland Manuscript*, I'll discuss in the next chapter. The second manuscript is an extremely important one, a copy of Essex's famous *Apologie*. Unfortunately, I have no information on the provenance or present whereabouts of this book and have seen nothing except the fragmentary notations with the poet's initials reproduced in Clara de Chambrun's *Shakespeare Rediscovered* (1938). In that reproduction the portions of Shakespeare's writing are so fuzzy or truncated that I cannot make out the poet's complete thoughts. The first two lines allude to "men of Acc[ti]on . . . men of warre" and line 4 mentions "of his owne p[ro]fession, the—." Whoever owns this manuscript copy of Essex's *Apologie* has reason to pop a cork, for the script is surely Shakespeare's. The notations may provide a valuable insight into the poet's opinion of Essex and his "rebellion." Perhaps Shakespeare also annotated or corrected some pages of the manuscript.

In a July 1936 *Scribner's Magazine* article entitled "The Book Shakespeare Used—a Discovery," the Countess Clara Longworth de Chambrun announced that she had turned up Shakespeare's own copy, with his marginal annotations, of Raphael Holinshed's *Chronicles of England* (1587), a second edition of the book that inspired the dramatist's great English historic plays. The first edition of Holinshed (1577) is often called "the Shakespeare edition" because it is believed to be a major source for Shakespeare. The poet certainly did use the first edition—Holinshed lived in the hamlet of Packwood near Shakespeare and very probably he and the poet were friends—but there is no doubt that the countess had latched on to Shakespeare's own copy of the second edition.

The countess had traced the three-volume set back to Sir Francis Skipwith's library at Newbold Revel in Warwickshire, near Rugby. The set remained in the family until the death of Sir Paton d'Estoteville Skipwith, whose bookplate, dated 1889, appears in the books. When Sir Paton died the set was acquired by Arthur Henry Bullen of Stratford-upon-Avon, a Shakespearean scholar. Bullen died in 1920 and B. H. Newdigate got the copy, which a few years later he sold to Captain William Jaggard, owner of the set in 1938, at the time the countess last examined it. In the space of one hundred and fifty years the set of Holinshed passed through six different hands, always remaining close to Shakespeare's birthplace.

The colophon page of Shakespeare's copy of Holinshed's *Chronicles* is adorned with scribblings and designs that incorporate the poet's initials. On the left side of the page, two-thirds of the way down, are three handsome lines in italic, which were not written

[139] Shakespeare's initials from the *Northumberland Manuscript*. It is possible that although Shakespeare apparently did not sign his books, he may have jotted his initials in some of them.

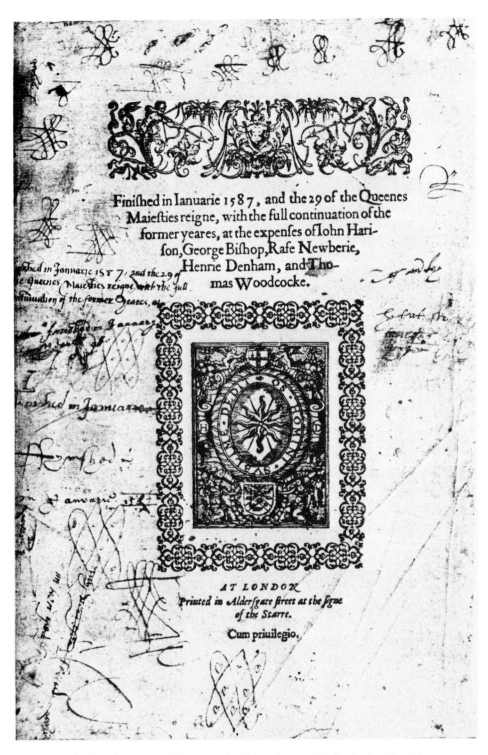

Finished in Ianuarie 1587, and the 29 of the Queenes Maiesties reigne, with the full continuation of the former yeares, at the expenses of Iohn Harison, George Bishop, Rafe Newberie, Henrie Denham, and Thomas Woodcocke.

AT LONDON
Printed in Aldersgate street at the signe of the Starre.

Cum priuilegio.

[140] Colophon page of the second edition (1587) of Holinshed's *Chronicles* revealing a few scattered words penned by the poet, as well as some of his ornately interwoven initials

[141] Three elaborately contrived initials of Shakespeare from the colophon page of his copy of Holinshed's *Chronicles* (1587)

[142] Interwoven initials of Shakespeare from his copy of the *Northumberland Manuscript* (about 1592–1597). Apparently Shakespeare used these elaborate designs incorporating his initials to identify his books.

by Shakespeare. The rest of the pen-and-ink perambulations appear to be in the poet's hand. In addition to the artistic designs that intertwine Shakespeare's initials, there are two heart designs which cleverly conceal a *W* and an inverted *W.* "A fanciful figure also in lighter ink shows two hearts," the countess writes, "one upright, the other reversed, cleverly forming the initial *W,* the spaces between the transverse lines are dotted in one case—for it is twice repeated—with tiny *o*'s, in the other with hearts, and might have stood for the name William Hart set down to amuse this nephew. . . ."

The heart designs are laboriously penned and appear to be in a different handwriting. I suspect they were drawn by William Hart, the son of Shakespeare's sister. (I mention this trifling point to preclude the possibility of some idle psychiatrist writing an article on "Shakespeare's narcissus complex.")

Concerning the elaborately contrived cabalistic initials, the countess observes that they are "of a style called in French 'Griffe de Notaire' and formed in such a fashion that the pen never leaves the paper until completion but makes the device in one stroke."

The marginal notations in the books were heavily cropped by a Victorian binder who, as if to memorialize his misdeed, encased the three-volume set in a "blackish" leather. To transcribe the annotations, the countess studied the volumes for six months, aided by Dr. G. B. Harrison and "some of the best experts from the Ecole des Chartes, Bibliothèque Nationale, Archives and Affaires Etrangères." Confronted by these specialists, I chose to present verbatim the countess's transcriptions for the illustrated marginalia (*illus. 143*).

Of special interest in this marvelous book, which I long to hold and caress, is a recipe for curing swollen joints in horses: " 'Black' soape, pigge-meat and honny mingled together, good for a horse's legge swollen." Of this remedy, the countess writes: "This recalls Sir William Davenant's affirmation, which there is no possible reason to doubt [in my opinion, all statements Davenant ever made about his alleged father, William Shakespeare, are open to doubt], that the Stratford youth on arriving penniless in London, was constrained to accept the first work offered to him by James Burbage and turned his rural knowledge of horse-flesh into account by taking care of the gentlemen's mounts who rode to the theater."

Chronicles of England

[1] [2] [3] [4] [5] [6]

[143] Page of Holinshed's *Chronicles* (1587) covering the reign of Richard II, with marginal notations in Shakespeare's hand. The notations read: "Wickedness of Northfolk men [de]stroye all [reco]rds" [2] "So the lawes of [England] should [com]e forth of one [crea]turs mouth" [3] "wate tiler" [4] "the wicked d[eeds] of rebell" [5] "The Kinge giveth a[n] abbayae" [6] "the intent of the rebels"

The two-line inscription in Shakespeare's handwriting at the bottom is the prescription on the index page for curing swollen joints in horses.

The third volume of the set is heavily worn and thumbed between the reigns of Richard II and Henry VII, but otherwise almost untouched. There are pointing fingers used to indicate passages that were used in the plays.

In the Folger Library is a copy of the first edition of Holinshed's *Chronicles*. Worn and stained and without a cover, it contains a few index fingers pointing to passages in the lives of Cymbeline and Macbeth, but the passages that deal with Lear were torn from the volume. I suspect that if Shakespeare owned this copy, he simply ripped the pages out and carried them around in his doublet until he'd memorized their contents. He was apparently heedless of whether he spilled "the precious lifeblood of a master spirit," so long as he had first drunk his fill of it.

Without having looked at the Folger copy of Holinshed I wouldn't care to venture any opinion as to Shakespeare's ownership. One thing is certain: Shakespeare did utilize both the first and second editions of Holinshed. Not only used them, but plundered them. He breathed life and beauty into the pedestrian prose of the Packwood historian. From the chronicler's pages Shakespeare filched phrases and even whole paragraphs and the great themes of *King John, Henry IV, VI* and *VIII, Macbeth, King Lear, Cymbeline* and *Richard II* and *III*. In return for all he borrowed, Shakespeare made Holinshed immortal.

There is, so I hear, in the Folger copy of Holinshed a tiny index finger pointing at the passage about Little John and Robin Hood. Perhaps Shakespeare wrote a "lost" play about the famed outlaw of Sherwood Forest. If I thought I had one chance in ten million to find the manuscript I'd follow the pointing finger through Shakespeare's old haunts for the rest of my earthly sojourn.

[144] Three pointing fingers, from the
Northumberland Manuscript, possibly drawn by
Shakespeare

XIV

GHOSTWRITER FOR
FRANCIS BACON

THE south reading room of the New York Public Library is not unlike the city morgue. However, the readers and students in the library are not stiffs; they merely appear so. One August day in 1983, I sat in the approved posture of simulated rigor mortis as I slogged through the collotype of a 350-year-old document known as the *Northumberland Manuscript.* This document had been printed in facsimile in 1904 on heavy paper that disintegrated at the touch of my fingers. The "folios," as the once elegant pages were called, had all broken loose from their heavy binding. Whenever I turned a fresh folio the old book silently regurgitated a deposit of rotting paper into my lap.

I had a very good reason for examining this reproduction. I'd just decided that the charred cover of this famous manuscript comprised, as several scholars had maintained, a mass of unrelated doodles and scribbles mostly in the hand of William Shakespeare.

Now and then, as you know, some researcher exhumes an "unknown manuscript of Shakespeare" that, upon a sober, second examination by an expert paleographer, turns out to be an impostor. Such brief candles light up the news for a day or two, then flicker out. The *Northumberland Manuscript* was one of these trumpeted discoveries, and it had barely survived the initial impact of academic skepticism.

In 1867, a badly scorched manuscript turned up in Northumberland House, the ancestral home of the Duke of Northumberland. The manuscript contained "Bacon's discourse in prayse of his Soveraigne" and "Bacon in prayse of Knowledge," as well as lengthy portions of a notorious political diatribe, *Leycesters Commonwealth.* The *Northumberland Manuscript* was described in detail by James Spedding, a noted Bacon scholar and rabid Baconian. Spedding was impressed with the frequent scribbling of Shakespeare's name on the front page (or makeshift cover) of the manuscript. Spedding did not, however, attribute the writing to Shakespeare. But the mention of several works by Shakespeare, with an allusion or two from the poet's writings on the cover of this volume that contained writings of Bacon, led Spedding to conclude he had discovered fresh evidence that Bacon wrote the plays and poems of Shakespeare.

Nearly seventy years later, in April of 1925, William Thompson (not to be confused with the eminent Shakespearean scholar, Sir Edward Maunde Thompson) made a detailed study of the jottings on the cover of the *Northumberland Manuscript* and opined (in *The Quarterly Review*, No. 484) that "the results of an examination of the scribblings are almost conclusive, that only Shakespeare himself could have written them. . . ." William Thompson follows this statement with an analysis of Shakespeare's signatures as they appear on the cover. In my opinion, he is correct in his belief that the *William* and the capital *S* of *Shakespeare* look like the poet's writing. Although some of Thompson's arguments (he had only the famous six signatures of the poet for comparison) are open to dispute, I concur with his final remark: "Should the conclusions I have set out be accepted, I think it may reasonably be stated that this partially burnt sheet of paper will be considered one of the most valuable documents in the world."

Acceptance of Thompson's views was not forthcoming from the higher echelons of scholarship. Edmund K. Chambers, a noted Shakespearean expert, dismisses the manuscript with little more than an imperial tsk-tsk. In Volume I of his *William Shakespeare: A Study of Facts and Problems,* he writes: ". . . a recent attempt [obviously Thompson's] to ascribe the jottings on the *Northumberland MS.* in which his [Shakespeare's] name and titles of some of his plays occur, is negligible." In Volume II of this critical biography, Sir Edmund amplifies his remark, describing and illustrating the disputed page, and ascribing it to one "Adam Dyrmonth." Although Sir Edmund discusses in some detail the genealogical origin of the Dyrmonth name, he does not come up with any biographical information about Adam, of whom nobody before or since has found any record. Sir Edmund concludes by hurling down an Olympian damnation: "A suggestion that the scribbler was Shakespeare is absurd." Sir Edmund's opinion is the view now held by virtually all Shakespearean scholars.

With this background, and with my own conviction that the writing on the cover page was in fact Shakespeare's I had decided to give the entire collotype a critical examination. Promptly at ten o'clock, when the library opened, I began a study of the book. As I pored over page after page of tedious transcripts of Bacon's work penned by a scribe my eyes grew very tired. I'd started work that morning at four o'clock, as I often do during the summer. It was now past noon and I hadn't paused long enough to eat breakfast. My mind was starting to meander. The previous day my secretary, Dianne Barbaro, who is very solicitous about my health, had expressed alarm over a small island of blood adrift in my right eye. Still, when I'm hard at work and rattling along at top speed I don't give a chipped aggie whether school keeps or not. If my nose fell off I'd just let it lie and pick it up later when I had time.

I tried to be meticulous in my examination of the *Northumberland Manuscript* but I found myself rushing through the collotype. The manuscript was like an endless, rolling

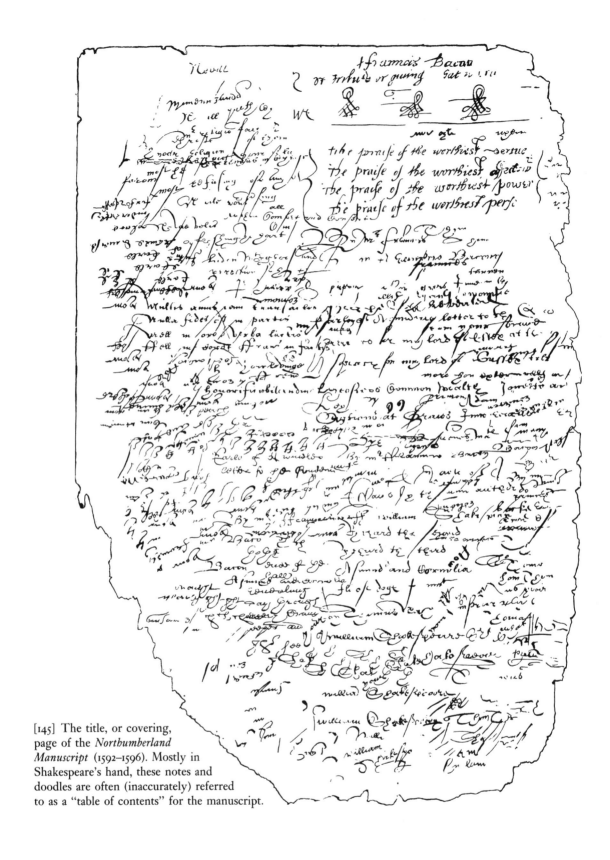

[145] The title, or covering, page of the *Northumberland Manuscript* (1592–1596). Mostly in Shakespeare's hand, these notes and doodles are often (inaccurately) referred to as a "table of contents" for the manuscript.

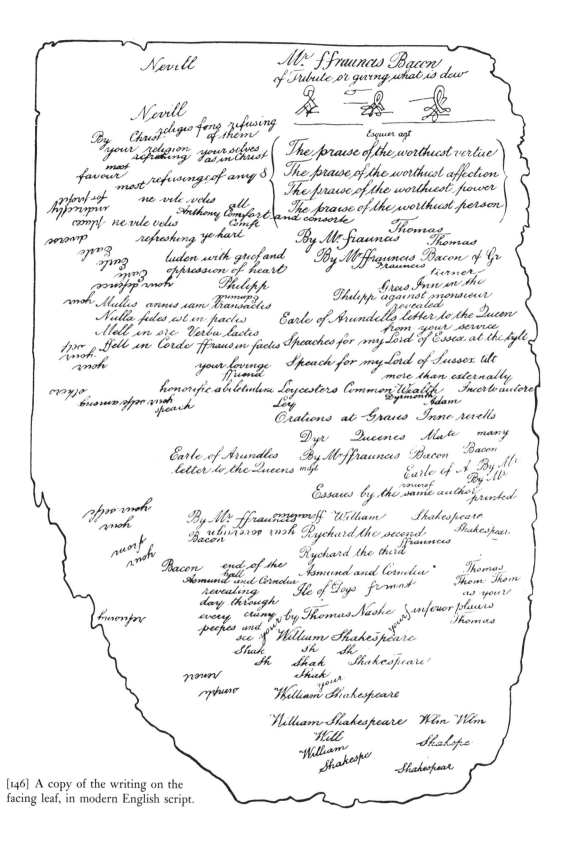

[146] A copy of the writing on the facing leaf, in modern English script.

desert of closely penned, undistinguished clerical script. Finally, with my eyes blurring, I slammed the volume shut and rose to return it to the library desk. As I did so, a free-spirited page near the end of the volume slithered away from its fellows and peeked from the binding. I perceived on it three or four words in Shakespeare's hand. In my joy and astonishment I shattered the solemn silence of the reading room by bursting out with the Saviour's name. The great occasion demanded the use of His full name, so I included the middle initial. It was probably the first time in fifty years that anyone had thus violated the silence in that baronial reading room, where every head was perpetually bowed in silence over a book.

My unexpected discovery drove me instantly back into the manuscript and, despite diminished vision from my now bloodshot eyes, I scrutinized the one and a half pages in the hand of the poet with ferocious zeal. I'd lucked into something I'd been looking for since beginning this book—a concrete link between Bacon and Shakespeare. I knew it was only a matter of hours, or at most a few days, before I'd be in a position to hazard a tenable guess on the relationship between these two great writers.

First I decided to find out precisely what writings were included in the manuscript. The cover page had an alleged "table of contents" that listed: "Mr. [Master] Frauncis Bacon's *Of the tribute or giving what is dew, The praise of the worthiest vertue, The praise of the worthiest affection, The praise of the worthiest power, The praise of the worthiest person, Philipp against Monsieur, Earle of Arundell's letter to the Queen, Speaches for my Lord of Essex at the tylt, A speach for my Lord of Sussex tilt; Leycester's Commonwealth, Incerto autore, Orations at Graie's Inne revells, Queene's Ma[jes]te . . . By Mr. Frauncis Bacon, Essaies by the same author; Rychard the second, Rychard the Third, Asmund and Cornelia, Ile of dogs.*"

Most of the more exciting material mentioned is not in the manuscript. In my opinion, it never was. The manuscript now contains the following: the outer page or makeshift cover, on which appear Shakespeare's and Bacon's names, many jottings and a supposed list of contents, folios 1–2; Bacon's *Of Tribute, or giving what is due*, folios 3–25; Bacon's *Of Magnanimitie or heroicall vertue*, folios 25–26; *An Advertisement touching private Cansure* (destroyed by fire) folios 26–29; Bacon's *An advertisement touching the controversies of the Church of England*, folios 29–44; Bacon's *A letter to a French gent. touching ye proceedings in Engl. in Ecclesiasticall causes, translated out of French into English by W.W.*, folios 44–45; a blank page, folio 46; *Speeches spoken in a 'Device' before Queen Elizabeth in 1595* (The device was presented by the Earl of Essex and the speeches were allegedly written by Bacon); *Bacon's speaches:* i. *The Hermitt's fyrst speach;* ii. *The Hermitt's second speach;* iii. *The Soldier's speach;* iv. *The Secretarie's speach;* v. *The Squyre's speach*, folios 47–53; *For the Earle of Sussex at ye tilt, an: 96*, folios 53–54; *Letter to Queen Elizabeth, dissuading her from marrying the Duke of Anjou*, folios 55–61; a blank page, folio 62; *Leicester's Commonwealth* (incomplete at the beginning and at the end), folios 63–90.

If you compare the list of the actual contents with the list on the cover, you will find that four items now present are not even mentioned on the alleged title page, all by Bacon: *Of Magnanimitie, Advertisement touching private censure, Advertisement touching the controversies of the Church* and *Letter to a French gent. touching Ecclesiastical causes in England.*

On the other hand, of the original supposed contents nine items are not present. These include Bacon's *Essays,* Shakespeare's plays of *Richard II* and *Richard III,* an unidentified manuscript entitled *Asmund and Cornelia,* Thomas Nashe's play *The Ile of Dogs,* and the missing portions of *Leicester's Commonwealth.* In my opinion, these additional writings, if present, would extend the volume far beyond the possible confines of a single manuscript. This suggests to me that the table of contents is nothing but aimless scribbling and the *Essays* of Bacon and two plays by Shakespeare were never in the volume.

Bacon's first volume of *Essays* was printed in 1597, as were Shakespeare's *Richard II* and *Richard III,* so it would be pointless for any clerk to go to the enormous pains of writing them in a manuscript volume after that date. Shakespeare's two plays were in print at sixpence the copy. The last date that appears in the manuscript is in the speech "For the Earle of Sussex at ye tilt, an: 96." Thus it is feasible to fix the date of writing of the *Northumberland Manuscript* between 1592 and 1596. Edmund K. Chambers, who accepts the scribbled "contents page" as bona fide (although he accepts nothing else on the page), holds a different view of the date. In Volume II of *William Shakespeare: a Study of Facts and Problems,* he writes: "The date cannot be earlier than 1597, when Nashe's *Isle of Dogs* [not present and in my opinion never present in the manuscript] was suppressed and *Rich. II* and *Rich. III* [both not present and in my opinion never present in the manuscript] printed, and is probably not earlier than 1598 when *Love's Lab. Lost* was printed." There is an abbreviated version of a humorous sesquipedalian word from *Love's Labour's Lost* penned by Shakespeare on the cover of the *Northumberland Manuscript* but I can see no reason why his writing of this word would have to await the publication of the play. It seems strange, too, that Sir Edmund does not question the feasibility of copying out two entire plays of Shakespeare's that were then in print at a trifling cost.

The Countess Clara de Chambrun defied the accepted academic opinion that the scribblings on the makeshift cover were not in Shakespeare's hand. In *Shakespeare Rediscovered,* the countess discussed the cover of the *Northumberland Manuscript:*

The . . . ornamental monograms representing 'W.S.' on the Northumberland manuscript . . . are more individual than a mere signature, and being in two cases identical with two among the six designs of the same letters on the Holinshed colophon page might well indicate Shakespeare as the possessor of both. Happily, however, the monograms do not stand alone, there is a mass of writing on the same page, names, phrases, scraps of verse, and as any inscription which may be attributed to such a pen is interesting in itself, whether or not we can declare just why and wherefore it was set down, I will list all the scribblings. Many were obviously merely trials to see whether the writer's quill worked well or needed trimming, but certain of them clearly refer to his own work . . .

'Honorificabilitudine,' here preserved, is taken up and elongated in 'Love's Labour's Lost' becoming 'honorificabilitudinitatibus' . . .

[147]

[147] Shakespeare's handwriting on folios 64 and 65 in the *Northumberland Manuscript*. The bottom half of folio 64 and all of 65 are in the hand of Shakespeare. They constitute a portion of the manuscript copy of *Leicester's Commonwealth*. In the top half of folio 64,

meticulously penned by a clerk, Shakespeare
made two interlinear additions with a
dull-nibbed quill. In the center of line 7 he adds
the words "by the tyme" and between lines 14
and 15 he interpolates the phrase "for your
instrucco̅" [for your instruction].

[147A]

As well apeared in his late marriage w^th *Dame Essex*, wch albeit y^t was celebrated twyce : firste att *Killingworth*, and secondly att *Wansteede* (in the psence of the Earle of *Warwick*, L. *Northe*, Sir *Fraunce Knowells* and others) and this expectly known to the whole courte, wth the very day, the place, the witnesses, and the mynister thatt marryed them togeather ; yet durst no man open his mouth to make her Ma^ty privy therevnto, vntill Mounsuer *Simiers* disclosed the same, (and thereby incurred his highe displeasure) nor yet in many dayes after for feare of *Leicester*. W^ch is a subiection most dishonorable and daungerous to any P[rince] lyvinge, to stand att the devocon of his subiecte, whatt to heare or not to heare, of things that passe w^thin his owne [Realm.] And hereof y^t followeth that noe sute can pvayle in [Court, be it] never soe meane, excepte he firste be made a[cquainted] therew^th, and receave not onely the thanks, but also [bee admitted] vnto a greate pte of the gayne and comodetye th[ereof. Which] as yt is a greate inivry to the suter : Soe is y^t [far] greater to the bounty, honor and securety of the [Prince, by] whose liberallity this man feedeth onely, and [fortifieth himself,] deprivinge his souaigne of all grace, thank[s and goodwill of th]e same. For wch cause he giueth onl [ordinarily, to every suit]er, thatt her Ma^ty is nighe and Par[simonious of herself, and] very difficill to graunt any sute, [where it is not only upon his] incessant solicitacon. [Whereby he fillith his owne purse the more, and emptieth the hearts of such as receive benefit, from due thankes from their Princes for the sute obtained.

Hereof also ensueth, that no man ma/ bee preferred in Court (bee hee otherwise never so well a deserving servant to her Majesty) except hee bee one of *Leycester's* faction]

or followers : none can be advaunced, excepte he [bee liked and] pferred by him : none can receave grace, excepte he [stand in his] good favoure, noe one may lyve in countenance, or qu[iet of life,] excepte he take yt, vse yt, ane acknowledge yt fr[om him, so as all the favoures, graces, dignityes, pfer, riches & [rewards,] wch her Ma^ty bestoweth, or the Realme can yeld : in [must serve] to purchase this man private frends, and favoure [onely to] advance his pty, and to fortyfie his faction. W^ch [faction if] by theis meanes y^t be greate, (as in deede y^t [is :) you] may not marvaile, seeinge the riches and wealth, [of so] worthie a comon weale, doe serve him but for a [price to] buy the same. W^ch thinge himselfe well knowing, [frameth] his spyrits of pceadinge accordingly. And first, upon confydence thereof, is becom soe Insolent and [impotent of his ire that noe man may beare the same, how [justly] or vniustlie soever yt be conceived : for albeyt he [begin to] hate may, vpon bare surmise onely (as comon[ly it falleth] out, Ambition beinge alwayes the mother of [suspicion)] yet he pscuteth the same, wth suche implac[able cruelty,] as there is noe longe abidinge for the ptye [in that place. As mighte be shewed by the examples [of many] whome he hathe chased from the courte, [upon his] onely displeasure w^thoute other cause, being [known to be otherwise moste zealous Protestants. As [Sir *Jerome*] *Bowes*, Mr *Gorge Scote*, and others that we [could name.] To this insolency is alsoe joyned (as by nature [it followeth) moste absolute and pemptory de[aling] in all thinges wherof y^t pleaseth to dispose, w[ithout] respecte either of Reason, order, due, righte, s[ubordination, custome, conueniency, or the like : whereof not[withstanding] Princes them selues are wonte to haue regarde [in] disposicon of theire matters : As for example a[mong the servants of the Q Ma. household, y^t is an a[ncient] and most comendable order and custome, that [when] a place of highere rowmes falleth voide, he that in succession is nexte, and hath made pfe of his [worthiness] in an inferior place, shold rise and possesse th[e same,] (except it be for som extraordinary cause) to [the end that noeman vnexperienced or vntried, shold [be placed] in the higher Rowmes the fyrste [day, to the prejudice] of others, and difference of the [Prince. Which most rea]sonable custome, this man [contending and breaking at] his pleasure, [thrusteth into higher rooms any person whatsoever, so he like his inclination or feel his reward : albeit he neither be fit for the purpose, nor have been so much as clerk in any inferior office before. The like he uses out of the court, in all other places where matters should pass by order election or degree : as in]

There is still a stronger reason to connect the writer with the author of *Lucrece* printed by Richard Field in 1594 and dedicated to Lord Southampton, for the opening lines of the 165th stanza of this poem are set down, but in such a manner as to indicate that the author was still experimenting with his rhymes. The verse in its printed form reads:

> Revealing day through every cranny spies
> And seems to point her out where she sits weeping;
> To whom she sobbing speaks: O eye of eyes,
> Why pry'st thou through my window? leave thy peeping,
> Mock with thy tickling beam eyes that are sleeping;
> Brand not my forehead with thy piercing light,
> For day hath naught to do what's done by night.

but here, on the Northumberland manuscript, we find:

> Revealing day through every cranny peeps
> And see . . .

At this point the line breaks off.

Frank J. Burgoyne, in *Collotype Facsimile and Type Transcript of an Elizabethan Manuscript . . . at Alwick Castle (Northumberland Manuscript)* thinks the line from *The Rape of Lucrece* is "revealing day through every cranny peeps and—see Shak" is a suggestion to look at Shakespeare's poem for the rest of the stanza. He mentions the doodle "Mr. Frauncis William Shakespeare," which is, I think, suggestive in view of the probable association between Bacon and Shakespeare. Burgoyne's reason for printing the manuscript in facsimile was because it contained several important essays by Bacon. He had no suspicion, evidently, that the cover page or any part of the manuscript might be in the hand of Shakespeare.

[149] An original holograph line from Shakespeare's *Rape of Lucrece*. Apparently a draft, it differs in one word from the version published in 1594. The lines here read: "Revealing Day through every Crany peepes/ And see[ms]. . . ." In the published version the lines are: "Revealing day through every cranny spies/ And seems. . . ."

[148] Transcription of Shakespeare's writing on folios 64 and 65 in the *Northumberland Manuscript*. These pages, from the burned-away portions of *Leicester's Commonwealth* in the poet's hand, are reconstructed from another complete copy of the manuscript. The brackets enclose portions missing from Shakespeare's pages.

Burgoyne points out that Bacon was constantly on the lookout for talented young men to assist him in his literary work and as copyists. The penman who wrote the bulk of the *Northumberland Manuscript* was a neat scribe, possibly trained as a lawyer's scrivener. He was probably recruited by Bacon to transcribe manuscripts. Almost certainly, the *Northumberland Manuscript* was one of scores of such manuscript volumes copied in Essex's mansion, Essex House, where Bacon, secretary and adviser to the Earl of Essex, had set up a regular workshop of young writers. On January 25, 1594, Bacon wrote to his brother Anthony: "I have here an idle pen or two . . . I pray send me somewhat to write out." Anthony was the supervisor of the literary undertaking. A distinguished member of the task force was Ben Jonson, busy with other writers translating some of Bacon's works into Latin.

In her chapter on the *Northumberland Manuscript* in *Shakespeare Rediscovered*, the Countess de Chambrun notes that "the so-called Northumberland manuscript was certainly a document belonging to a person or persons in close touch with the [Robert Devereux, Earl of] Essex faction. . . .

"Shakespeare *may* have been hired to work for the attorney's [Bacon's] brother Anthony, while both were under the Earl of Essex's direct patronage.

"The suggestion that William Shakespeare might have had an entry to this workshop directed by Anthony Bacon even more naturally than Ben Jonson, through the protection he enjoyed between 1590 and 1597 from Southampton and Essex himself, is reasonable. . . ."

The countess did not realize she was on the brink of an important discovery and dropped the matter here, without again alluding to the possible relationship between Bacon and Shakespeare.

James Spedding is quoted by Frank J. Burgoyne in his Introduction to the *Northumberland Manuscript* as speculating that "Anthony Bacon appears to have served [Essex] in a capacity very like that of a modern under-secretary of state; receiving all letters, which were mostly in cipher; in the first instance, forwarding them (generally through his brother Francis's hands) to the Earl, deciphered and accompanied with their joint suggestions; and finally, according to the instructions thereupon returned, framing and dispatching the answers. . . ."

Several skilled writers must have been required to carry out this work. If Shakespeare were employed as a secretary and literary assistant to Bacon, which I consider probable, there may exist letters in the poet's hand bearing the signature of Francis Bacon or Lord Essex. Such a letter would be one of the world's supreme literary prizes. What could be more intriguing than a missive in Shakespeare's script signed by Francis Bacon? It would be far more exciting, I think, than other known letters of a similar nature, such as an epistle in the beautiful italic hand of the noted scholar Roger Ascham signed by his famous pupil, Elizabeth I. Or a letter of Oliver Cromwell's penned by his Latin secretary John Milton; or a missive in the squarish, legible and handsome script of Jonathan Swift, signed by his employer Sir William Temple; or a letter of Martha Washington's in the beautiful, urbane penmanship of her husband and erstwhile secretary, George; or a letter

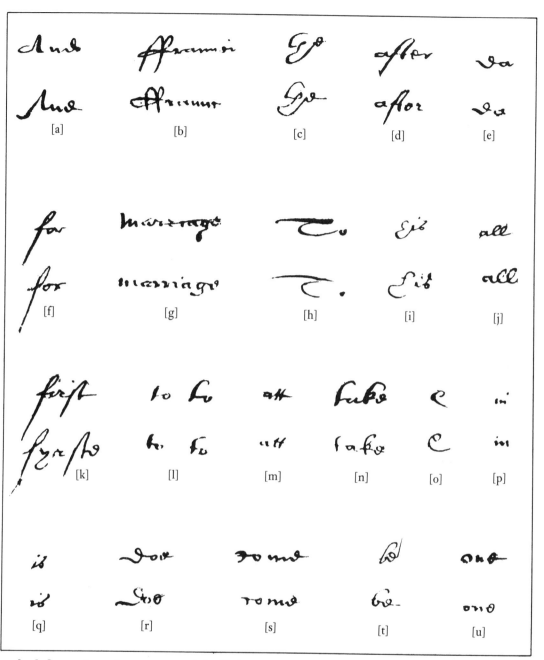

[150] Comparison of common words in Shakespeare's will, 1616 (top line in each set) with common words in Shakespeare's writing, between 1592 and 1596, in the *Northumberland Manuscript*

[a] And	[h] To	[o] & (ampersand)
[b] Frauncis/Fraunc[e]	[i] his	[p] in
[c] the	[j] all	[q] is
[d] after	[k] rst/fyrste	[r] Doe
[e] Do	[l] to/to (variants)	[s] come
[f] for	[m] art	[t] be
[g] marriage	[n] take	[u] one

[a]   [b]   [c]

[151] Comparison of Shakespeare's corrections—three of scores of changes—in the text of the *Northumberland Manuscript (bottom line in each set)* with words or parts of words from Glossary of Shakespeare's Words (Chapter 17)

[a] act   [b] And   [c] compelled

of Lincoln's attorney-general, James Speed, penned in the very black and very bold script of his postwar secretary, Walt Whitman.

Of the eighty-nine pages of the *Northumberland Manuscript* only one and a half pages are in Shakespeare's hand. They occur on folios 64 and 65 of the twenty-seven surviving pages of *Leicester's Commonwealth*. Apparently, the clerk who was copying the manuscript became weary and Shakespeare relieved him for an hour or two. Shakespeare's script is, as usual, tumultuous and ebullient. Although indited with punctilious care, it moves swiftly and beautifully across the page. It is the poet's chirography at its fairest,

[152] Handwriting of Bacon and Shakespeare on the same page. In this page of the transcript of *Leicester's Commonwealth*, a book banned in Elizabethan England by the censors, there occur several small corrections in the hand of Shakespeare and an observation on a quotation from Aristotle by Francis Bacon. Two of the words written by Shakespeare are legible and easily identifiable as his script. In the upper left corner of the manuscript, at the start of the first line, Shakespeare has penned the word be. In line 15, about two thirds of the way across the page, Shakespeare has crossed out a word and added a supralineal *agent*. The intrusion of the upper stem of a *d* in the deleted word necessitated a very tiny space between the poet's writing of *e* and *n* in *agent*. Also, in Shakespeare's hand is an easy-to-read portion of *yett* in the margin at the left of line 10. The first part of this word is too faded to be legible.

The writing of Francis Bacon comprises four short lines in the left margin, about a third of the way down the page. It is difficult to make out because some of it is badly faded and does not show up in the reproduction. The recognizable words are: line 1, *a philosophicall;* line 2, *arg[u] m[e]nt fo——;* line 3, *w[i]th intent to.*

This is the only example of Bacon's hand I've found in the entire manuscript and, as might be expected, it does not constitute a change in the text but, rather, a philosophical observation. No doubt Bacon was convinced that he need not reread his own essays after Shakespeare had gone over them. Although the amount of writing in Bacon's hand comprises fewer than a dozen words, many of them faded and illegible, and is almost insufficient for positive identification, the note has the feel of Bacon's informal script. The letters and words that are readable match Bacon's handwriting. While I should like to examine the original and positively confirm my belief that this is Bacon's script, I shall have to leave that pleasant task to others.

Shakespeare's changes in *Leicester's Commonwealth* are of a trifling nature, mainly corrections of quill slips. His changes in Bacon's essays in the manuscript are more substantive and involve questions of literary style and modes of expression.

each letter formed with copybook precision. Yet it has none of the prissy precision of the clerical hand that precedes and follows it.

In addition to the page and a half in Shakespeare's hand, I found in the *Northumberland Manuscript* some far more important notations: numerous interlinear corrections in Shakespeare's hand, particularly in the compositions of Francis Bacon. Written with a quill that often wanted sharpening, the corrections are in Shakespeare's hurried script. There is little pretense to elegance in them. In many cases these hurried interpolations are changes that clarify Bacon's meaning and polish his style.

The most logical explanation for the poet's corrections is that Shakespeare was in Bacon's employ, perhaps supervising the copyists in Bacon's literary factory. Except for Shakespeare's brief contribution, and half a page of obscenities in the childish script of a much later writer, the manuscript is almost entirely in the same, monotonous, unshaking, precise hand. It bears a number of small corrections by the copyist himself, clearly rectifications of his errors in transcription. There are many marginal corrections and some pointing fingers, all, I believe, in the hand of Shakespeare. The substantive alterations in the text, those which explain or elucidate remarks in Bacon's essays, are nearly all in the script of Shakespeare. The essays of Bacon, incidentally, bear no corrections in the author's hand.

Here are some of the changes in Shakespeare's handwriting that are characteristic of

[a]   [b]   [c]

[153] Comparison of Shakespeare's corrections on leaf from *Leicester's Commonwealth (bottom line)* with words or portions of words by Shakespeare taken from the Glossary (Chapter 17).

[a] be   [b] ett   [c] agent

[154] Bacon's handwriting in this leaf compared with Bacon's handwriting from his notebook (British Museum). The feel of the handwriting is the same in both. The two scripts have an easy, flaccid quality that belies the great intellect of the writer.

[a] Bacon's note in *Leicester's Commonwealth*
[b] Bacon's writing from his notebook

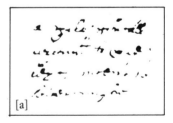

the emendations he makes in the essays of Bacon: In folio 19, part of Bacon's essay *Of Tribute,* Shakespeare changes "in tender regard towardes that young king" to read "in tender regard towardes *ye fortune of* that young king"; in folio 20 he alters the line "What shall I speake of the offering Don Ant. to his fortune" to "What shall I speake of *her endeavour to settle* Don Ant. *in* his fortune"; in folio 21, Shakespeare changes *disfortunes* to *misfortunes;* in folio 30 of Bacon's *An avertisement touching the controversies of the Church of England,* Shakespeare changes "if we would observe amongst Christians" to "if we would observe *yt league* amongst Christians"; in folio 34, he substitutes *low* for *foulee* (foully) in the phrase "stumbled too low"; and at one point, in folio 35, Shakespeare becomes the strict constructionist and gives Bacon a grammatical lesson when he alters the phrase "they shall inferr the sollicitacon of ye peace" to "they *will* inferr the sollicitacon of ye peace."

Quite naturally, I searched avidly for Bacon's handwriting in the manuscript. I discovered only one marginal note in his hand, an almost indecipherable scrawl next to a quotation from Aristotle in *Leicester's Commonwealth.* On the same page were several tiny corrections in Shakespeare's script.

The handwriting of these two celebrated authors in the same manuscript and on the same page is certainly indicative of their close association, and virtually confirms my belief that Shakespeare was employed by Bacon. We can easily surmise how this literary intimacy occurred.

Let's start with their patrons. The patron and employer of Francis Bacon was Robert Devereux, second Earl of Essex, handsome, clever, generous but far from wise. The young Essex was the favorite of the aging Queen Elizabeth, very probably her lover, and, as a result, one of the most powerful men in England. The patron of Shakespeare was the young and handsome Henry Wriothesley, Earl of Southampton, intimate friend of Essex's and possibly Shakespeare's lover, to whom the poet was soon to dedicate *Venus and Adonis* (1593). Ben Jonson, a drinking companion of Shakespeare's, was at work translating Bacon's writings into Latin. A century later, Anthony à Wood wrote that Jonson "did with Dr. Hacket (afterward Bishop of Lichfield) translate into Latin the Lord Bacon's Essays. . . ." The bonds of friendship, politics and cultural tastes thus intimately linked Shakespeare, Bacon, Jonson, Essex and Southampton.

[155] Three words or portions of words from Bacon's notebook compared with similar portions of the marginal note. *(Left to right) w[it]h, fo, lo.* Compare *w[it]h,* first word of line 3 in the note, with the same word from Bacon's notebook. The letters are similarly formed.

In both writing samples the words are swiftly penned in an easy, loose manner. The lines are approximately the same distance apart. And, despite the limited marginal space available, Bacon has spaced his words rather far apart, as in the notebook. The lines in the marginal annotation descend at the end, as do those in the notebook. Finally, the marginal comment is precisely the sort of remark one would expect from Bacon.

ROBERT DEVEREUX EARL OF ESSEX 1601

J. Oliver pinx.   In the collection of Sr. Robert Worsley Bart.   J. Houbraken Sculp

Impensis J. & P. Knapton London 1738.

[156]

184

[157] Henry Wriothesley, Lord Southampton (1573–1624). This handsome portrait shows Shakespeare's friend and patron in the Tower of London. The young lord had been condemned to death because of his participation in the Essex Rebellion but the sentence was set aside in 1603, by James I, because of his youth. Southampton's boyish face, effete pose and earnest gaze (much like that of his cat) are most interesting and provocative. It was to Southampton, a courageous soldier and lavish supporter of the arts, that Shakespeare dedicated his two lengthy poems *Venus and Adonis* and *The Rape of Lucrece.*

[156] Robert Devereux, second Earl of Essex (1566–1601). This rare portrait bust includes his decapitated head. Shakespeare may have lived for a time in Essex House during the plague (1592–1594)— while assisting Essex's secretary, Francis Bacon, as a ghostwriter—and possibly continued to work for Bacon periodically until the failure of the Essex Rebellion on February 7, 1601. The former favorite of Queen Elizabeth, Essex was beheaded on February 25, 1601. The night before his execution, Shakespeare and his company entertained the queen.

By 1592 Shakespeare was already a famous poet, dramatist and actor. Only twenty-eight, he had achieved a great reputation in literary circles and was well on his way to attaining riches as an actor when plague struck the city of London. The theaters closed (with rare, brief openings) for nearly two years and Shakespeare's income as an actor and playwright was cut off. He found himself without a job and, very likely, without money. At this point he turned to poetry for an occupation, but in those days, as now, the word poet was almost a synonym for poverty. Although poets "live on love and air," they cannot do so for long. Not until two centuries after Shakespeare (if one excepts Pope), in the era of Scott and Byron, did rimes put sovereigns into a man's pocket. Without doubt, Shakespeare looked to his friend and patron, Southampton, for financial aid, for in those days it was the custom for the poet to ask his patron for help, and it was the custom for the patron to pitch a few shillings to his protégé. I think Southampton did more than this, however. I think he got Shakespeare a job as literary assistant and secretary to Essex's right-hand man and assistant, Francis Bacon.

Bacon had more great and exalted ideas than he had time to put upon paper. He may have found an important use for Shakespeare, perhaps furnishing the young poet with rough notes and letting him do the writing. Obviously, Shakespeare was a master of language. He could write the argot of the gutter or the exalted speech of princes. He could also use the staid, ponderous style of the philosopher. He was an ideal amanuensis, too, for his script, as can be seen in the two folios reproduced in this chapter, was fluid and easy *(illus. 146)*.

Is it not quite possible that during the two years the plague raged in London and Shakespeare had no employment as an actor he lived with Essex and Bacon, assisting Bacon both in his correspondence for Essex and and in turning out the massive amount of writings that poured from the indefatigable philosopher and author of the *Essays*? At the very time when Shakespeare found himself jobless, in 1592, Bacon was starting work on the essays that were to circulate in manuscript for some years before the first installment was published in 1597. Did Shakespeare help to write the *Essays*? It seems likely that he did. Almost certainly he at least polished them for Bacon before they went to the printer. I hope that some enterprising scholar will go over the surviving papers of Bacon and cull out those in the hand of, or bearing notes by, William Shakespeare. And I suspect there may be quite a few. The Bacon papers in the British Museum would be a good place to start.

It was during the period of the poet's probable employment with Bacon (1592–1596) that Shakespeare utilized his knowledge of the law most brilliantly in his plays. I have a hunch that Bacon, the most adroit legal mind of his age (more so than Coke, I think) may have helped the poet in attaining his profound interpretation and understanding of the law. Bacon may have been of help when Shakespeare was working on the legal aspects of "the pound of flesh" scene in *The Merchant of Venice* (published 1598).

As a lawyer, Bacon would have delighted in the company of Shakespeare, a fellow spirit. They may often have dined together, perhaps with Ben Jonson, then chatted and bantered the evening away. Their collaboration would be almost inevitable. Shakespeare,

[158] A Francis Bacon handwritten signed letter, 1595, showing his sedately handsome formal style. An informal note or manuscript from his agile quill, on the other hand, reveals the power and verve one expects from perhaps the most brilliant thinker of his age.

[159] Quickly penned script by Francis Bacon,
from a notebook in the British Museum

[160] Bacon's customary script, unhurried, informal

[161] Bacon's signature as Lord Verulam

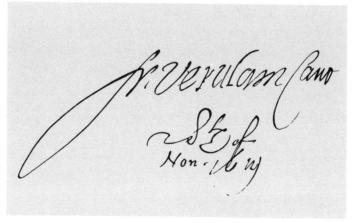

fierie and eager inuectiues, and in some fond mi...
reuerend behauior towardes their persons, to the last
exposeth them to derision and obloquie by libells, the are
perswaded the whole syde. neither dothe that othe...
ous practised by the worst sorte of them which is to doa...
to their aides certaine ordinarie bandes which mi...
other Ecclesiasticall dignities to haue the spoyle of the
liuinge of those that cannot speake to handle. It is an
betweene Jncendiaries and robbers, the one to fire the...
to rifle it. The 4th point wholie pertaineth to the...
the present Ecclesiasticall gouernm who allthough the...
cutt themselues of from the Communion of the Chur...
affect certaine ceremonies and disorderes whe...
make Correspondence amongst themselues and to the...
others and it is truelie said tam sunt mores quidam sch...
dogmata schismatica. thus they haue impropried vn...
the names of zealous sincere and Reformed, as is all...
Gold, mingles of godlie and prophane thinge, and f...
yea be a man indued with great vertues and fruitfu...
workes yett if he Concurre not fullie with them they...
derogaton a Ciuell and morrall man, and Compar...
Correttes, or some heathen philosopher. whereas the...
of the scriptures teacheth vs otherwise, to iudg and de...
religious according to their workes of the second tab...
they of the first were often Counterfaited and pro...
-potrishe So St Jhon saith that a man doth beiuelie...
god whom he neuer saw if he loue not his neighbor...
seen. and St James saithe this is true religion to visitt...
and the widdow. so as that which is with them but philoso...
morrall is in the Apostles phrase true religion and...

And as in affection they Challendge the said vertues of ze...
so in knowledge they attribute to themselues light and...
they saw the Churche of England in K. Ed. time, and i...
of her make raigne was but in the Cradle. and the...
in those times did somewhat for daie-breake, but t...
fulnes of light proceded from themselues. so Cabi...
irlea a Neuredomian said, that the staigers in the...
but infante and ignorant men. that the...
in their derwees as to Refuse that t...
oate Concealed:

only three years younger than Bacon, could turn out for Essex's adviser the political or religious epistles, and occasional speeches demanded by Essex's post. Above all, he could assist Bacon in his philosophical writing.

It must be remembered that in Shakespeare's time, only two or three centuries away from the Middle Ages, the individual was often anonymous and glory was reserved for God. I doubt if Shakespeare cared a crooked stile whether or not his name was affixed to anything he wrote for Bacon or Essex.

If Shakespeare was a ghostwriter for Bacon, as I believe, it would not have bothered either one of them. When it came to going over Bacon's essays or treatises and making changes and corrections, Bacon may very well have told Shakespeare: "Do whatever you think is necessary to make my writing clearer. Delete or change any words or phrases that do not entirely make sense." And this is exactly what the dramatist has done, as a perusal of Bacon's essays in the *Northumberland Manuscript* shows. What part, if any, of these essays were originally written for Bacon by Shakespeare I don't know, but would it not be odd if Bacon passed up the services of a man whom he surely knew to be a great writer?

[163] Sir Francis Bacon (1561–1626), philosopher, statesman, essayist. Shakespeare may have written speeches and essays for Bacon and Lord Essex.

[162] Folio 41 of Bacon's essay "An advertisement touching the controversies of the Church of England," with corrections by Shakespeare. The poet wrote three interlinear words or parts of words and added a fourth word, *And,* in the margin. His text corrections are *libells* (line 3), *aries* (correction over end of *Incendiaries*), and *table* (line 25). There is a pointing index finger in the margin that seems aimed at the change in *incendiaries.* Possibly, Shakespeare wished to call Bacon's attention to the alteration.

[164] Woodcut from the title page of Thomas Dekker's plague pamphlet *A Rod for Run-awayes, Gods Tokens* (1625). At the top center is the lightning of God's wrath. At the left are corpses, and on the right are the people of London fleeing from the scourge, which covered the bodies of its victims with black spots.

Certainly Bacon would not have crayfished at putting his own name on the work of a ghostwriter like Shakespeare. Recall that Bacon was an opportunist long on brains but short on scruples. He personally conducted the prosecution and obtained the treason conviction of his friend and benefactor, Lord Essex, who was subsequently beheaded. Years later (1621), as Lord Chancellor of England, Bacon was convicted of accepting bribes. He admitted it, offering as an excuse that he had double-crossed those who bribed him, since he had never allowed the bribes to influence his judgment.

In his introduction to the speeches spoken at the tilt of Lord Essex, Frank J. Burgoyne (editor of the *Northumberland Manuscript*) observes: "These are speeches written by Bacon to be spoken in a Masque or Device, given by the Earl of Essex in 1595. In the Lambeth Palace library there is a paper in Bacon's handwriting, without date, containing the rough drafts and notes of portions of the speeches now printed, and a second paper containing a fair copy of the last four of them."

Burgoyne misunderstood the meanings of the words masque and device. They are not the same thing. A masque is an allegorical play; a device is a slogan, ornament or coat

The bubonic plague—known as the Black Death—raged in London between 1592 and 1594. When the theaters were officially closed, Shakespeare lost his job as an actor. He turned to writing poetry, from which there was little or no profit except the open purse of his generous patron, Lord Southampton. During this period he wrote his narrative poems *Venus and Adonis* (published 1593) and *The Rape of Lucrece* (published 1594)—both dedicated to Southampton—and, apparently, most of his sonnets (not published until 1609).

[165] Burial trench for plague victims in London. Most of the bodies were shoveled into the earth naked or draped only in a shroud. A few were buried in coffins. This woodcut is from a rare poster.

[166] Scene in a churchyard near London during an outbreak of the plague. This view, from an old poster, depicts the horrors of the disease, which sometimes wiped out a fourth of a country's population when it struck. The plague was carried by fleas on rats aboard ships returning from the Orient. Its cause was unknown in Shakespeare's day and was variously attributed to God's vengeance against a sinful mankind, stray dogs (who were butchered by the thousands during plague visitations) or to Jews, who, in some countries, were accused of having induced the plague to destroy Christianity and were burned alive.

of arms. Here's how the word was used by that impeccable grammarian and professor of modern languages at Harvard, Henry W. Longfellow: "A youth who bore, 'mid snow and ice, a banner with the strange device, *Excelsior.*"

In Chapter XI, I mentioned that in 1613 Shakespeare and Burbage, both experts in heraldry and tilts, were paid forty-four shillings apiece in gold for making an impresa for Francis Manners, sixth Earl of Rutland, to wear in a tilt at an anniversary celebration of James the First's accession to the throne.

According to Burgoyne, on November 22, 1595, four days after the Essex tilt, Rowland Whyte wrote to Sir Robert Sydney: "My Lord of Essex's device is much commended in these late triumphs." If, as I have conjectured, Shakespeare was at this period still employed part-time by Bacon, is it not feasible that the poet and his artist friend Richard Burbage prepared the impresa?

Of more interest are the notes and rough drafts of portions of the speeches preserved in the Lambeth Palace Library. As mentioned, I believe that Shakespeare wrote essays and speeches for Bacon based upon rough drafts supplied by the great philosopher. I'd trade my rights to reread *Titus Andronicus* for a one-second glance at the fair copy of the last four of the speeches. It could be in Shakespeare's hand.

As I am merely a lover of Shakespeare, and not an expert on his stylistic quirks, I must leave the critical examination of Bacon's writings to others. I especially commend to the Shakespeare experts an examination of the speeches written for Essex at the tilt. The style seems to me more flexible than Bacon's. The ideas, too, are in my opinion not those of the great thinker. Bacon's essays are little gems and, like his philosophical writings, mathematically structured, hard, compact, brilliantly cut, like the glass of a prism. It would be difficult to imagine the icy-souled, unemotional Bacon as a lover of poetry, or even comprehending the reason for poetry. Yet Bacon's speeches for Essex at the tilt are beautifully written and imply the vision of a poet. Take this little passage from the "Hermitt's second speech": "But the gardens of the Muses keep the privilege of the golden age; they ever flourish and are in league with time. The monuments of witt survive the monuments of power: the verses of a poet endure without a syllable lost, while states and empires pass. . . ." Does this not suggest Shakespeare's Sonnet 55, probably written about the same time or perhaps several years earlier:

> Not marble, nor the gilded monuments
> Of princes, shall outlive this powerful rhyme. . . .

If Bacon wrote the passage I've just quoted, then it was certainly a departure from his usual mode of thinking and expression.

In a sense, the prolific Bacon reminds one of the enormously productive writers of France. Dumas père, for instance, employed a whole stable of authors to turn out scores of novels to which he put his name. The number of Bacon's published works, considering the demands of his public life, is colossal. And so prolific a writer was Shakespeare that with little or no aid he could very likely have appeased the almost insatiable appetite of Bacon for new material. Perhaps this duo of authors was aided by the erudite Ben Jonson in research and checking the classical allusions.

Bacon and Shakespeare would have been perfect foils for each other: Bacon, the Renaissance philosopher, constantly probing *de rerum natura* in quest of truth; and his witty companion and literary assistant, William Shakespeare, the master of fantasy, with an astral imagination that could ricochet from star to star. I like to think they may have enjoyed glorious conversations of a cold winter's eve over a cup of hot sherry or buttered rum. In 1592 Shakespeare was twenty-eight, Bacon thirty-two. In these two young men would be vested much of the glory, beauty, and power of English literature.

In my opinion, the *Northumberland Manuscript* was prepared for Bacon. It probably was scheduled to be bound up and placed in his library, at which time the scribbled-on cover would be jettisoned and replaced by parchment or calf. For some reason this was never done.

The question that now confronts us is not "Did Bacon write Shakespeare's plays?" but "Did Shakespeare write Bacon's essays?"

[167] Signatures of William Shakespeare

[a] Practice signatures from the cover of
the *Northumberland Manuscript*, 1592–1596
[b] Italic signatures from the text of Shakespeare's
draft applications for a coat of arms, 1596–1599
[c] From the Quiney-Mountford deed, December 4, 1612
[d] From the text of the Welcombe Enclosure Agreement
between Shakespeare and Repplingham, October 28, 1614
[e] From the text of the last will and testament,
March 25–April 23, 1616
[f] Signature from the last page (3) of the will, mid-April, 1623

XV

NOTES ON SHAKESPEARE'S PENMANSHIP

SHAKESPEARE's handwriting is volatile. Sometimes it flows sweetly across the page in a rolling succession of sensual curves and swirls, with the swinging bellies of the lower loops of *b*'s and *y*'s voluptuous hinges for his other letters in an almost copybook script. At other times, his pen seems to explode with such vehemence that all fripperies and curlicues are abandoned, portions of words and the long tails of *f*'s and *s*'s are jettisoned, leaving a flat, almost indecipherable text.

The slant of the poet's script varies according to inspiration or mood. His favorite style is upright, with a very slight lean to the right, but sometimes, as in the Welcombe Enclosure Agreement, the forward lean is more pronounced. A page in his hand may then look like rows of wheat touched by a summer zephyr. My surmise is that Shakespeare was right-handed, possibly ambidextrous.

Shakespeare invariably focused on ideas and paid little attention to his penmanship. When his thoughts outsped his quill, then goodbye to the copybook script! Edward Maunde Thompson, the literary detective who first provided strong evidence that Writer D, author of three pages in *The Booke of Sir Thomas More,* might be Shakespeare, noticed the poet's penmanship varied in accordance with shifts in dramatic mood. In *Shakespeare's Handwriting,* Sir Edward writes:

There is a decided distinction between the writing of the first two pages and that of the third page. The text of the former is evidently written with speed . . . The rapid action of the hand is indicated, for example, by the prevalence of thin, long-shafted descending letters (*f* and long *s),* which are carried down often to unusual length and end in a sharp point, and by a certain dash in the formation of other letters, both in the text and in the marginal names of the characters.

These signs of speed generally slacken in the course of the second page, in the second half of which the long-shafted descending letters give place to some extent to a more deliberate and heavier style of lettering. This change seems to be coincident with the change in the character of the composition—the change from the noisy tumult of the insurgents to the intervention of [Sir Thomas] More with his persuasive speeches, requiring more thought and choice of language on the part of the author. The full effect of this change in the style of composition is manifest in the more deliberate character of the writing on the third page.

I have frequently mentioned that handwriting should be tested for authenticity by feel, rather than by a minute scrutiny of the formation of individual letters and words. However, I do not mean to impeach the validity of examining individual words (which, incidentally, may vary greatly from line to line) but such an individual-word examination should be auxiliary and subsequent to the more important feel, or overall impression. Some of the early paleographers, Dr. Samuel A. Tannenbaum, for example, a controversial scholar with special acumen in ferreting out evidence, was frequently wrong in his judgments. He filled reams of paper to prove that Writer D in *Sir Thomas More* was not Shakespeare (*The Booke of Sir Thomas Moore*, 1927) and in the end seemed to doubt his own conclusions. He invested perhaps months of painstaking effort to establish that the spurious signature in Montaigne's *Essays* (which I shall discuss in detail later) was genuine ("Reclaiming One of Shakspere's Signatures"). He should have perceived in a second that the feel of the Montaigne signature was totally different from that of the six other known Shakespeare signatures. Tannenbaum correctly divined that Shakespeare's first application for a coat of arms was a draft copy and even hinted that the poet had a hand in preparing it. But after he had piled all the evidence for a great discovery into the palm of his hand, he failed to clench his fist on it. With a sharper feel for the script in the draft application, he might have linked it successfully with Shakespeare's six signatures. Never did fate throw so many opportunities into the path of a scholar and then in the end deny him the triumph of the ultimate discovery—what Shakespeare's handwriting really looked like.

Throughout this book I have provided a few charts illustrating the similarity of key words—basic, common, often-repeated words—in certain documents penned by Shakespeare but whenever possible I have carefully avoided the use of individual letters. I am convinced that letters alone are sometimes misleading and inconclusive. A full word, even a very brief one, or a portion of a word, often conveys the feel of a manuscript. It would be easy to take all the holographic documents of Shakespeare I've discussed, pick out individual letters from each, and establish what would appear to be an air-tight case for Shakespeare's parenthood. But far more conclusive is the movement and slant of a script, the size of the handwriting, the position of dots over the *i*, the spacing between the words and between the letters in the words, the *je ne sais quoi* that is "feel."

Shakespeare the penman is not bound by rules. He is an orthographic madman. His spelling is fugacious and unpredictable. This and other inconsistencies proclaim his creative independence. He was not a man who lived or thought within narrow confines. True, he was bigoted in his views of religion and certain aspects of morality, and no doubt believed in witches, ghosts, and demons. But in all other respects he could soar. I suspect that the term "gentle Shakespeare," now rather fashionable with bardolaters, is an egregious misnomer. Get Will out for a night on London town and I'll bet a golden angel against a counterfeit half-groat that he was a wild one!

In Shakespeare's day Latin was taught in school and its spelling was regulated and precise. English, on the other hand, was regarded mainly as a spoken tongue. Any orthography that got across the meaning was acceptable. If they'd held an English spelling bee in Stratford when Shakespeare was a boy, the judges would've been carted off to Bedlam and every entry proclaimed a winner. There are some pretty confusing aspects to the poet's spelling. He often dropped the terminal *e* from a word, thus risking a misunderstanding. Clearly, if it were the *e* from *come,* as it often was, there was no problem. But if an *e* were dropped from *made* the change could alter his meaning. Another feature of his handwriting is the almost interchangeable use of *l* with *ll, m* with *mm,* and *i* with *y.* The single and double consonants or vowels are varied with no apparent reason. The poet wrote Stratford-*upon*-Avon and Stratford-*uppon*-Avon. *Gold* turned into *gould,* and *would* into *wold.* When it came to capital letters, Shakespeare left the decision to spontaneous inspiration.

Shakespeare's abbreviations may throw you at first, but after a while you'll get used to them. He always put a tittle (a straight or curved umbrella) over the portion of the word he abbreviated, often drawing it the full length of the word. He used a looped letter that looks something like a noose to indicate a terminal *es,* especially after a *d.* He frequently employed a contraction for *per* or *par* or *pro* in a longer word. His most common abbreviations are *mr* (master), *Mtie* (Majestie) and *wth* (with).

Shakespeare not only constantly altered his spelling and the slant of his script; he also exploits to the fullest the flexibility of the secretary hand. From word to word, from line to line, his quill exhibits the virtuosity that gives his penmanship unusual gusto and power. During my initial examination of his holographic will I was amazed at the chirographic variations compressed in only three pages. No clerical script this! Here is the fiery, undisciplined intellect of the world's supreme poet set upon paper. To get an idea of the variations in Shakespeare's penmanship in a single document, just examine the twelve different ways he writes the letter *g* in the will (*illus. 168*).

These varieties of *g* occur over and over again in the various manuscripts of Shakespeare illustrated in this book. I suppose, in the end, we are reduced to describing Shakespeare's handwriting with a conceit: The only consistent thing about it is its inconsistency.

[168] Variants of *g* used in Shakespeare's holographic will

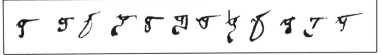

XVI

THE POET AND THE PRINTERS

WHAT a literary butcher was the Elizabethan printer! He often came down on Shakespeare's manuscripts like the wolf on the fold. Occasionally he disemboweled the poet's thought with typographical blunders, then violated his inspiration with eccentric punctuation. Shakespeare was truly the victim of "compositor's curse." No doubt, however, he deserved it, as I shall shortly point out. Shakespeare's early quartos, in which many of his plays were first published, fell victim to printers who could not decipher his script.

In *The Scholar Adventurers*, Richard D. Altick gives a capsule description of the situation: "As everyone knows, the text of Shakespeare's plays is full of perplexities. Largely because of the careless copying of the manuscript that went to the printer, and the equally careless typesetting of the first editions, there are thousands of lines which have had to be corrected, one way or another, by every editor." H. T., a nineteenth-century writer whose full name no man knows, writes in *Was Shakespeare a Lawyer?*: "It has often been a matter of wonderment with students of the Plays how the innumerable errors and gross absurdities which are patent in the early texts, could have crept into existence." Then he presents an interesting theory: The early printers were mainly imported from Germany and when they weren't able to make out a word, or didn't know where to put a comma, they simply improvised. An early editor of Shakespeare and a great poet himself, Alexander Pope complained two hundred and fifty years ago of Shakespeare's printers, noting: "It is impossible to repair the injuries already done him."

There's not much doubt that many of Shakespeare's plays were printed from the poet's manuscripts, or at least from prompt books. Alfred W. Pollard wrote an essay for *Library*, "The Manuscripts of Shakespeare's Plays," in which he declares: ". . . we submit that it is bibliographically probable that some of the First Quarto editions of Shakespeare's plays were printed from the author's own autograph manuscript, which had previously been used as a prompt-copy; that the actors replaced their manuscript prompt-copy by a copy of the printed Quarto. . . ."

A few of the offending printers of the Elizabethan era, those who were meddling varlets, should have been marched straightaway to the local inquisitors for a turn of the thumb-screw. The more conscientious printers, however, and those of them who worked on Shakespeare's manuscripts especially, merit more sympathy than censure. I am inclined to toss a bouquet or two to the printers who triumphed over Shakespeare's often execrable penmanship. For when the poet wrote creatively at top speed the result was a cascade of slurred words. His originality in devising abbreviations almost equaled that of his creative genius. And his vile habit of scrawling letters that looked alike—*e*'s that resembled *c*'s; *a*'s that were ringers for *u*'s; *v*'s that seemed twins to *a*'s; *d*'s and *e*'s that were cousins germane; and *u*'s and *n*'s that could trade places and fool their creator—must have mightily distressed compositors. Worse yet, Shakespeare's custom of jettisoning terminal *e*'s when they were required by edict, as in *Fraunc*[e] and *deceas*[e], and thrusting *e*'s in where they weren't needed or wanted, as in *paied* and *saied*, must have driven printers to the nearest pub for a tankard or two of humming ale.

In one of the most brilliant examples of detective work in the history of scholarship, Professor J. Dover Wilson uncovered the fact that mistakes in spelling, especially the use of archaic forms of words, were often attributable to the authors, not the compositors. In *The Manuscript of Shakespeare's* Hamlet *and the Problems of Its Transmission*, Wilson writes: "I set out to discover what sort of a wild ass had perpetrated the ridiculous (quarto) text of 1603. . . ." Wilson eventually became convinced that the quarto was printed direct from Shakespeare's manuscript. In my opinion, this would not be possible if the manuscript used for the bad quarto (1603) were the same manuscript from which the good quarto (1604) was printed. No compositors, however inept or myopic, could so outrageously misread even the galloping, abbreviated speed writing of the poet.

Many scholars now explain the bad quartos (abbreviated versions with mangled texts)

[169] Confusing Letters in Shakespeare's Script
(Columns are in descending order.)

[a] *o, e,* terminal *s* in: unt*o,* th*e,* Decea*s*
[b] *p, x* in: *p*ence, u*p*on, ne*x*t, *p*oundes, si*x*e
[c] *e, t, c* in: th*e* /th*e,* y*t* /a*t,* *c*ountie, De*c*eas, followe*i*ng
[d] *v, a* in: De*v*ided, m*a*les, gy*v*e
[e] *a, u* in: t*a*ken, D*u*ring, s*a*ye, Fo*u*rth
[f] terminal *es, &* (ampersand), *l* in: pound*es*/*&,* hand*es,* Hal*l,* Russel*l*
[g] *d, e* in: gard*e*ns, unpai*e*d, sai*e*d, pay*ed*
[h] *n, w, u, o* in: *n*ewe, *w*elcombe, here*u*nto, gr*o*undes
[i] *r, v* in: hund*r*ed, ha*v*e, he*r*
[j] *o, u, n* in: L*o*nd*o*n, to b*u*y him A Ri*n*ge
[k] *n, u* in: *n*at*u*rall, Da*u*ghter, Pou*n*des

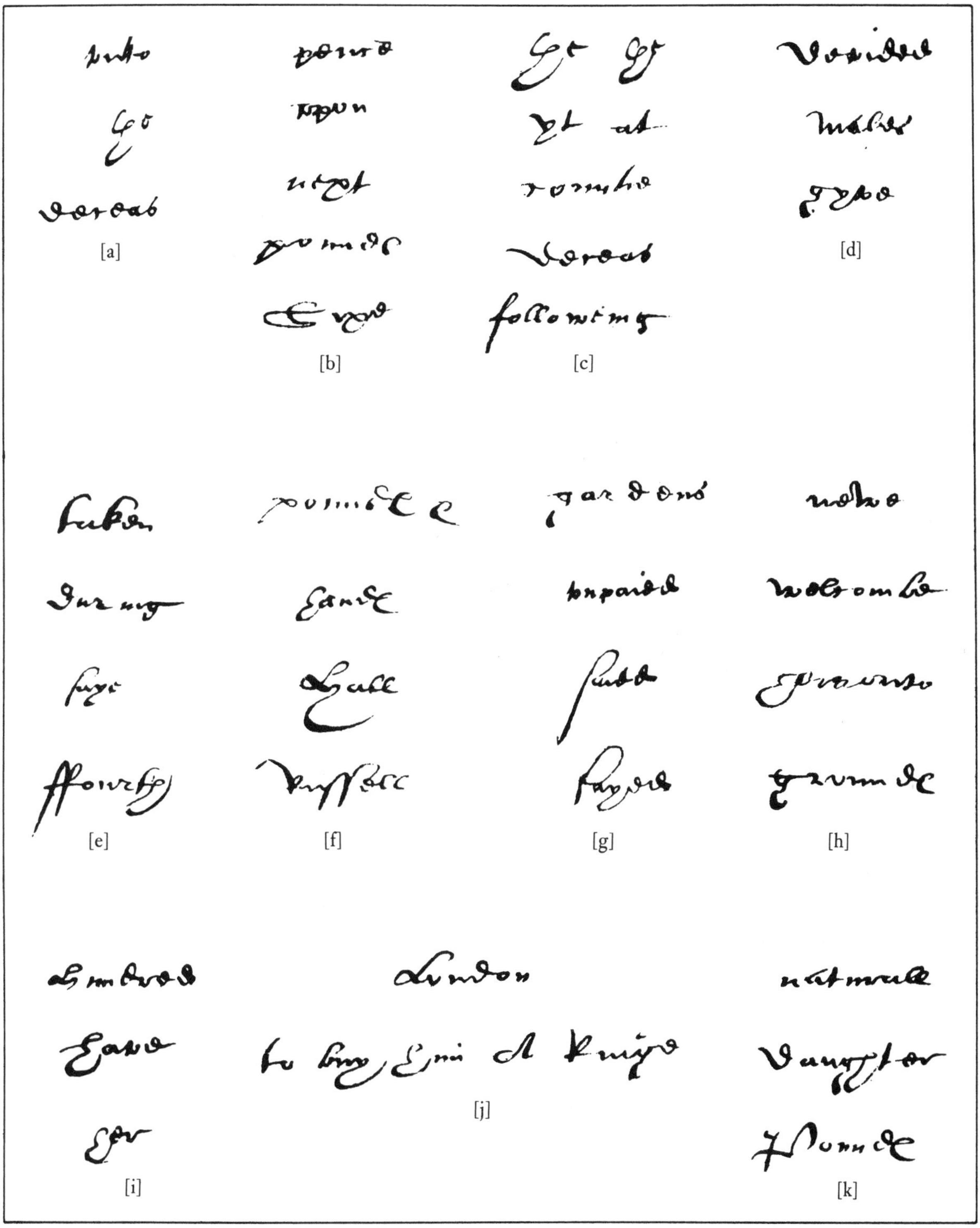

[a]

[b]

[c]

[d]

[e]

[f]

[g]

[h]

[i]

[j]

[k]

by the rather implausible supposition that such versions were, as Stanley Wells states in *Shakespeare: An Illustrated Dictionary*, "probably put together from the memories of a few of the actors." It seems most unlikely to me that any actor, even the most insensitive or amnesic, could forget such powerful phrases as "the slings and arrows of outrageous fortune" or "take arms against a sea of troubles." Earlier experts (and a few still cling to this theory) contended that the pirated *Hamlet* (1603) and other bad quartos were compiled from defective shorthand notes furtively taken during performances of the plays.

Professor Wilson's view that the bad text of *Hamlet* was set up from Shakespeare's manuscript by printers who could not read his writing and thus botched up the lines would be tenable only if the manuscript text they composed from were different from the subsequent good (complete and reasonably accurate) text. I think it far more probable that the bad quarto of *Hamlet* was based upon an early manuscript draft of the play, an original version that Shakespeare later jettisoned. Admittedly, there is evidence for the popular belief of scholars that Shakespeare was an inspired poet who made very few changes in his manuscripts. To support this view, we have the three fluid, almost uncorrected pages of Shakespeare's in *The Booke of Sir Thomas More*, which appear to furnish an example of the poet's tumultuous method of composition. We also have in evidence the remarks of Heminges and Condell, editors of Shakespeare's plays ("wee have scarce received from him a blot in his papers") and Ben Jonson's remark from *Timber* (1641), likely cribbed from Heminges and Condell ("whatsoever he penned he never blotted out [a] line"). My opinion is, however, that Shakespeare may have written one or more preliminary drafts of *Hamlet*, conceivably dashing off a rough working text in a few weeks. Like the other bad quartos, the 1603 *Hamlet* is much shorter than the final version, another evidence that it may be an early, trial draft. *Hamlet* was greatly increased in size in the good quarto published in 1604. The scarce-a-blot manuscripts examined and used by Heminges and Condell may have been fair copies, punctiliously indited by Shakespeare for use as prompt books. It is also possible that the three holographic pages in *Sir Thomas More* are Shakespeare's fair copy of a much reworked original draft.

[170] Hamlet's soliloquy "To be, or not to be . . ." as printed in the "bad" quarto of 1603 (reproduced here from Stanley Wells's excellent handbook *Shakespeare: an Illustrated Dictionary*, 1978). A glance will show that the text is quite different from the moving lines familiar to us today. Here, the blank verse is atrocious, some lines mocking all rules of prosody. It is difficult to believe that such itinerant iambs came from the quill of the quintessential dramatist. Some of the blame must fall upon the compositor; yet there is enough similarity between this text and the modern one to suggest that the quarto was printed from a draft of the play as the poet first wrote it. If we shift the scrambled iambs and trochees a little, the passage yields a nomadic pentameter and makes more sense:

To be or not to be—aye, there's the point.
To die, to sleep. Is that all? Aye, all? No!
To sleep, to dream, aye, merry, there it goes,
For in that dream of death, when we awake,
And borne before an everlasting Judge
From whence no passenger ever return'd—
The undiscovered country, at whose sight. . . .

If we accept the premise that Shakespeare was like most other authors, and wrote and rewrote a manuscript many times before he attained the perfection he sought, I think we can then consider two possibilities: Shakespeare wrote a hasty, rather crude, working draft of *Hamlet*. He later pitched it out, but it was salvaged from his papers by some miscreant, and printed in 1603, without his knowledge or authority. The second possibility is that Shakespeare used a shorter, working draft to test audience reaction to his new play by performances mostly outside of London. The bad quarto was advertised as having been "divers times acted by his Highness' servants in the City of London, as also in the Universities of Cambridge and Oxford, and elsewhere." This seems to add weight to the suggestion that Shakespeare, like most modern dramatists, tried his play out of town before placing it before the critical audiences of the Globe. The bad quartos, which include *King Lear*, would thus represent early "test" vehicles that were subsequently overhauled, greatly amplified and transformed into the great plays we now know.

There is, in my opinion, another possible explanation for the strange text in the bad quarto (1603) of *Hamlet*. The spectacular success of Shakespeare's play in 1602 may have

Ham. To be,or not to be, I there's the point,
To Die, to sleepe,is that all? I all:
No,to sleepe,to dreame, I mary there it goes,
For in that dreame of death, when wee awake,
And borne before an euerlasting Iudge,
From whence no passenger euer retur'nd,
The vndiscouered country, at whose sight
The happy smile,and the accursed damn'd.
But for this,the ioyfull hope of this,
Whol'd beare the scornes and flattery of the world,
Scorned by the right rich,the rich curssed of the poore?

The widow being oppressed,the orphan wrong'd,
The taste of hunger, or a tirants raigne,
And thousand more calamities besides,
To grunt and sweate vnder this weary life,
When that he may his full *Quietus* make,
With a bare bodkin, who would this indure,
But for a hope of something after death?.
Which puzles the braine, and doth confound the sence,
Which makes vs rather beare those euilles we haue,
Than flie to others that we know not of.
I that, O this conscience makes cowardes of vs all,
Lady in thy orizons, be all my sinnes remembred.

inspired the bad-quarto publishers Nicholas Ling and John Trundel to issue and ascribe to Shakespeare an earlier, popular version of the Hamlet drama (now lost and known to scholars as the *Ur-Hamlet*), probably written by Thomas Kyd in 1589. Ling and Trundel may have printed their text from a prompt book or manuscript of Kyd's shorter drama.

Not just the bad quartos are stunted. *Macbeth* is the shortest of Shakespeare's tragedies. So short, in fact, that it's often regarded as a cut version for some special performance, perhaps at court. However, I think it equally plausible that the first printing of *Macbeth* (by Heminges and Condell in the First Folio of 1623) was based upon an early, working manuscript of Shakespeare's. The two editors may have amplified a shorter "trial" text, the only copy available to them, by drawing additional lines from their own memories or the memories of other actors who had performed the play in a subsequent, more polished and elaborate version.

In pursuing his research, Professor Wilson discovered in the good quartos many parallels to the archaic spellings in the three pages by Shakespeare in *The Play of Sir Thomas More*. Then Wilson went further. In "Bibliographical Links between the Three Pages and the Good Quartos" (*Shakespeare's Hand in the Play of 'Sir Thomas More,'* 1923), Professor Wilson describes a method by which mistakes in the early printings of Shakespeare can be ferreted out:

> Lists were . . . made of all the obvious misprints (i.e. misprints which have been corrected in all modern editions), and of the abnormal spellings which occur in the Good Quartos. By 'abnormal spellings' is meant such spellings as a reputable compositor of Shakespeare's day is not likely to have wittingly introduced into the text himself. . . . When in dealing with the fifteen Good Quarto texts, produced by some nine or ten different printing-houses over a space of twenty-nine years, we find the same types of misprint and the same peculiarities of spelling recurring throughout, it is safe to attribute them to one constant factor behind them all—the pen of William Shakespeare.

> The constant confusion between *e* and *d* in the quartos proves that the copy from which they were printed was in English [secretary script], in which these two letters are formed on the same pattern; to have found, then, that the Addition [the three pages by Shakespeare in *Sir Thomas More*] was written in an Italian hand would have been disconcerting, to say the least. Or again, one of the bibliographical features of the quartos is the frequent and whimsical appearance of an initial capital *C,* in a way which shows that Shakespeare's pen was fond of using this letter in place of the minuscule. It was therefore encouraging to note that every initial *c* on p. 1 of the Addition was a capital. . . ."

Wilson cites a few examples of how Shakespeare's penmanship led to a corrupted text:

> . . . Shakespeare's habit of sometimes leaving the top of his *a* open, or conversely of curving the initial minim of his *u* so that it appears to be an ill-formed *a*. Thus *Othello* gives us 'coach' for 'couch' and 'heate' for 'hint' (spelt 'hente'); *Troilus* 'seat' for 'sense'; *Hamlet* 'heave a' for 'haven' and 'raine' for 'ruin'. . . . In English script minim-letters are *m, n, u, i, c, r, w;* and the large number of conpositor's errors in words containing such letters prove that Shakespeare must have been more than ordinarily careless in the formation of them, that he did not properly distinguish

between the convex and concave forms, and that he often kept no count of his strokes, especially when writing two or more minim-letters in combination. For example, we have 'game' for 'gain' *(Othello)*, 'might' for 'night' and 'string' for 'stung' *(Lear)*, 'sanctity' for 'sanity,' and 'the most' for 'th'inmost' *(Hamlet)* . . . 'where' for 'when' *(Othello* and *Lear)* . . . 'arm'd' for 'a wind' *(Hamlet).* . . .

Dr. Samuel A. Tannenbaum followed up on Professor Wilson's discovery by writing "Some Emendations of Shakspere's Text," a chapter in his book *Shaksperian Scraps and Other Elizabethan Fragments* (1933). Tannenbaum demonstrates in detail how a careful study of the secretary script can explain "most of the errors" in Shakespeare's text.

The difficulties encountered by Professor Wilson and Dr. Tannenbaum were largely the result of the very small amount of Shakespeare's handwriting they had to work with. The glossary in the next chapter will, I hope, make the work of scholars easier. By working backwards (starting with the pages of the published plays) and noting all obscure phrases or words that do not precisely make sense, and comparing these phrases or words with the handwriting illustrated in the glossary, a skilled student of bardography can deduce precisely what the printer's mistakes were and how to rectify them. I have added some additional confusing letters, which Professor Wilson did not point out because of the limitations of the Shakespeare manuscript he was working from.

By using the glossary, or similar and more detailed charts, an imaginative scholar can visualize what Shakespeare's manuscript looked like, precisely how a harried compositor might go about setting it up, and what blunders he might make in the process. He can then examine the modern text of Shakespeare with a critical eye and search out printer's errors almost as though he held Shakespeare's original manuscript in his hands.

XVII

GLOSSARY OF
SHAKESPEARE'S WORDS

THE glossary that follows comprises over five hundred different words written by Shakespeare, taken from five principal holographic sources: the poet's will, the Welcombe Enclosure Agreement, the legible page from the three folio leaves in *The Booke of Sir Thomas More,* the three heraldic documents concerning Shakespeare's coat of arms, and the one and a half pages in the *Northumberland Manuscript.* All five documents employ different vocabularies and together cover a time span of almost twenty-five years.

In addition to all the key words that are usually similar or identical in the five manuscript sources, I have included a few unusual words that give an idea of the great range and power of the poet's vocabulary and the variety of his spellings. Also illustrated are his more common abbreviations: the symbol for the terminal *es* used to pluralize certain nouns; the symbols for *par, per* and *pro;* and the tittle, a supralineal flourish or umbrella to indicate the omission of a letter or letters from a word *(illus. 171).* The tittle varies in shape, from a long straight line (see *William*—written *Willm* by Shakespeare —in the Glossary) to a tiny curve or circle. When Shakespeare uses the tittle at the end of a word and the abbreviation requires no explanation, I have not indicated the tittle's use, but if the tittle is used medially and could be obscure or misunderstood, I have put the missing letters in brackets in the modern English equivalent of Shakespeare's word. I have also bracketed the missing letters when the poet uses the symbols for *par, per* or *pro.*

For no apparent reason, Shakespeare uses *y* and *i* interchangeably. Also frequently interchanged are his *u* and *v,* and *i* and *j.* The switching of these letters is a hangover from old Roman days. The Roman alphabet contained no *v* (as *v* was actually their letter for *u*) and no *j* (the letter *i* was a substitute for *j*). When the Romans wrote the name

JULIUS, for example, it came out IVLIVS. It's a good idea to remember that, whether in London or Stratford, Shakespeare did as the Romans did.

The variations in Shakespeare's script are amazing, and will most likely continue to plague scholars for the next two or three centuries. Look up the word *be* in this glossary —there are five different ways the poet wrote it. All five are from the poet's will and not, as might be presumed, written at different times. Notice the two variants of the word *body*; both come from the will. The variants of the word *wings* (which the poet spells *winges* and *wynges*) appear to be written by different persons, yet all three occur in Shakespeare's applications for a coat of arms.

The major problems I had in selecting words for the glossary were created by the assaults time had made on the old manuscripts, sometimes eroding away portions of words, and by Shakespeare's own ebullient style of writing—the pendulous pen-and-ink bellies that swing from his *b*'s into the line beneath and the lengthy tails of his *f*'s and long *s*'s that often impale the words under them. In a very few cases I strengthened minuscule portions of lines that had almost disappeared from Shakespeare's writing because of the disintegration of the original documents, but all of the words appear exactly as Shakespeare wrote them.

When the poet's handwriting is on good behavior, as in his will and the portion of *Leicester's Commonwealth* that he copied into the *Northumberland Manuscript*, it is more easily read and more easily recognizable. Although the pages of the *Northumberland Manuscript* date from about 1592 or 1593 (in my opinion) and the will was penned in 1616, almost a quarter of a century later, the writing is strikingly similar. I suppose this is because when Shakespeare wished to be especially punctilious about his script he reverted to the copybook penmanship he had learned in the Stratford Grammar School.

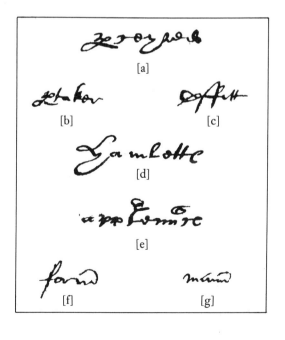

[171] Abbreviations commonly used by Shakespeare: the *per* symbol to mean both *per* and *par*; the *pro* abbreviation; the terminal *es* (after the second *t* in Hamlettes); medial tittles (app[*ur*]tenn[*an*]ces), and terminal tittles (form[*er*], mann[*er*]).

[a] p[er]ceyved (perceived)
[b] p[ar]taker
[c] p[ro]ffitt (profit)
[d] Hamlettes (hamlets)
[e] app[ur]tenn[an]ces (appurtenances)
[f] form[er]
[g] mann[er]

GLOSSARY OF SHAKESPEARE'S WORDS

1. a		18. ancient	
2. abode		19. And	
3. above		20. and	
4. accord		21. (ampersand)	
5. according		22. Antecessor	
6. accustomed		23. any	
7. advanced		24. appear	
8. afford		25. appeared	
9. after		26. appertaineth	
10. against		27. Appoint	
11. agree		28. appropriate	
12. All/all		29. approved	
13. also		30. Argent	
14. always		31. Arms	
15. Ambition		32. Articles	
16. Amen		33. As/as	
17. Amongst			

34. assigned		54. body	
35. assuredly		55. bowl	
36. at		56. breaking	
37. Avon		57. broad	
38. Bailiff		58. But/but	
39. barbarous		59. buy	
40. bare		60. by	
41. barns			
42. bastoneth		61. Called	
43. be		62. calls	
		63. can	
44. bearing		64. Capital	
46. become		65. captain	
47. been		66. case	
48. before		67. causes	
49. being		68. certain	
50. believing		69. Chartered	
51. Bend		70. chased	
52. better		71. Child[r]en	
53. between			

72. Chivalry		90. cut	
73. clement		91. Dame	
74. Coat		92. Danger	
75. Cognizance		93. Date	
76. come		94. Daughter	
		95. Day	
77. commend		96. Decease	
78. commodity		97. Default	
79. Commonweal		98. Defender	
80. conceived		99. degrees	
81. consideration		100. Demonstratio[n]	
82. convenient		101. Depicted	
83. Country		102. Deposited	
84. County/county		103. Depriving	
85. court		104. Descend	
86. credible		105. descents	
87. credit		106. desperate	
88. Crest		107. detested	
89. custom/Custom		108. Difference	

109.	Dignify		127.	Eight	
110.	Disclosed		128.	either	
111.	Dishonor		129.	elements	
112.	Displayed		130.	endorsed	
113.	Dispositions		131.	England	
114.	Divided		132.	English	
115.	Divulged		133.	entreat	
116.	Do		134.	Equal	
117.	dogs		135.	error	
118.	doing		136.	Esquire	
119.	Dominions		137.	estate	
120.	done		138.	everlasting	
121.	down		139.	example	
122.	During		140.	except	
123.	Dwell		141.	exercises	
124.	Dwelleth		142.	expenses	
125.	Earl		143.	extraordinary	
126.	earth/Earth		144.	facts	
			145.	faith	

146. faithful	*faithfull*	165. forever	*for ever*
147. Falcon	*Falcon*	166. forgiven	*forgiven*
148. families	*families*	167. form	*form*
149. famous	*famous*	168. form[er]	*form*
150. fastened	*fastened*	169. forth	*forth*
151. feet	*feet*	170. forty	*forty*
152. field	*field*	171. foul	*foul*
153. Fields	*Fields*	172. four	*four*
154. fifth/Fifth	*fifth Fifth*	173. Fourth	*Fourth*
155. Fifty	*Fifty*	174. France	*France France*
156. figure	*figure*	175. friend	*friend*
157. find	*find*	176. friends	*friends*
158. first/First	*first First*	177. from	*from*
159. Five	*Five*	178. fun[e]ral	*funeral*
160. flanders	*flanders*	179. gain	*gain*
161. follow	*follow*	180. 'gainst	*gainst*
162. follower	*follower*	181. gardens	*gardens*
163. following	*following*	182. gent.	*gent gent gent gent*
164. for	*for for fo fo*	183. gentlemen	*gentlemen*

212

184.	Gentleme[n]		203.	he
185.	give/Give		204.	headed
186.	given		205.	health
187.	giving		206.	heirs
188.	go		207.	helmet
189.	god		208.	her
190.	gold		209.	hereof
191.	good		210.	heretofore
192.	goods		211.	hereunto
193.	grace		212.	hideous
194.	gra[n]t		213.	highness
195.	granted		214.	him
196.	great		215.	himself
197.	greetings		216.	hindrance
198.	grounds		217.	his
199.	had		218.	hold
200.	hands		219.	hoping
201.	hath		220.	hound
202.	Have/have		221.	household
			222.	houses

223. how	242. John
224. Hundred	243. Joined
225. I	244. kill
226. if	245. kindred
227. In	246. king
228. in	247. kingdoms
229. incident	248. kneel
230. indifferent	249. knees
231. informed	250. knives
232. injury	251. known
233. insolency	252. Lady
234. interruption	253. lands
235. into	254. last
236. intreat	255. late
237. Ireland	256. law
238. is	257. lawful
239. issue	258. Laws
240. it	259. lead
241. Jewels	260. Leases

261.	lent		280.	marvel
262.	lets		281.	master
263.	life		282.	matters
264.	lift		283.	may
265.	like		284.	mean
266.	living		285.	memory
267.	London		286.	men
268.	lying		287.	merit
269.	made		288.	might
270.	magistrate		289.	minds
271.	magnanimity		290.	money
272.	ma[jes]ty		291.	monument
273.	make		292.	moor
274.	males/Males		293.	most
275.	man		294.	mother
276.	mano[r]		295.	must
277.	margent		296.	my
278.	marks		297.	name
279.	marriage		298.	Names

299. Nations		318. One		
300. natural		319. only		
301. nature		320. or		
302. near		321. Orchards		
303. needs		322. ordain		
304. new		323. orator		
305. next		324. others		
306. no		325. own		
307. noble		326. owed		
308. Noble		327. our		
309. nor		328. paid		
310. not		329. parents		
311. now		330. p[ar]taker		
312. obey		331. party		
313. October		332. p[ar]ts		
314. of		333. pence		
315. office		334. p[er]ceived		
316. on		335. p[er]emptory		
317. one		336. p[er]fect		

337. perpetual			355. produce	
338. p[er]son			356. progenitors	
339. p[er]sons			357. p[ro]vince	
340. p[er]taining			358. put	
341. place			359. Q[ueen]	
342. plate			360. Queen	
343. play			361. Queens	
344. pleasure			362. Rate	
345. point			363. Realm	
346. Poor			364. reason	
347. possess			365. rebels	
348. posterity			366. Received	
349. pounds			367. reign	
350. Pounds			368. Remain	
351. praised			369. remembrance	
352. preceding			370. report	
353. privileges			371. reputation	
354. p[ro]cure			372. Rest	

373. Revoke

374. Ring

375. rout

376. rule

377. Sables

378. said

379. same

380. Saviour

381. say

382. Seal

383. Seals

384. service

385. set

386. Seventh

387. shall

388. shall be

389. shewed

390. shield

391. Shields

392. shillings

393. silver-gilt

394. single

395. singular

396. sing[u]lar

397. Sister

398. Six

399. Sixth/sixth

400. slip

401. so

402. solicited

403. some

404. son

405. Soul

406. souls

407. sound

408. sov[er]eign

409. spain

410. stables

411. stand	*stand*	430. ten	*ten*
412. standing	*standing*	431. ten[emen]t	*tenement*
413. still	*still*	432. term	*term*
414. strangers	*strangers*	433. testam[en]t	*testament*
415. Stratford	*Stratford Stratford*	434. testimony	*testimony*
416. street	*street*	435. That/that	*That that that that that*
417. stuff	*stuff*		
418. subjection	*subjection*	436. the	*the the the the the the the*
419. Submit	*Submit*	437. the[e]end	*theend theend*
420. such	*such*	438. their	*their their*
421. sufficient	*sufficient*	439. them	*them them*
422. suitor	*suitor*	440. themselves	*them selves*
423. surmise	*surmise*	441. th[e]only	*theonly*
424. Surrendering	*Surrendering*	442. there	*there*
425. Sword/sword	*Sword sword*	443. thereof	*thereof thereof*
426. take	*take*	444. thing	*thing thing*
427. taken	*taken*	445. think	*think*
428. tears	*tears*	446. third	*third*
429. temper	*temper*	447. thirteen	*thirteen*

448. this		467. until		
449. Thomas		468. unto		
450. those		469. untried		
451. threats		470. up		
452. three		471. upon		
453. throats		472. upward		
454. throne		473. us		
455. thus		474. use		
456. To		475. valiant		
457. to		476. village		
458. Tokens/tokens		477. violence		
459. Tombs		478. virtue		
460. Town		479. virtuous		
461. towns		480. warwick		
462. traitor		481. was		
463. trespass		482. wash		
464. true		483. we		
465. two		484. well		
466. unexperienced		485. we'll		

486. were

487. what

488. whatsoever

489. when

490. where

491. wherefore

492. wherein

493. whereof

494. w[hi]ch

495. whilst

496. whose

497. why

498. wife

499. will

500. Will[ia]m

501. wings

502. wit

503. w[i]th

504. w[i]thout

505. witness

506. won't

507. worthiness

508. worthy

509. would

510. wreath

511. written

512. ye

513. Year/year

514. yet

515. you

516. y[o]u

517. you'll

518. your

519. Arabic numeral dates: 1599, 1614, 1616

520. Roman numerals (for day of month or monetary sums) 8, 26

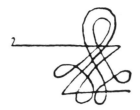

XVIII

FAKES AND IMPOSTORS

NOT long ago, a man telephoned me with some news that put a quaver in his voice. "I've just read an article about you in *The Saturday Evening Post*," he said. "I notice you're offering a million dollars for a signature of Shakespeare's. I've got one and I'm ready to sell for cash."

I started to caution my caller about forgeries and printed facsimiles, but he would hear none of my warning words.

Within an hour he rang the doorbell of my gallery. He struggled into my office with a swollen briefcase that made his spare frame list as he walked. His face glistened with perspiration. His hands trembled and there was a glitter in his eyes, the same glitter that betrays a poker player whose stony visage cannot hide a gleam of triumph when he fills an inside straight.

With the man was a uniformed official who wore a shiny badge and a holstered pistol. He was introduced by the man with the suitcase: "This is Joseph. He's here to see that nobody steals my Shakespeare signature."

The man opened his suitcase. Inside was a massive archive of stapled reports on top of which lay a slender envelope. From the envelope he tenderly extracted an engraved signature of Shakespeare's, the same that is on page 3 of the will. He placed it reverently in my hands.

I said: "What is this?"

His voice was hoarse with emotion. "An original signature of Shakespeare's."

"I'm truly sorry," I said, "but this is a signature cut from a portrait in a volume published about 1880. It's engraved. You can feel the raised writing."

My visitor allowed himself a little smile. "I've had it authenticated. Passed on by *real* experts. Look!" He pointed to the briefcase that bulged with papers. "Here are full reports on the ink. It dates from the seventeenth century. Reports on the paper, too, a variety used in Shakespeare's day . . . the chemical examination of the ink all in detail. Everything's here. I'm afraid you were hasty, Mr. Hamilton."

I often am hasty. So I looked again. It required only a second's glance to see that the paper was not more than a hundred years old. And that the ink was not more than a hundred years old. And that the chemists who carried out the ink and paper tests were probably two hundred years old and should have been laid to rest a century ago.

In addition to the tests by ink and paper specialists, there was a sheaf of letters from English professors who had examined the signature. Unanimously they acclaimed it as a literary discovery of major importance.

I glanced through the tests. They were full of charts and graphs and breakdowns of chemical compositions. They were also very lengthy and elaborate, crammed with technical gibberish and the high-toned language used by people who don't know what they're talking about.

I asked: "How much did this adventure with chemists set you back?"

"Over a grand."

I was forced to tell this man that he'd been had. I broke the news as gently as I could, but it still pained him.

It pained me, too, because it left me just where I'd started about sixty years ago. Still looking for a genuine Shakespeare. Such disappointments are not unusual. At least two or three times a year I'm offered "genuine" autographs of the great poet that "have been in our family for over a hundred years."

I don't have too much confidence in modern machinery when it comes to judging the age or authenticity of handwriting. So far as I know, modern scientific methods, such as chemical analyses of ink, ultraviolet, infrared and fluorescent lamps with special filter cameras and microscopes, have never yet produced any important or sensational literary or historic result. It is the human eye attached to the human brain that makes the great discoveries.

Perhaps I am foolish to doubt modern archival methods and question the value of sophisticated equipment. It can and often does set me at odds with other specialists. There is, for instance, *The Revels Account* (Malone MS 29) in the Bodleian Library *(illus. 172, 173)*. This strange document, an alleged record of plays performed by the King's Men (Shakespeare's company of actors) before James I in 1604–1605, attracts attention not only because of the bizarre spelling of Shakespeare's name (Shaxberd) but by its curious script. I'd have made book that it was a fake; yet critical examination has "established" its chemical authenticity. To me, however, the handwriting does not resemble Elizabethan script. It is devoid of delicacy and beauty, a gauche effort to create the fragile shading of the goose quill. To turn the quill deftly while writing and thus produce a handsomely shaded chirography requires years of practice *(illus. 174, 175)*.

The spelling is strange for the Jacobean period and creates the impression that the scribe took his degree from the University of Bedlam. The penmanship is labored and

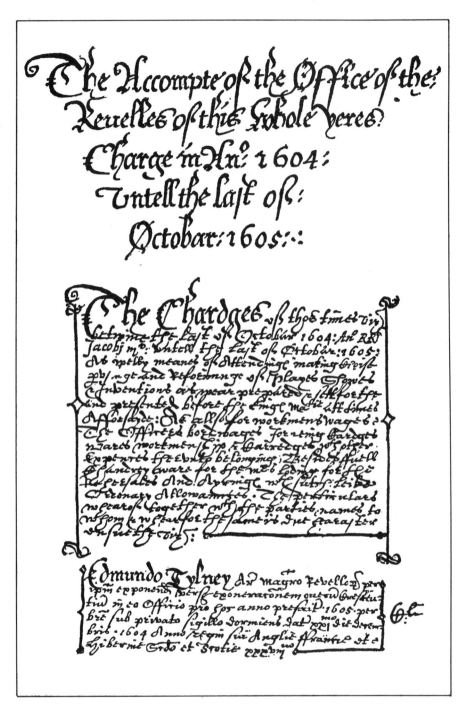

[172] First page of *The Revels Account*, a record of plays performed by the King's Men at court between 1604 and 1605. Crudely penned in imitation of Jacobean script. Possibly forged by Peter Cunningham, son of the noted poet, but more likely by John Payne Collier.

[173] Page from *The Revels Accounts,* showing Shakespeare's name as "Shaxberd."

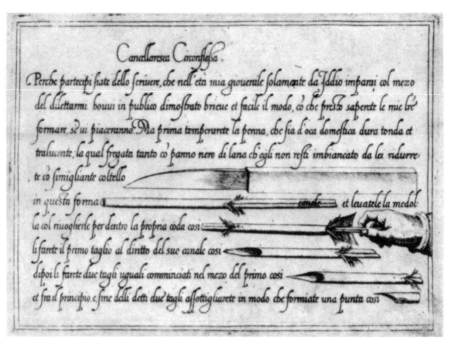

[174] Illustrated instructions for the proper method of cutting and trimming a quill to make a pen. (From *La Scrittor' Utile et brieve Segretario*, G. A. Hercolani, Bologna, 1574.)

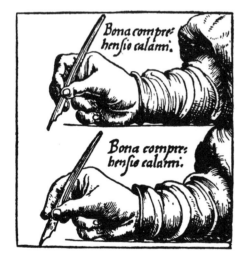

[175] Method of grasping the quill for writing. The bottom illustration shows the correct pen grip, still in use today. In writing the cursive secretary script Shakespeare pulled and pushed and sidled his strokes. He made the hairline by a horizontal movement of his quill; for the downstroke, he flexed his fingers and thumb, a maneuver that splayed the nib and left a bold, wide track. These two primary strokes and their variants, executed with natural and easy movements, resulted in Shakespeare's beautiful, fluent handwriting.

the lines weave, showing that the writer was concentrating on the formation of individual letters rather than on words or lines, a characteristic of forgeries. In *William Shakespeare: a Documentary Life*, Professor Schoenbaum notes that this curious document has "received corroboration . . . on the basis of . . . chemical and microscopic examination." Cagey old Halliwell-Phillipps did not tumble for this strange creation but, since the ink has met the acid test, Professor Schoenbaum is, I presume, justified in reporting that "the matter now appears to have been settled."

Old ink, however, is extremely hard to date by chemical analysis or microscopic examination. If you will look at the illustration of a recipe for ink (*illus. 176*) written about the middle of the eighteenth century, you will see the characteristic recipe that survived almost unchanged for three centuries. Almost every literate family kept a manuscript recipe book. Recipes often remained in use for hundreds of years, since manuscript recipe books for food, cures, paints, inks and so on were transmitted from generation to generation and highly valued by the owners. Favorite recipes were widely copied. Many old recipe books, some of them dating back to the early years of the seventeenth century, have passed through my hands. They often contain dated recipes that cover a span of more than a century and are penned in a variety of old hands. Even when they are undated, one can pretty closely fix the time span by looking at the type of handwriting used in the entries.

Most people prepared their own ink. The ingredients varied a trifle from recipe to recipe and from century to century, but the bases of home-style ink were usually oak galls, also known as gallnuts or nutgalls (excrescences caused by insect eggs on the leaves

[176] "To Make Black Ink," from a manuscript recipe book dating from the middle of the eighteenth century, probably copied from a seventeenth century recipe book. Thousands of such books survive from the early days in England, when every family kept a manuscript book of recipes for food, cures, paints and inks. Most ink in Shakespeare's day was homemade.

The recipe reads: "Take four Ounces Nutt Galls beaten & infused a Week in One Scots pint of Rain or River Water Set in the Sun or near the fire, and Shaken or Flared frequently after which add half an Ounce Green Coperas and a fourth of an Ounce Roman Vitriol, one Ounce Gum Arabic and a few specks of Logwood. N.B. too much Coperas makes the Ink Black at first but it soon grows Brown Upon the paper but with the above preportion it always grows Blaker & never degenerates."

or twigs of oak trees), copperas (a compound of copper and ferrous sulfate), and gum arabic. These bases were used from the sixteenth century until the middle of the nineteenth century. Excellent early inks were often compounded, too, from chimney soot, lampblack, kettle-black or gunpowder. Aniline dye, the base of our modern, fast-fade, easy-wash-away ink, was not widely employed in Europe until about 1860. Certainly John Payne Collier's ink (about 1830–1860), especially if mixed by Collier himself from a family recipe, would likely contain much the same ingredients as the inks of Shakespeare's time.

Old paper is, as might be expected, very easy to come by. I often run across manuscript account books that date back three centuries or more and contain hundreds of unused folio sheets. But even a forger who does not have access to such manuscript bonanzas can abstract a blank flyleaf from a worthless sixteenth-century volume if he has a mind to add a Shakespeare fabrication to his wares. He should, of course, size or glaze the porous old paper before applying ink, otherwise the ink may feather or fuzz and betray his forgery. A friend of mine, a prominent author of books and articles on historical hoaxes like the two Will Wests and the Shroud of Turin, has a genius for imitating old scripts. At his request, I've supplied him with antique ink recipes and ancient paper so that he can turn out some of his merry jests. His superbly executed fakes are instantly apparent to me, and would be to any manuscript expert who has invested many years in handwriting studies, but I doubt if his fabrications could be exposed by chemical or microscopic analysis. The paper and ink would both check out. Test tubes and microscopes and ultraviolet machines perform their tasks in a robotlike manner and do not profit from study, observation, intelligence or experience.

Genuine old ink with a nutgall base (containing tannin) bites into paper and can withstand a prolonged immersion in water without blurring or fading. In a previous chapter I mentioned that two of the three folios in Shakespeare's hand in *The Booke of Sir Thomas More* were mutilated by an archivist who pasted tissue paper over the handwriting in the belief that it would aid in preservation. If I could borrow those two precious pages of Shakespeare's writing for half an hour, I'd plunge them into a bathtub half full of lukewarm water and totally divest them of their raiment. They might then be readable and easy to photograph.

A final remark about modern methods of analysis. Certainly all documents that were forged prior to 1860, especially those suspected to be by Collier or Jordan, should be examined with great cunning and without undue reverence for the evidence of chemical, microscopic, and ultraviolet examinations. However, strong magnification or ultraviolet examination can be useful in exposing forgeries if the fabricator has first prepared his fake in pencil, traced over it in ink, and afterwards erased the pencil markings. Collier sometimes resorted to this amateurish trick.

As for a writing tool, it's not difficult to cut or trim a quill. Any barnyard where turkeys gobble or geese cackle will provide a supply of stout feathers. The problem really starts after you whittle the quill, for you will at first find it hard to write without almost immediately exhausting your quill's supply of ink. It is a nuisance to redip the pen after every sentence. You will also find it awkward to oscillate the pen slightly to put the delicate shading in your strokes. The quill may squeak like a frightened rodent. Its nib demands constant attention; when it is too sharp, for instance, it may snag the paper and catapult a tiny shower of ink droplets over your page. Writing with a quill is truly an art that can be mastered only by long practice. Some writers of modern times have preferred the quill to the steel-nibbed pen. Joaquin Miller, the American poet, put his jingles on paper with a stubby, fat goose quill. Lord Dunsany, the Irish author, indited his verses and letters with an eagle feather. His heavy, flamboyant strokes can be recognized clear across a room.

It is to be hoped that forgers of the future, for whom I have here provided some good tips, will not trouble scholars with crude fabrications like those of John Jordan, William Henry Ireland and John Payne Collier.

The dawn of the final decade of the eighteenth century found scores of bardolaters scouring England in search of Shakespeare relics, anything he had owned or touched and especially documents about him or signed by him. The seat of the poet's alleged chair in his birthplace had to be replaced every few years because of the vast concourse of admirers who wished to position their derrières in the exact spot once occupied by the poet's. As for autographs, there was not a quill scratch to meet the demand.

Whenever a great man passes into legend there is always a proliferation of his "personal" relics. Consider that any old quill pen, of which quite a number have survived, is likely to be "the one used by Jefferson to write the Declaration of Independence" or "found on Shelley's desk after he was drowned." Only a few years ago, a top hat made in Springfield about 1860 and "said to be Lincoln's" was sold at Sotheby's. The hat was not Lincoln's size, but no matter. It fetched $10,000. Which brings me to one of the most delightful of hoaxes—the mulberry tree "said to have been planted by Shakespeare." A legend grew up in the mid-eighteenth century about this old mulberry tree on his New Place property, a legend probably invented and fostered by the subsequent owner of the land, Sir Hugh Clopton. Sir Hugh used to show with great pride to all his visitors "the mulberry tree planted by Shakespeare." Clopton sold the property to an atrabilious prelate, Francis Gastrell, who abhorred bardolaters and, in 1753, cut the mulberry tree down. He later tore down New Place, too. The felled mulberry tree was hauled off as lumber by a clockmaker named Thomas Sharpe. Within a few months, Sharpe had built a thriving business selling souvenir objects carved from Shakespeare's mulberry tree.

The Borough of Stratford was one of Sharpe's best customers. In August 1760, he sold for twelve shillings enough wood to make a tea chest. Perhaps it was from this purchase that T. Davies, of Birmingham (at a cost of fifty-five pounds), carved the celebrated casket presented to David Garrick in 1768 by the Borough of Stratford (*illus. 177, 178*). The casket featured on the front panel an excellent carved portrait of Shakespeare. So many goblets, caskets, snuffboxes and other items were carved from the old mulberry tree that rumors flew about that Sharpe was replenishing his supply of wood from other trees. He emphatically denied this and took an oath on his deathbed that all the wood, and all the relics made from the wood, were as represented. The hoax continues even today, and

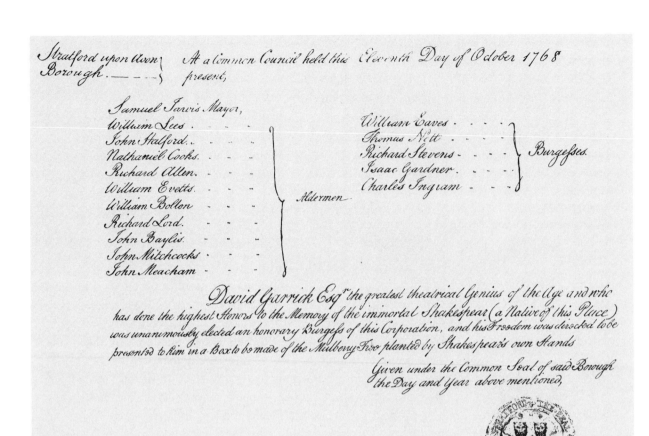

[177] Certificate from the Borough of Stratford to David Garrick, presenting him with the "mulberry tree casket," 1768

[178] Casket said to be made by T. Davies, of Birmingham, from the wood of "the mulberry tree planted by Shakespeare." It featured a carved portrait of the poet.

carved objects from the mulberry tree frequently turn up at auction, where they sell for modest prices.

The first man to cater to the market for manuscript delicacies was John Jordan (1746–1809), a self-educated wheelwright born at Luddington, near Stratford. Jordan published a volume of verses, *Welcombe Hills* (1777). It was a failure. Fifteen years passed before he discovered that the path to success lay in fabricating documents by and about Shakespeare. William Henry Ireland, his successor in the Shakespeare business, met Jordan about 1794. Young William and his father, Samuel Ireland, a prominent antiquarian, were in quest of any vestiges of Shakespeare. In his *Confessions* (1805) William Henry Ireland records his father's meeting with Jordan:

On Mr. Samuel Ireland's arrival at Stratford-on-Avon, he entered with the utmost avidity upon every research which might tend to throw any new light upon the history of our dramatic bard; and in these excursions he was joined by a very honest fellow of the name of Jordan, who was bred up a carpenter, but having, or conceiving himself to possess, a spark of the Appolonian fire, he had dedicated himself to the Muses, and was commonly denominated 'the Stratford Poet.' This civil inoffensive creature had not been idle, on the score of Shakespeare; and had made frequent visits to the neighboring villages and ancient houses, endeavouring if possible to glean any new anecdote or traditionary tale.

Apparently, Ireland was utterly deceived by the disingenuous Jordan, who had launched his career as a forger about 1790 by tossing some "newly discovered" manuscript material about Shakespeare right into the lion's mouth. That is, he sent the manuscripts to the great Edmund Malone, exposer of Chatterton (1782) and later (1796) William Henry Ireland. Malone viewed the material with some skepticism but helped Jordan financially. He accepted as genuine the will of John Shakespeare, the poet's father, and printed it in 1790. Later, in 1796, he rejected it. Sir Sidney Lee believes that Jordan forged the will. So do I. It was certainly a great achievement for Jordan to fool the canny Dubliner Malone for even a few years, but his victim soon got as wary as a corbie. Jordan "uncovered" in an old "chest of drawers that formerly belonged to Mrs. Dorothy Tyler, of Chattery, near Stratford" a ballad about Sir Thomas Lucy, whose deer were allegedly poached by young Shakespeare. The supposition was that Shakespeare had written the jingle, of which I will quote the first stanza:

> A parliment member, a justice of peace
> At home a poor scarecrowe, in London an asse,
> If Lucy is Lowsie as some volke miscall it
> Synge Lowsie Lucy whatever befall it.

The were seven more quatrains in the same vein. Jordan sent the poem to Malone, who was not gulled. Malone replied that he hadn't much confidence in it and detected a modern appearance in the handwriting.

Although Jordan was never able to score with his elaborate fakes, he did trouble scholarly waters with his forgeries of Shakespeare's signature in books. Of all autographic fakes, a signature in an old volume is the most difficult to detect. The paper is "right," the date of the fabrication is "right," and to duplicate nothing more than a signature requires from the forger minimal effort and carries a minimal risk of detection. For these reasons a volume allegedly signed by Shakespeare or any other celebrated person is automatically suspect.

Jordan's forgeries of Shakespeare's signature are competent. The capital *S* is excellent. The capital *B* in *Booke* represents a careful effort to mimic the *B* in *By me* at the conclusion of the third page of the poet's will. However, as can be seen *(illus. 180)*, the *h* is wrong, and so, in fact, is every letter, except *S* in the poet's surname.

The first forger to market Shakespeare fakes in a big way was the seventeen-year-old youngster William Henry Ireland. Young Ireland fooled the British Museum and a lot of literary bigwigs, but he did it in the eighteenth century, when bardography was in

[179] Epitaph composed by Shakespeare's friend John Combe, for himself. This interesting variant of a similar quatrain in John Aubrey's *Brief Lives* is in John Jordan's handwriting.

[180] John Jordan forgery (about 1790) in a 1605 edition of Bacon's *On the Advancement of Learning*. In 1829 this forgery belonged to Thomas Fisher of the East India House. It was first reproduced in John Gough Nichols's *Autographs of Royal, Noble, Learned, and Remarkable Personages*, 1829.

[181] Forgery of Shakespeare's signature (about 1790) in an old copy of *Bartholomeus*. A well-executed fake by John Jordan (1746–1809), based on Shakespeare's signature on page 3 of his will.

its infancy and knowledge about handwriting, and Shakespeare's handwriting in particular, was in short supply. To delight his father, who had spent much of his life in quest of a genuine Shakespeare autograph, Ireland decided to "discover" one for him. He played the sedulous ape to the five signatures of Shakespeare then known to exist. In his *Confessions* (1805) Ireland tells the story:

Having cut off a piece of parchment from the end of an old rentroll . . . I placed the deed before me of the period of James the First, and then proceeded to imitate the style of the penmanship as well as possible, forming a lease between William Shakespeare and John Hemings with one Michael Fraser and Elizabeth the wife, whereto I affixed the signature of Shakespeare, keeping the transcript of his original autographs before me, while the superscription of Michael Fraser was executed with my left hand, in order the better to conceal it as being from the same pen.

The contents of the lease being finished, and the signatures subscribed, I found much difficulty in annexing the seals, which, at the period of James the First, were not similar to those of the present day, being formed of malleable wax, and stamped upon narrow pieces of parchment hanging from the deed directly under the signatures. . . . At length I adopted the expedient of heating a knife, with which I cut an old seal in two without its cracking, and having with a penknife carefully scooped a cavity on the opposite side to that bearing the impression, I therein placed the strip of parchment pendent from the deed, and having heated some wax of less ancient date, I placed it when hot within the remaining part of the cavity, and thus formed a back to the seal. . . .

It was about eight o'clock, being after my evening's attendance at chambers, that I presented the deed in question . . . I drew it forth and presented it, saying—'There, sir! what do you think of that?'

The elder Ireland nearly collapsed from joy. Here at last was an authentic relic of the world's greatest poet! The next day he spread the good news. Scholars came to see the find and pronounced it authentic. Quite by accident, young Ireland had adorned Shakespeare's signature with a seal depicting the quintain, a tilting device used in practice by knights, and antiquarians at once proclaimed this to be the original family crest of *Shake-speare.*

How did the young rascal explain his discovery? Very simply. He had met a man in a pub who shared Ireland's obsession and who had invited the boy to help himself to a cache of old documents, but the man insisted upon remaining anonymous. The elder Ireland accepted this tale. So did most of the scholars who looked at his fabrication.

Emboldened by success, Ireland forged a "confession of faith" for Shakespeare. This also won wide acceptance in critical circles and Doctors Parr and Wharton, both noted scholars, went into ecstasies over this fabrication in which they discerned every characteristic of Shakespeare's style.

Young Ireland now gave himself up to the great bard, and out of his wonderful imagination re-created, in that year of 1795, the world of Shakespeare as it had existed two centuries earlier. From his facile pen came letters of Queen Elizabeth, Lord Essex, Francis Bacon, William Shakespeare—even the complete, original manuscript of *Lear,* with select fragments of *Hamlet.*

The British Museum displayed the rare treasures. The great James Boswell came to the Ireland home and, fortified by a tumbler of brandy, knelt and kissed the manuscript of *Lear,* and then blubbered his gratitude for the privilege. Wrote Ireland:

On the arrival of Mr. Boswell, the papers were as usual placed before him: when he commenced his examination of them; and being satisfied as to their antiquity, as far as the external appearance would attest, he proceeded to examine the style of the language from the fair transcripts made from the disguised handwriting. In this research Mr. Boswell continued for a considerable length of time, constantly speaking in favour of the internal as well as external proofs of the validity of the manuscripts. At length, finding himself rather thirsty, he requested a tumbler of warm brandy and water; which, having nearly finished, he then redoubled his praises of the manuscripts; and at length, arising from his chair, he made use of the following expression: 'Well; I shall now die contented, since I have lived to witness the present day.' Mr. Boswell then, kneeling down before the volume containing a portion of the papers, continued, "I now kiss the invaluable relics of our bard: and thanks to God that I have lived to see them!' Having kissed the volume with every token of reverence, Mr. Boswell shortly after quitted Mr. Ireland's house: and though I believe he revisited the papers on some future occasions, yet that was the only time I was honored with a sight of Mr. James Boswell.

Later, Ireland confessed: "Fired with the idea of possessing genius to which I never aspired, and full of the conviction that my style had so far imitated Shakespeare's . . . I paid little attention to the sober dictates of reason, and thus implicitly yielded myself to the snare which afterwards proved to me the source of indescribable pain and unhappiness."

The history of forgeries abounds with tales of audacious rogues—enterprising deceivers who would dare almost anything. One crafty fellow even forged a letter in which Columbus described the discovery of America, the very letter which Columbus had sealed in a cask and thrown overboard during a storm that threatened to sink his homeward-bound Santa Maria. Still, for sheer, unabashed gall the palm must go to William Henry Ireland.

Perhaps Ireland had duped so many famous scholars that he finally came to believe his own story. Their testimonials were given with such confidence that Ireland may have begun to confuse his identity with that of Shakespeare's. But whether he was supremely naïve or had merely lost touch with reality, the young rogue ultimately surrendered to the irresistible temptation—he wrote a play for Shakespeare.

This was the most daring fake of all time—an original manuscript play of William Shakespeare. Ireland created the plot, developed the characters, and wrote every line of blank verse without aid. When it was completed, he titled it *Vortigern and Rowena.* And what's more, he found a lot of people who were convinced that Shakespeare wrote it.

It was the find of the century. Covent Garden and Drury Lane vied for the honor of producing it. The manager of Drury Lane, Richardson, paid an unprecedented price for the drama—three hundred pounds down and half the receipts of the house for the first sixty nights of the performance, after expenses.

[182] Edmund Malone (1741–1812), Shakespearean scholar and literary detective of the late eighteenth century. Malone was the first to condemn William Henry Ireland's Shakespeare forgeries.

[183] William Henry Ireland (1775–1835), notorious forger of Shakespeare and other Elizabethan figures

With John Philip Kemble playing the lead, Vortigern, the play was presented under the management of Richard Brinsley Sheridan. Although the acting was excellent, the poetry was rotten and the plot was worse. In the fifth act there was this line: "And when this solemn mockery is o'er . . ." which, according to the author, convulsed the house with laughter: "No sooner was the above line uttered in the most sepulchral tone of voice possible . . . than the most discordant howl echoed from the pit that ever assailed the organs of hearing. After the lapse of ten minutes, the clamour subsided; when Mr. Kemble, having again obtained a hearing . . . in order to amuse the audience still more, redelivered the very line above quoted with even more solemn grimace than he had in the first instance displayed" (*The Confessions of William Henry Ireland,* London, 1805).

But the failure of his drama and the devastating condemnation of his forgeries by Edmund Malone did not mark the end of Ireland's deceptions. True, his forgeries were no longer accepted by scholars as authentic relics. But since the notorious fakes quickly became collector's items, there were not nearly enough *Lear*s and *Hamlet*s to supply the market, and Ireland quickly set about to meet the demand by forging his own forgeries!

Today it is quite a trick to spot an original forgery from a forged forgery. The pale ink used by Ireland and his very inaccurate Elizabethan spelling are easily recognizable. Most libraries and collectors who own examples of Ireland's work are acquainted with the spurious natures of their property.

The ultimate irony. In 1841 the last original Shakespeare signature ever to appear for sale changed hands at £145. In 1982 a small packet of Shakespeare forgeries by Ireland sold at auction fetched £12,000.

It had always been a desire of Ireland's to add Holinshed's *Chronicles* to his self-reckoned eighty or so forged signatures of Shakespeare in old books (Dr. Tannenbaum said he had located seventy-nine of them!). But "I in vain endeavoured to procure [a copy] with margins sufficiently broad to enable me to affix manuscript notes. . . ."

Nearly a century and a half ago another forger, still unidentified, was lucky enough to run into the second volume of Holinshed. This redoubtable odd volume, which the forger improved by adding a weird signature of Shakespeare on page 1437, dated back

[184] Forgeries of Shakespeare's Signature in Books

[a] In a 1577 copy of volume 2 of Holinshed's *Chronicles*

[b] Pasted in John Ward's copy of the Second Folio (1632)

[c] By William Henry Ireland in a book owned by the Rylands Library

[d] By John Jordan in a copy of Pliny's *Historie of the World* (1579). Notice the spastic tremor in the double *l* of *William* copied by Jordan from the signature on page 3 of Shakespeare's will.

[e] In a copy of the *Florentine History* of Brutus (1562)

[f] By John Jordan in Warner's *Albion's England* (1612). (Original in the British Museum.)

[g] In a copy of Rastell's *Statutes*. This forgery is clearly by the same person who signed Florio's *Montaigne*, now in the British Museum.

[h] In a copy of North's *Plutarch's Lives* (1612)

[i] In a copy of North's *Plutarch's Lives* (1579)

[j] In a copy of *Plutarch's Lives* owned by the Boston Public Library. Because Plutarch's *Lives* and Holinshed's *Chronicles* were important sources for Shakespeare, they are favorites of forgers.

[a]

[b]

[c]

[d]

[e]

[f]

[g]

[h]

[i]

[j]

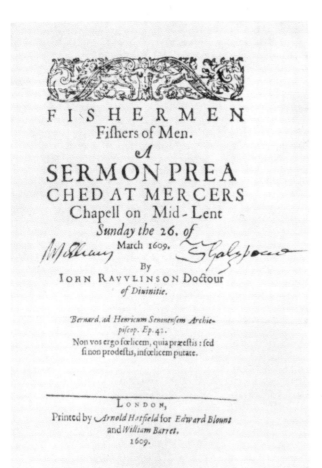

FISHERMEN
Fishers of Men.
A
SERMON PREA
CHED AT MERCERS
Chapell on Mid-Lent
Sunday the 26. of
March 1609.
By
IOHN RAVVLINSON Doctour
of Diuinitie.

Bernard. ad Henricum Senonensem Archie-
piscop. Ep. 42.
Non vos ergo fœlicem, quia præestis : sed
si non prodestis, infœlicem putate.

LONDON,
Printed by *Arnold Hatfield* for *Edward Blount*
and *William Barret.*
1609.

WILLIAM HENRY IRELAND FORGERIES
EXECUTED ABOUT 1795

[187] *(Top):* Script Ireland invented for his bogus letters and documents of Elizabeth I and *(bottom)* the actual alphabet the queen used. Note the delicacy and beauty of her italic hand. This chart was worked out by Edmund Malone.

[188] Holographic letter of Shakespeare's patron, the Earl of Southampton

[189] Ireland forgery (about 1794) of a letter by the Early of Southampton.

[185] Forged Shakespeare signature by William Henry Ireland in an old pamphlet. Ireland created scores of such forgeries. Notice how he imitated the spastic *l* (the first *l* in William) found in the final signature Shakespeare made on his will, written when the poet was dying.

[186] Forgery by William Henry Ireland of the first page of the manuscript of Shakespeare's *King Lear*

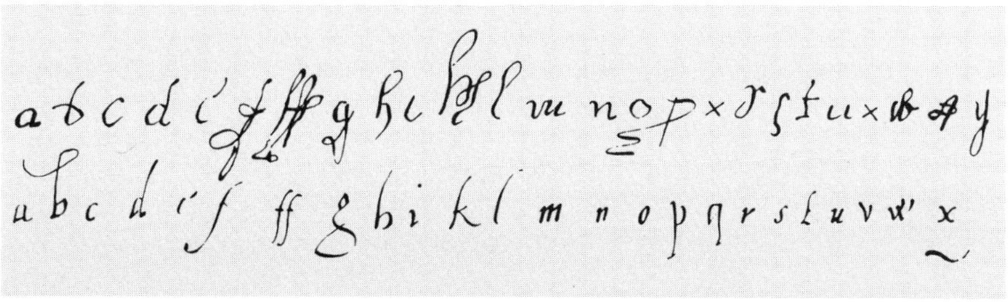

[187]

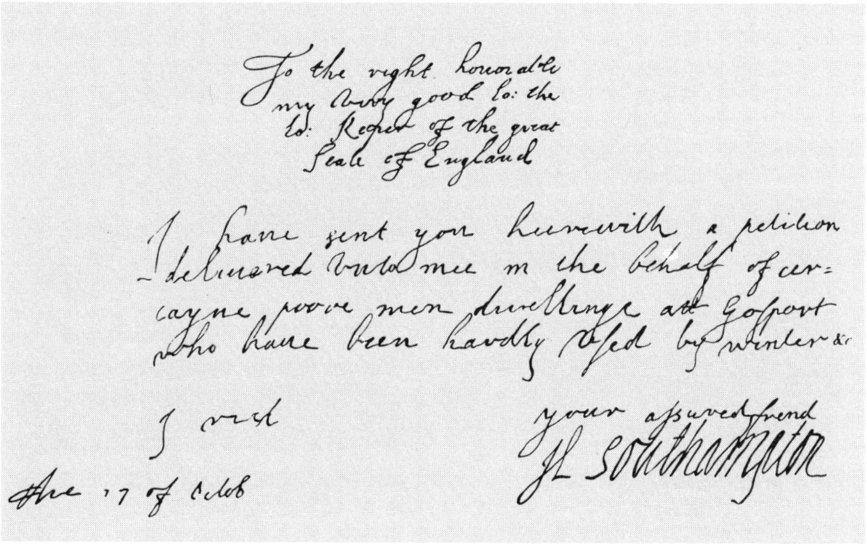

To the right honorable
my very good lo: the
Lo: Keeper of the great
Seale of England

I have sent you herewith a petition
delivered vnto mee in the behalf of cer-
cayne poore men dwellinge att Gosport
who have been hardly vsed by winter &c

I rest

your assured frend
H: Southampton

the 17 of Octob

[188]
[189]

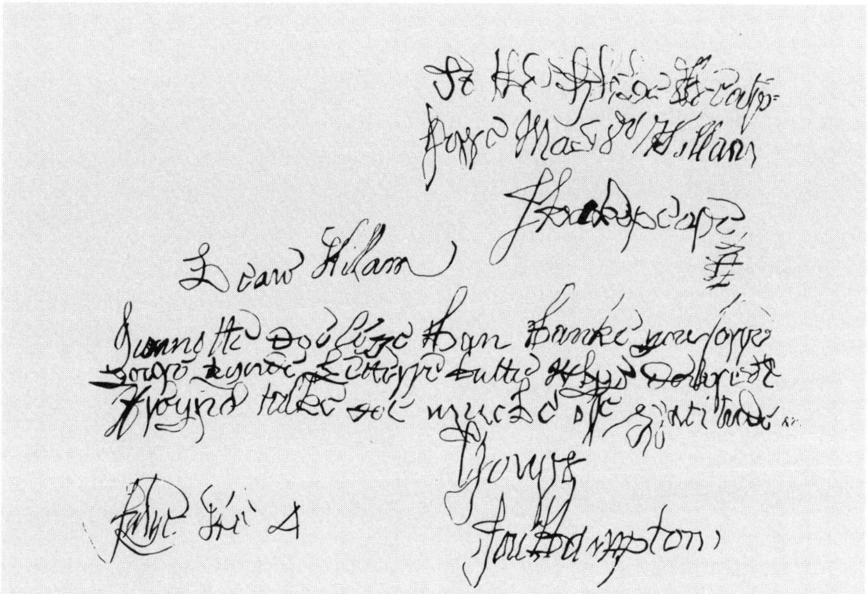

239

to 1577. It was sold by the book dealer Elkins, on Lombard Street in London, together with Volume I from another set, to Thomas Powell. Powell noticed that the profusion of notes that cascaded down the margins were mainly concerned with the reign of Richard III. The margins of the book had been trimmed in rebinding. The new owner discovered the signature *W. Shakspere ejus* and suggested that the trimmed portion of the margin had contained the word *liber,* so that the original signature had read (in translation), *William Shakspere his book.* I have not looked at the marginal annotations, but if they are in the same hand as the signature, I can dub them forgeries without a second thought. The alleged signature of Shakespeare looks nothing at all like the poet's writing. Not a single letter of the name bears any similarity to his script.

In the great Folger Library in Washington, D.C., is a water-damaged volume, *Archaionomia,* a paraphrase of Anglo-Saxon laws by William Lambarde. Inside is a note: "Mr Wm Shakespeare lived at No 1 Little Crown Street Westminster. NB near Dorset steps St James Park." The note, it is said, is penned in an eighteenth-century hand. Also in the book, on the title page, just above the top of the ornamental border and extending into it, is a very pale signature that appears to read, "W. Shakspere," but it is so hard to make out that I can't be sure of the spelling *(illus. 190).* However, the pale ink is not pale enough to conceal the bastard birth of the signature. The *W* is incorrectly formed. The *S* seems to be an effort by a writer unfamiliar with the secretary hand: he merely pieced it together, penning a modern *S,* then adding at the top an adventitious stroke. The *h* and *a* are not joined by a swinging loop in Shakespeare's usual manner, and both are laboriously and clumsily penned. The writing suggests the fabrications John Jordan executed around 1790. However, the script was tested at the National Archives and the results conclusively established that the ink was of the Elizabethan era. My opinion is that the signature is a forgery, or else was written by someone with a name similar to Shakespeare's.

Whenever a forgery is embellished with a romantic tale about its origin, especially a tale enveloped in mystery, it has a special appeal for gullible collectors and archivists. In 1926, an "occasional gardener" named H. C. Rogers, of Langley, Buckinghamshire, England, discovered an ancient map in the bottom of an old chest. The map was accompanied by a letter dated 1818 that described how some of Shakespeare's original manuscripts were buried to keep them from falling into the hands of the forger William Henry Ireland. The map showed exactly where the treasure was buried. Rogers dug at the indicated spot and uncovered a casket containing manuscripts which, if genuine, would be worth many millions of dollars.

It was a sensational find. The only hitch was that, as genealogists were quick to point out, Shakespeare's granddaughter, Elizabeth Hall, from whom the casket had descended to Rogers, had never had any children.

Did this put an end to the hoax? Not a bit of it! Despite the clear evidence of fraud, a lot of people remained convinced that the bogus manuscripts were genuine.

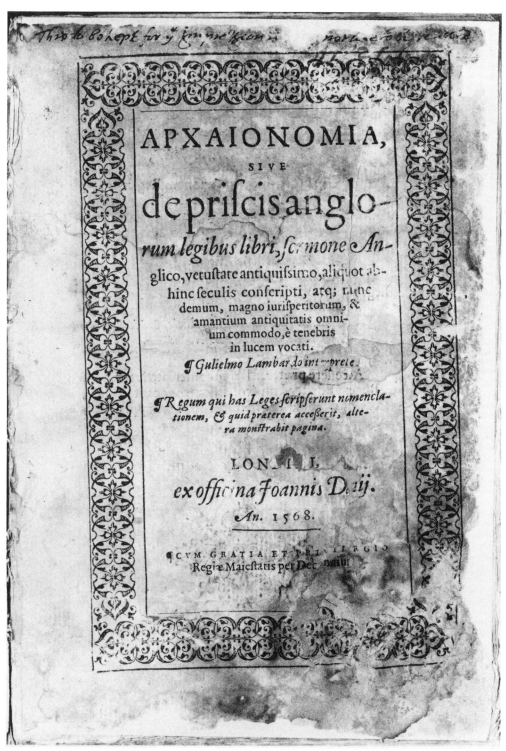

APXAIONOMIA,
SIVE
de priscis anglo-
rum legibus libri, sermone An-
glico, vetustate antiquissimo, aliquot ab-
hinc seculis conscripti, atq; nunc
demum, magno iurisperitorum, &
amantium antiquitatis omni-
um commodo, è tenebris
in lucem vocati.

¶ Gulielmo Lambardo interprete.

¶ Regum qui has Leges scripserunt nomencla-
tionem, & quid praeterea accesserit, alte-
ra monstrabit pagina.

LONDINI,
ex officina Joannis Daij.
An. 1568.

¶ CVM GRATIA ET PRIVILEGIO
Regiae Maiestatis per Decennium

[190] Forgery in a copy of William Lambarde's *Archaionomia* (1568).
The faint ink of the fabricated signature is partially visible at the top
right of the page, slightly impinging upon the ornamental border.

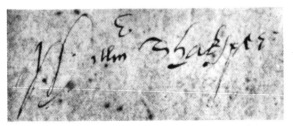

[191] Forgery in a copy of Florio's translation of Montaigne's *Essays*

[192] The Montaigne forgery magnified to reveal all its defects. This celebrated fake was done by the same forger who wrote Shakespeare's signature in Rastell's *Statutes*.

Among the ersatz treasures of the British Museum is a somewhat battered copy of Montaigne's *Essays* "Englished" by John Florio. Its loose flyleaf is adorned with a strange signature of Shakespeare that has, over the past two centuries, won accolades from many scholars (*illus. 191*). The Florio book was published in 1603, and its first known owner was the Reverend Mr. Edward Patteson, of Smethwick in Staffordshire, not far from Shakespeare's birthplace. Patteson used to show it to friends ("before 1780") as a curiosity, never failing to note that the signature "challenges and defies suspicion." Students of *The Tempest* may recall that Shakespeare pilfered a passage from Montaigne and transformed it into a dialogue of rich poetry. This fact would naturally enhance the value of this quaint copy.

The book attracted a lot of attention right from the start. It was sold at auction by Evans's of Pall Mall to Pickering, a bookseller, on May 14, 1838, for £100. The enormous price was no doubt inspired by the reassuring tale of its provenance. Pickering sold it at a £20 advance to the British Museum. The next morning one of the London papers announced that the nation had just bought "Shakespeare's own copy of Marmontel's *Tales,* with his autograph." Only three years later, the book was something to brag about. A member of the Corporation of the City of London boasted that "the city of London might be proud to have in its library the real signature of William Shakespeare, the immortal author of *Venice Preserved.*"

It would be hard to find an autograph more deserving of such unintentional gibes. Yet I must mention that the signature was immediately acclaimed and authenticated by Charles Knight, editor of the popular pictorial edition of Shakespeare, and Sir Frederick Madden, a distinguished scholar, whose sober *Observations on an Autograph of Shakspere* (1838) it would be advisable to peruse only after a few martinis. So enthusiastic was Sir Frederick that he opted at once for a change of spelling in the poet's name: "To these five [genuine signatures] we have now to add the autograph before us, in Florio's volume, which so unquestionably decides in favour of Shakspere, that in this manner I shall beg

242

leave to write it; since I know no reason why we should not sooner take the poet's own authority in the point, than that of his friends or printers." Other scholars rallied to Madden's support. W. C. Hazlitt, a most competent scholar, cast a vote in favor of authenticity. Sir Sidney Lee vacillated and Hamilton Wright Mabie said: "Maybe."

Before I disembowel this celebrated signature, I'd like to quote Samuel A. Tannenbaum on the subject. You will perhaps recall that Tannenbaum and Edward Maunde Thompson had an ongoing feud over the authenticity of the three pages in *The Play of Sir Thomas More* that were attributed to Shakespeare. The battle was renewed by Dr. Tannenbaum when Sir Edward, after an extended analysis of the signature in Florio's *Montaigne,* declared it an "undoubted forgery." Tannenbaum's defense of the signature, *Reclaiming One of Shakspere's Signatures* (1925), runs to twenty-five pages. The doctor offered an eloquent argument:

The pictorial impression made by 'Montaigne' is one of unquestionable genuineness; there is about it that naturalness, boldness, abandon, freedom, directness, straightforwardness, which one associates with genuineness. The writing strokes have the smoothness, directness, uniformity and continuity of genuineness. There is no sign of the hesitation, deliberation, doubt, patching, mending, or drawing which we associate with forgery and which are so strikingly and unequivocally apparent in the abbreviated 'signature' in the Bodleian Library's copy of the 1502 edition of Ovid's *Metamorphoses.* The 'Montaigne' not only looks genuine but does not even remotely suggest that it might have been modelled on or copied from another signature; it is sufficiently unlike the known genuine signatures not to be an imitation of them, and yet it is sufficiently like them to give an impression of genuineness. There are none of those suspicious and unnatural joinings, unusual stops, artificial shadings, concern about imperfections resulting from failure of the writing movements to register, and fear of introducing new features, which characterize a forgery. And it must be especially noted that the shading—one of the most significant elements in any writing—has the smoothness and directness that are infallible characteristics of genuineness. In speed, movement, pen pressure, and line quality, there is that uniformity and normalcy throughout which are never found in forged writing.

These are cogent reasons for accepting the Montaigne signature, or any other signature, as genuine. They fail only because the signature is not in Shakespeare's handwriting. The forgery is based upon the signature at the bottom of page 2 of the will. The *W* is much too large for the rest of the signature. It falls far below the *i* of *Willm* and rises far above the *S* of *Shakspere.* The terminal downstroke of the *W* even sweeps under the initial in a manner unlike any capital letter that Shakespeare ever penned. The *illm* is defective on several counts. Nearly always, when Shakespeare wrote a double-*l,* the second fell a little below the first. In this case, the second *l* is much taller than the first. There is a spastic jerkiness to the *l*'s that we find only in the last signatures of Shakespeare signed on his will. The *h* in *Shakspere* is badly formed and is not in position to swing its lower loop up to join the *a,* as would be the case if Shakespeare had written it. The *a* is badly formed, and the terminal downstroke should hug the oval of the *a,* but instead there is a clear space between the downstroke and the rest of the *a.* The *k* and medial *s* are quite different from Shakespeare's. The *s* should descend in a straight, unwavering

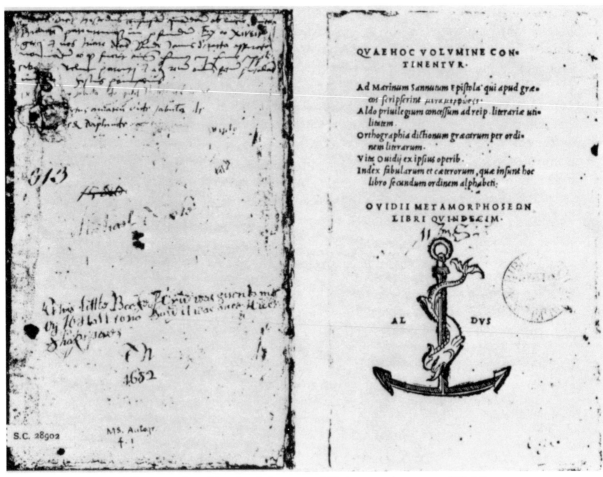

[193] Forgery of an abbreviated signature of Shakespeare in a copy of Ovid's *Metamorphoses* (at top of anchor). On the left-hand page, two thirds of the way down, is a prior owner's forged note.

[194] Photograph of the forgery in Ovid of Shakespeare's abbreviated signature

[195] Forgery in Ovid magnified to reveal its numerous defects

line, whereas the forger's *s* is tremulous and bends back at the base like a hockey stick. The *p* is totally unlike any *p* that the poet ever wrote. Its tail is much too elongated. The final *re* of the signature is malformed, especially the *r*. Apparently, the forger was not familiar with the secretary script and did not know precisely how the letters should be written. My opinion is that the signature in Florio's *Montaigne* is a forgery.

Almost tied with the Montaigne signature in notoriety is the alleged signature of the poet in a 1502 Aldine edition in Latin of Ovid's *Metamorphoses*. I have no doubt that Shakespeare read this Latin classic, but not this particular copy. The signature of Shakespeare is abbreviated to *Wm Shre* and appears on the title page just above the famous anchor of Aldus. On the opposite page is a crude imitation of the secretary script that reads: "This little Book of Ovid was given to me by W. Hall who sayd it was once Will. Shakspers. T.N. 1682" *(illus. 193)*.

In *A Catalogue of the Shakespeare Exhibition Held in the Bodleian Library,* the bogus signature of item 105 is illustrated under the heading "The Supposed Shakespeare Autograph." According to the Bodleian, the book was bought at a London auction in 1864, when the stock of a bookseller named W. H. Elkins was sold. The catalogue reads:

In favour of the signature are the considerations (1) that he would be an exceptionally bold forger who ventured on an abbreviated signature—a rare occurrence in Shakespeare's time, though found in such books as the University Verses of the period; (2) that the forgery (if it be one) would seem to be earlier than the golden age which began about 1760, before which scientific fraud, such as could deceive a critic of Victorian times, is hardly found; (3) that an early forger could hardly have had sight of the genuine signatures attached to the Will of 1616, which alone (of the six undoubted signatures) resemble the present one. Sir Edward Maunde Thompson has decided that both signature and note are forgeries, but until his proofs are published it is still allowable to regard the signature as perhaps genuine.

The signature was authenticated by Dr. Von F. A. Leo, in the *Jahrbuch der Shakespeare-Gesellschaft* (Band XVI, 1881). Dr. Leo, the editor of this prestigious yearbook, subsequently (1882) disputed J. C. Jeaffreson's assertion that Shakespeare's will was holographic.

The abbreviated signature in the *Ovid* book is a credit to the ingenuity of the forger, who, by writing only a few letters of Shakespeare's name, risked less chance of exposure. Unfortunately, he used as a model the script of the dying poet, copying the name almost without change from the signature at the end of page 3 of the will. The Bodleian explains this by noting that the signature was signed late in life. Much too late, I fear. My opinion is that it is a forgery.

As long ago as January 1917, Edward Maunde Thompson poked fun at these fakes in *The Library:* "Of the many spurious signatures of Shakespeare there are two [the *Montaigne* and *Ovid*] which have enjoyed a longer career than their fellows owing to their good fortune in having found hospitality and a lasting abode in two of our great public libraries. In the opinion of some they still hold up their heads as genuine autographs; and they may continue to do so, endowed, as such productions often are, with vigorous constitutions that defy attacks of criticism and only succumb in extreme old age."

Quite right, Sir Edward! These abominable fakes have lived longer than Old Parr. Many of you, I am sure, are weary of their false faces peering from almost every biography of Shakespeare. I therefore pronounce them both officially dead and urge that their respective owners launch them into Valhalla with a funeral pyre in the old Viking manner.

XIX

A SUMMARY OF THE EVIDENCE

I had described only a few of the discoveries chronicled in this book to a noted expert on Shakespeare when he interrupted me: "Frankly, I'm skeptical."

This was precisely the reaction I'd expected. I sensed that the expert looked upon me as an interloper; not even an establishment hanger-on but a rank iconoclast bent on toppling the tenets based upon more than two centuries of scholarship.

Not a bit of it! Most of the statements in this book are based upon my own field of expertise—handwriting. As a historian, however, I have reserved the privilege of occasionally probing into Shakespeare's life. Whenever I have trod in other areas, I have qualified my remarks and made clear that my views are speculations. This is not an unusual posture. Most scholarly views of Shakespeare are admittedly pure hypothecations and often change from generation to generation.

It is amazing, I think you'll agree, that no professional handwriting expert has ever before made an examination of the Shakespeare documents. True, a few museum or university paleographers, specialists in deciphering old scripts, and a few professorial dabblers in autographs have reconnoitered some of the documentary evidence on Shakespeare's life and writings. But these distinguished scholars were not handwriting experts who earned their living year after year by examining and authenticating tens of thousands of documents.

Consider the necessary credentials of the professional handwriting expert, of whom there are fewer than a dozen in the world. He must have a rich knowledge of history and literature. He must have an intimate acquaintance with old watermarks, ink, paper and, above all, the handwriting of noted persons in all fields. He must be able to read difficult scripts speedily and judge quickly and accurately the authenticity of the documents before him. He must know how to spot and expose a forgery at a glance. He cannot afford to make errors, either, because his clients—archivists, curators, librarians, authors and other specialists—would quickly discover his fallibility. His talent for making swift and correct judgments is partly instinct and partly the result of decades of daily experience in the examination of old handwriting.

Before embarking upon the examination of Shakespeare's own handwriting, I offered, in Chapter II, a brief review of the various types of Elizabethan scripts to give some idea of the handwriting styles of the poet's era. I hoped to demonstrate beyond question that Shakespeare's chirography is very different from that of any of his noted contemporaries.

Another necessary preliminary was to show conclusively that the handwriting of the same individual in the Elizabethan age often changed dramatically in different documents, as demonstrated in the handwriting of Elizabeth I and Sir Francis Bacon (Lord Verulam). I also tried to prove that the variations in the six previously known signatures of Shakespeare are not so great or so unusual as is generally supposed by illustrating similar—and even more dramatic—variant examples of the signatures of Napoleon, Kennedy and Nixon. I might also have included Hitler, for his signature varied from a huge, audacious, paranoid scrawl to a tiny, unreadable blot, not unlike a crushed insect.

I digressed briefly to demolish the claims of Bacon to the authorship of Shakespeare's plays. The Bacon chapter, between you and me, was really designed to establish the authenticity of the six previously known signatures of Shakespeare and pave the way for a discussion of his will.

In the first chapter of this book, I explained how I accidentally discovered that Shakespeare's will, long believed to be in the handwriting of his attorney, Francis Collins, or Collins's anonymous scrivener, is actually in the poet's hand. The will itself is incredibly mangled and mixed up, probably because Shakespeare was dying when he completed it: The poet makes the same bequest to two different persons, forgets the name of his nephew, alludes to his granddaughter as his niece, and so on. All these blunders were previously blamed upon Collins. The plain truth is that there is not, and never was, any evidence that either Collins or his scrivener wrote the will; yet many biographers have uncritically repeated this groundless assertion generation after generation. It has been repeated so often that even intelligent scholars have come to believe it. There were, I must mention, a few bardophiles who thought the will was holographic but lacked the evidence to prove it. So that you can judge the handwriting for yourself, I reproduced examples of Francis Collins's writing—totally unlike that in the will—and the alleged handwriting of Collins's clerk, also very different from the script in the will.

In Chapter VI, I furnished a chart showing that the handwriting in the will, long regarded as very different from the six known signatures, could, in fact, be matched very closely with the script of the signatures. I reconstructed the six signatures with letters and portions of words taken from the body of the will so that you could be see how closely the writing in the will resembles that of the six signatures.

Even this powerful evidence that the will was in Shakespeare's hand could not be considered unchallengeable until the script was matched with other writing of the poet's.

The chart in Chapter IX shows some key words from the will in juxtaposition with the same common words from the three pages generally believed to have been written by Shakespeare in *The Booke of Sir Thomas More,* a prompt book dating from about the year 1593. Although more than two decades separate these two specimens of handwriting, I think you may agree they are virtually identical and were written by the same person. In 1916, and more expansively in 1923, Edward Maunde Thompson determined *almost* conclusively that the three pages from *More* were in Shakespeare's hand. His belief was bolstered by the investigations of his contemporaries, R. W. Chambers and J. Dover Wilson. To strengthen the evidence that the poet wrote both the will and the three pages from *More,* I set up twenty-six lines in alternate four-line excerpts from the *More* prompt book (1593) and the will (1616), so that you could get the feel of the writing and see for yourself that the script is the same in both documents.

May I here digress and point out that the word *feel*, by which I mean to indicate the general over-all appearance of handwriting, is an old term that has been current among manuscript experts for over a hundred years. I suspect it is partly because the earlier investigators into the Shakespearean documents judged possible authenticity by a study of the formation of individual words, and not by feel, that they failed to learn what Shakespeare's handwriting was really like.

In Chapter VII, I proposed several theories, not one of them provable but all of them tenable. The first is that Shakespeare, as an afterthought, gave to the actors Burbage, Heminges and Condell a mourning ring for each, not as a memento of his long friendship with them, but as a token of gratitude for their willingness to undertake the preparation and publication of Shakespeare's works after his death. The second unusual bequest, much wrangled over by biographers of the poet, was the gift of his second-best bed to his wife. I believe this bequest was made because Shakespeare's daughter Judith, whom I think the poet despised, would have seized it for her new home if Shakespeare hadn't specifically left it to his wife. The interlinear words making this bequest were probably the last words the poet ever wrote, for they are wretchedly penned and the letters quiver vehemently. The final bequest was the result of slashing out of the will the name of a beneficiary, an old friend of Shakespeare's who had got involved in a financial peculation. I wished to establish that Shakespeare was a deeply religious man of impeccable morals, who was inclined to be judgmental.

A segment in this book that is certain to be controversial is Chapter VIII, in which I speculate on the possibility that Shakespeare was murdered. There is considerable evidence to support this speculation. As a very careful examination of the first page of the poet's will shows, the first half is penned in Shakespeare's familiar, easy-flowing script, but the handwriting begins to deteriorate as it passes the midpage mark. The poet makes errors in bequests and his pen blots and smears as he writes. Obviously he is in pain or in great mental distress. Two-thirds of the way down the page the poet is so unhinged that he leaves a trail of smudgy ink strokes. He crosses out, rewrites, blots and finally abruptly stops in the middle of a thought. When he again picks up his pen, his script is that of a broken old man—shaky, hard to read, smaller than usual, cramped. My suspicion that Shakespeare had suffered a stroke while rewriting his will led me to consult my old friend, Dr. Michael Baden, former chief medical examiner of New York City and often regarded as the world's leading medical forensic expert. He confirmed my view and ventured the opinion that Shakespeare had either injured his brain in a fall while celebrating in the alleged "merry meeting" with Ben Jonson and Michael Drayton or had been poisoned by arsenic. Dr. Baden stated that page 1 of the will followed precisely the pattern of notes left by suicides who died by poison. Subsequently, Dr. Baden showed the first page of the will to two other noted brain experts, both of whom concurred with his opinion that the writer of the will had suffered a cerebral stroke while penning it.

The evidence for Shakespeare's murder hinges upon the fact that the poet was rewriting the will to cut out a major bequest (that of his valuable silver) to his daughter Judith, and to render it impossible for his new son-in-law, Thomas Quiney, a ne'er-do-well and seducer, to wrench a single farthing from his estate. A vintner, Quiney had an unsavory reputation. He had almost certainly married Judith for her money. He had easy access to arsenic, known in Shakespeare's day as "the inheritance powder," ample opportunity, and a strong motive to kill Shakespeare, as did Judith. Shakespeare had perhaps announced that he was changing his will and leaving a minimum bequest to Judith. Quiney had gone into debt just before marrying Judith, in February 1616 (probably without Shakespeare's knowledge or permission). Quiney likely counted on getting a loan or an inheritance from Shakespeare. His judgmental father-in-law no doubt turned against him when he discovered that Quiney had got another woman pregnant before marrying Judith. If Shakespeare rewrote his will and cut Judith out, Quiney would be ruined.

To support the evidence that Shakespeare was poisoned or suffered a cerebral stroke while writing his last testament, I have provided you with a chart showing his handwriting in the will of identical words before and after the stroke. The difference in the scripts is appalling.

I also discuss my opinion that Quiney murdered by arsenic poisoning his former mistress, Margaret Wheeler, who died with her infant during childbirth in February 1616.

Once Shakespeare's handwriting in his will and in the three pages of *Thomas More* was positively identified it was not difficult to discover additional examples of his script, especially as I enjoyed an incredible run of serendipity. It was as though the documents written by Shakespeare were deliberately planted in my path. I am almost embarrassed to claim any sort of credit for discovering them.

There has long ranged a dispute (going back to Edmund Malone, the Shakespearean expert of the last two decades of the eighteenth century) as to whether Shakespeare was apprenticed to an attorney when a youth. A barrister himself, Malone felt positive that Shakespeare had studied law. Evidence to support this opinion, discussed in Chapter X, cropped up in the form of two important documents signed by Shakespeare: the first is the Welcombe Enclosure Agreement (October 28, 1614), by which the poet protected his rights against the enclosure of Welcombe township commons. In this case Shakespeare evidently acted as his own attorney. The Welcombe Enclosure document, the more important of the two, is clearly penned in Shakespeare's script, and docketed by a clerk as a copy, probably indicating that it was one of two or three such complete documents, all signed, as was this one, by four witnesses and then distributed to the principals in the Welcombe case. In my opinion, Shakespeare composed as well as penned this document. A second document, the Quiney-Mountford property transfer, appears to indicate that the poet acted as attorney for Elizabeth Quiney on December 4, 1612.

A spectacular trio of documents that opens fresh avenues of study on Shakespeare comprises the poet's applications to the College of Heralds on behalf of his father, John Shakespeare, for a coat of arms. The three applications, two dated 1596 and one dated 1599, are in Shakespeare's rapid-fire script. Despite the sloppy writing and the abbreviations, you should easily recognize the script as Shakespeare's if you examine the chart comparing key words from the applications with identical key words from the poet's will. The official grant of arms was apparently made to John Shakespeare and subsequently to his son. The data supplied in the applications was in part false, but it was customary at the time to exaggerate in such applications.

Many scholars have contended that the coat of arms applications were prepared on Shakespeare's behalf by Sir William Dethick, Garter-King-of-Arms at the College of Heralds. As you will see from the reproduction of a letter of Dethick's, there is not the slightest similarity between Dethick's script and the script in the applications.

One of the most significant things about the coat of arms applications is that each contains a sketch by Shakespeare, suggesting that the poet was a skilled amateur artist.

I discussed, too, a most interesting drawing of John Shakespeare's coat of arms, allegedly by Ralph Brooke, the York herald, an enemy of Dethick's and thus, presumably, of Shakespeare's also. Under the sketch appears a hand-lettered label, "Shakspear ye Player." The lettering in the label appears to be quite modern. It is certainly not Brooke's (for evidence, see the letter written by Brooke). The designation of the recipient as a "player" is quite incorrect. The award was made to John Shakespeare, who was a bailiff of Stratford. The sketch is extremely crude and is, in my opinion, a forgery, probably by John Payne Collier.

The sketches made by Shakespeare of his proposed coat of arms (a falcon fluttering his wings and shaking a spear clasped in one claw) suggest another facet of the poet's genius. In an attack upon Shakespeare, Robert Greene, a contemporary dramatist who died in 1592, dubbed the poet a "factotum." This is probably a correct appellation. Shakespeare generally took only small parts in his plays, but it was not because he lacked acting ability. It was likely because he was the director or assistant director, composer of drum and trumpet music, and designer of props and costumes for each of his plays. There exists a rare, undated sketch depicting a scene from *Titus Andronicus*, a drama attributed to Shakespeare and certainly in part written by him. Known as the "Longleat manuscript," the sketch is accompanied by a mixed-up text from the play, with two previously unknown lines. Scholars had previously dated the sketch 1595, because of a marginal forgery thus dated, and ascribed the page to Henry Peacham, an artist of the Elizabethan era whose forged signature also appears in the margin. After dispensing with these two misleading clues—the bogus date and the bogus signature—I dated the sketch around 1592 and attributed the variant text to the use of an earlier, unknown manuscript of the play. Scholars have long debated the purpose of this drawing and text. After presenting all the significant scholarly opinions on the subject, I ventured my own opinion that the sketch was made to illustrate for other acting companies who rented the drama the type of costume to be worn by the players. I attributed the sketch to Shakespeare, who, as we know from his heraldic applications, was an excellent artist. In my opinion, he probably designed the costumes for all his plays. There is one of the minor actors in the *Titus Andronicus* sketch who looks remarkably like the poet and I speculated that it might be a self-portrait.

Chapter XIII contains is a lengthy discussion of the books used by Shakespeare and the three volumes that are presently known to have survived from his library. Very possibly more such books will turn up, since we now know what the poet's handwriting looks like. The problem of identifying his books is slightly aggravated because he apparently did not sign them, except when testing a new quill or with a curious monogram that appears in two volumes he owned or used. Also described is the second edition of Holinshed's *Chronicles*, with its numerous annotations in Shakespeare's hand showing how he utilized this book for his British history plays.

In the 1930s the Countess de Chambrun, a Shakespearean enthusiast, identified the paper cover of a handwritten volume known as the *Northumberland Manuscript* as being in the hand of Shakespeare. The cover bears a number of florid practice signatures of the poet, together with several monograms that are almost identical with the monograms in Shakespeare's copy of Holinshed. Chambrun's ascription was disputed by E. K. Chambers and other leading experts. However, the *Northumberland* signatures of Shakespeare are very similar to signatures of the poet in other documents. Further, there are in the *Northumberland Manuscript* two pages in the poet's hand. The vast importance of the fifty-year-old research by the Countess de Chambrun is that it enables us to link Shakespeare with Bacon, for some of the writings in the *Northumberland Manuscript* are essays by Bacon, written in a clerical hand. These essays bear manuscript changes and corrections in Shakespeare's script. Why should Shakespeare be correcting Bacon's essays? Probably because he was employed as a secretary or assistant to Bacon during the period between 1592 and 1594, when the theaters were closed because of riots and plague. Shakespeare's patron was Southampton, and Southampton was an intimate friend of Bacon's patron and employer, Lord Essex. Ben Jonson also worked as a Latin translator for Bacon, who had a regular "literary workshop" at his disposal. Thus it was logical that the unemployed actor from Stratford should find employment as an assistant to Bacon. I was very punctilious about identifying the handwriting of Shakespeare in the *Northumberland Manuscript*, using a comparison with identical words from the will. You can see how little the poet's Sunday-go-to-meeting script changed in the course of more than two decades. The corrections in the essays of Bacon (and in other writings in the volume) are definitely in Shakespeare's hand, and I have linked them plainly to identical words in other documents of the poet. I suspect that an investigation of the manuscripts of Bacon, of which a fairly large number survive, will reveal other papers in Shakespeare's hand. The question now is not, "Did Bacon write Shakespeare's plays?" but "Did Shakespeare write Bacon's essays?"

After a discussion of the vagaries and quirks of Shakespeare's handwriting in Chapter XV, I turn to the subject of how the poet's text was mutilated by his printers. Professor J. Dover Wilson discovered many years ago that scholars can uncover textual errors by compositors through a study of Shakespeare's script. I had the advantage of many new examples of Shakespeare's writing and was able to record some additional letters that could easily be mixed up by printers. These are illustrated so that you can perceive for yourself the confusing similarity of many of the poet's letters, a similarity that led to outrageous typographical blunders, many not yet detected. I ventured the opinion that the "bad" quartos, those early printings of Shakespeare's plays that are rife with errors and omissions (thought by many scholars to have been compiled from shorthand notes illicitly taken down during performances or recorded from the memories of the actors), were possibly printed from early, unrevised drafts of the plays by Shakespeare or from the early texts of the plays as written by lesser dramatists before Shakespeare revised them.

The numerous forgeries of Shakespeare's signature are dealt with in Chapter XVIII. About most of them there is a unanimous concurrence among scholars, but a few, like the atrocious fakes in a copy of Montaigne's *Essays* and in Ovid's *Metamorphoses*, have been so widely acclaimed that they called for a demolition rather than just a curt dismissal. I trust we will not again have to look at their false faces whenever we open a new book about Shakespeare.

Let me conclude with the fervent hope that the years to come will bring a great renaissance in Shakespearean scholarship.

BIBLIOGRAPHY

GENERAL INTEREST

Adams, Joseph Quincy. *A Life of William Shakespeare.* Boston, 1923.

Altick, Richard D. *The Scholar Adventurers.* New York, 1950.

Aubrey, John. *Brief Lives.* London: The Folio Society, 1975.

Brooke, C. F. Tucker. *Shakespeare of Stratford: A Handbook for Students.* New Haven, 1926.

Chambers, E. K. *William Shakespeare: A Study of Facts and Problems.* 2 vols. Oxford University Press, Oxford, 1930.

Chute, Marchette. *Shakespeare of London.* New York, 1949.

Fido, Martin. *Shakespeare.* Maplewood, N.J., 1978.

Granville-Barker, H., and G. B. Harrison. *A Companion to Shakespeare Studies.* New York, 1934.

Halliwell-Phillipps, James O. *The Life of Shakespeare.* London, 1848.

———. *Outlines of the Life of Shakespeare.* 2 vols. 7th ed., London, 1887.

Hotson, J. Leslie. *I, William Shakespeare.* 1938.

Lee, Sidney. *A Life of William Shakespeare.* New York, 1899.

Lewis, Benjamin R. *The Shakespeare Documents.* 2 vols. Stanford, 1940.

Majault, Joseph. *Shakespeare.* Geneva, 1969.

Neilson, William A., and Thorndike, Askley H. *The Facts About Shakespeare.* New York, 1916.

Nicoll, Allardyce, ed. *Shakespeare Survey 4.* Cambridge: Cambridge University Press, 1951.

Norman, Charles. *The Muses' Darling.* Drexel Hill, Pa., 1950.

———. *So Worthy a Friend: William Shakespeare.* New York, 1947.

Pearson, Hesketh. *A Life of Shakespeare.* New York, 1961.

Quennell, Peter. *Shakespeare.* Cleveland, 1963.

Rowse, A. L. *Shakespeare the Elizabethan.* New York, 1977.

———. *William Shakespeare: A Biography.* New York, 1963.

Schoenbaum, S. *Shakespeare: The Globe and the World.* New York, 1979.

———. *Shakespeare's Lives.* New York: Oxford University Press, 1970.

———. *William Shakespeare: A Documentary Life.* New York, 1975.

Waleffe, Pierre. *Shakespeare.* Geneva, 1969.

Wells, Stanley. *Shakespeare: An Illustrated Dictionary.* New York, 1978.

Williams, Frayne. *Mr. Shakespeare of The Globe.* New York, 1941.

Wright, Louis B. *The Folger Library. Two Decades of Growth: An Informal Account.* Charlottesville, Va. 1968.

HANDWRITING AND FACSIMILES

Astle, Thomas. *The Origin and Progress of Handwriting.* n.p., 1784.

Dawson, Giles E., and Kennedy-Skipton, Laetitia. *Elizabethan Handwriting, 1500–1650. A Manual.* New York, 1966.

Flower, Desmond, and Munby, A. N. L. *English Political Autographs.* London, 1958.

Garnett, Richard, and Gosse, Edmund. *English Literature: An Illustrated Record,* vol. I. London and New York, 1903.

Greenwood, George. *Shakespere's Handwriting.* New York, 1920.

Greg, Walter Wilson. *English Literary Autographs, 1550–1650.* 3 vols. London, 1932.

Hector, L. C. *The Handwriting of English Documents.* London, 1958.

Madden, Frederic. *Observations on an Autograph of Shakespeare.* London, 1838.

Nichols, John Gough. *Autographs of Royal, Noble, Learned, and Remarkable Personages.* 1829.

Plimpton, George A. *The Education of Shakespeare.* London and New York, 1933.

Rawlins, Raymond. *Stein and Day Book of World Autographs.* New York, 1978.

Rosenbach, A. S. W. *Books and Bidders.* Boston, 1927.

Tannenbaum, Samuel A. *The Handwriting of the Renaissance.* New York, 1930.

Thurston, Herbert. "Shakespeare's Handwriting." *Month* 123 (London, 1914).

Wise, George. *Autograph of William Shakespeare.* Reprint. New York, 1974.

Wright, Thomas. *Court Hand Restored.* New edition. n.p., 1891.

THE BACON CONTROVERSY

Bacon, Delia. *The Philosophy of the Plays of Shakspere Unfolded.* Preface by Nathaniel Hawthorne. London, 1857.

Bostelmann, Lewis F. *Rutland.* New York, 1911.

Brune, Clarence Marion. *Baconian Theory Refuted. Shakespeare's Use of Legal Terms.* London, 1914.

Castle, Edward J. *Shakespeare, Bacon, Jonson and Greene.* London, 1897.

Durning-Lawrence, Sir Edwin. *Bacon Is Shakespeare.* London and New York, 1910.

Eagle, Roderick. *Forgers and Forgeries.* The Bacon Society. no place, no date.

Ewen, C. L'Estrange. *Shakespeare No Poet?* London, 1938.

Owen, Orville W. *The Tragical Historie of Our Late Brother Robert, Earl of Essex, by the Author of Hamlet, Richard III, Othello, As You Like It, etc. . . . Deciphered from the Works of Sir Francis Bacon.* Detroit, circa 1895.

Rendall, Gerald H. *Shake-speare: Handwriting and Spelling.* no place, no date.

SHAKESPEARE'S WILL

The Autographic Mirror. 4 vols. London and New York: Cassell, Petter and Galpin, 1864 to 66.

Eccles, Mark. *Shakespeare in Warwickshire.* Madison, Wisc., 1961.

Elton, Charles Isaac. *William Shakespeare: His Family and Friends.* London, 1904.

Green, A. Wagfall. "Shakespeare's Will," *Georgetown Law Journal,* xx (March 1932).

Hall, E. Vine. *Testamentary Papers.* 1931.

Jeaffreson, J. C. "A New View of Shakespeare's Will." *The Athenaeum* nos. 2844, 2847, 2848, 2906 (1882).

Stalker, Archibald. "Is Shakespeare's Will a Forgery?" *Quarterly Review* 274 (1940).

Staunton, H. *Memorials of Shakespeare Comprising the Poet's Will.* London, 1864.

Tannenbaum, Samuel A. *A New Study of Shakspere's Will.* Baltimore, 1926.

———. *Problems in Shakespere's Handwriting.* New York, 1927.

Yeatman, John Pym. *Is William Shakespere's Will Holographic?* no place, 1901.

SHAKESPEARE'S MURDER

Bond, Raymond T. *Handbook for Poisoners.* New York, 1951.

Brookes, Vincent J. *Poisons.* Huntington, N.Y., 1975.

Dreisbach, Robert L. *Handbook of Poisoning.* Los Altos, Calif., 1961.

Friswell, J. Hain. *Life Portraits of Shakespeare.* London, 1864.

Halliwell-Phillipps, James O. *An Historical Account of New Place, Stratford-upon-Avon.* London, 1864.

Hanley, Hugh A. "Shakespeare's Family in Stratford Records." *The Times Literary Supplement,* May 21, 1964.

Osler, Sir William. *The Principles and Practice of Medicine.* New York and London, 1916.

Rowland, John. *Prisoner in the Dock.* New York, 1960.

SHAKESPEARE, THE PLAYWRIGHT

Chambers, R. W. "The Expression of Ideas . . . in the 147 Lines . . . of Sir Thomas More." *Modern Language Review,* July 1931.

Croft, P. J. *Autograph Poetry in the English Language,* vol. 1. n.p., 1973.

Des Moineaux, Edwin J. *Manuscript Said to Be Handwriting of William Shakespeare Identified as the Penmanship of Another Person.* Los Angeles, 1924.

Greenwood, George. *The Shakspere Signatures and "Sir Thomas More."* London, 1924.

Greg, Walter W. *The Book of Sir Thomas More.* Oxford University Press, Oxford, 1911.

Pollard, Alfred W. "The Manuscripts of Shakespeare's Plays." *Library* 7, Series 3 (London, 1916).

Pollard, Alfred W., *et al. Shakespeare's Hand in the Booke of Sir Thomas More.* Cambridge, 1923.

Tannenbaum, Samuel A. *The Booke of Sir Thomas Moore.* New York, 1927.

———. *Shakspere's Unquestioned Autographs.* Baltimore, 1925.

———. *Shakspere and "Sir Thomas Moore."* New York, 1929.

Thompson, Edward M. *Shakespeare's Handwriting.* Oxford University Press, Oxford, 1916.

———. *Shakespeare's Hand in the Play of Sir Thomas More.* Cambridge: Cambridge University Press, 1923.

Wilson, J. Dover. *The Manuscript of Shakespeare's* Hamlet *and the Problems of Its Transmission.* 2 vols. Cambridge, England, 1963.

SHAKESPEARE'S LEGAL BACKGROUND

Barton, Sir Dunbar Plunket. *Links Between Shakespeare and the Law.* London, 1929.

Bentley, Richard. "Shakespeare's Law." *Canadian Law Times* 42 (1922).

Campbell, Lord John. *Shakespeare's Legal Acquirements Considered.* New York, 1859.

Devecmon, William C. "*In re* Shakespeare's Legal Achievements." Publication no. 12, The Shakespeare Society of New York.

Greenwood, George. *Shakspere's Law.* Hartford, 1920.

Heard, Franklin Fiske. *Shakespeare As a Lawyer.* Boston, 1883.

Hicks, Frederick C. "Was Shakespeare a Lawyer?" *Case and Comment* 22 (1916).

H. T. *Was Shakespeare a Lawyer?* London, 1871.

Keeton, George W. *Shakespeare and His Legal Problems.* London, 1930.

———. *Shakespeare's Legal and Political Background.* London, 1967.

Lybarger, Donald F. *Shakespeare and the Law.* Cleveland Bar Journal, Cleveland, 1965.

Mackenzie, J. B. "Was Shakespeare Bound to an Attorney." *The Green Bag* XIV, no. 2 (February 1902).

Martin, Milward W. *Was Shakespeare Shakespeare? A Lawyer Reviews the Evidence.* New York, 1965.

Noel, F. Regis. "Legal Influences in Shakespeare." An Address delivered before the Shakespeare Society of Washington, May 12, 1941.

THE SHAKESPEARE COAT OF ARMS

Assignment of Arms to Shakespeare and Arden. Introduction by Stephen Tucker. n.p., 1884.

Baker, H. Kendra. "Shakespere's 'Coat-of-Arms.'" *Baconiana* XXIV, no. 93 (April 1939).

Furnivall, F. W. "Shakspere's Signatures." *Journal of the Society of Archivists and Autograph Collectors,* no. 1 (June 1895).

Miscellanea Genealogica et Heraldica. Second series. n.p., 1886.

Stopes, C. C. *Shakespeare's Family.* London, 1901.

Tannenbaum, Samuel A. *The Shakspere Coat-of-Arms.* n.p., 1908.

———. *Was Shakspere a Gentleman?* New York, 1909.

Baynes, T. S. *Shakespeare's Studies.* n.p., 1893.

Bradley, Jesse Franklin, and Adams, Joseph Q. *The Jonson Allusion Book.* New Haven, 1922.

Burgoyne, Frank J. *Collotype Facsimile and Type Transcript of an Elizabethan Manuscript ... at Alnwick Castle (Northumberland Manuscript).* London and New York, 1904.

Chambrun, Clara de. "The Book Shakespeare Used—a Discovery." *Scribner's Magazine,* July 1936.

———. *Shakespeare Rediscovered.* New York, 1938.

Keen, Allan, and Lubbock, Roger. *The Annotator. The Portrait of an Elizabethan Reader of Halle's Chronicle.* New York, 1954.

McLaren, Moray. *By Me ... A Report upon the Apparent Discovery of Some Working Notes of William Shakespeare in a Sixteenth Century Book.* London, 1949.

THE TITUS ANDRONICUS ILLUSTRATION

Adams, Joseph Quincy. Introduction to Shakespeare's *Titus Andronicus* (First Quarto of 1594). New York and London, 1936.

Chambers, E. K. "The First Illustration to 'Shakespeare.'" *The Library* (fourth series) I, no. 1 (June 1924).

Wilson, J. Dover. "*Titus Andronicus* on the Stage in 1595" *Shakespeare Survey I.* Cambridge University Press, London, 1948.

SHAKESPEARE'S LIBRARY

Anders, H. R. D. *Shakespeare's Books. A Dissertation on Shakespeare's Reading and the Immediate Sources of His Works.* Berlin, 1904.

FORGERIES AND FAKES

A Catalogue of the Shakespeare Exhibition Held in the Bodleian Library. Oxford, 1916.

Hamilton, Charles. *Scribblers & Scoundrels.* New York, 1968.

Ireland, William Henry. *Confessions.* London, 1805.

Tannenbaum, Samuel A. "Reclaiming One of Shakspere's Signatures." *Studies in Philology* XXII, no. 3 (July 1925).

———. *Problems in Shakspere's Penmanship.* New York, 1928.

INDEX